Wandering the World

David G. Paul

WANDERING THE WORLD

Printed and bound by Blurb

First Printing, 2020

davidgpaul.co.uk

"The world is a book and those who do not travel read only one page"

— *St. Augustine*

1: Starting the Adventure

I never really had a plan to travel around the world. How many of us did ten or twenty years ago? In more recent years travel has gotten cheaper, and it's now more common. It wasn't always like this.

I grew up in a time when people would go on family holidays to Spain, Greece, or America - they were the normal places if you weren't holidaying around the UK. The only stories I'd hear of other places were from backpackers who had travelled the world in a single trip - though my exposure to these was mostly television.

People I knew that had taken a gap year before university said years later that it'd been a very memorable experience for them yet at the same time they found readjusting to life afterwards took considerable time. They had left everything and everyone they knew behind. We'd been told at college that universities would frown upon gap years in applications too. How true this was, I didn't know.

It wasn't something I'd found appealing anyway - I had no interest in taking a gap year, no interest in travel, and certainly no plans to visit every continent. I was mostly content to learn about places from books. Mostly. Sometimes I'd wonder what it was like to be in these different environments. What would it be like to trek across a great desert?

When I was growing up I found an interest in ancient history, and in particular the history of Egypt. I never thought it was somewhere I'd visit - it wasn't something I'd ever thought about. I'd spend most of the day in front of my computer screen, and almost shunned the outdoors. I was probably as inactive as you could imagine: a stereotypical computer scientist of the time.

I'd only been overseas a handful of times with my parents. We'd been to Spain's Balearic islands of Menorca and Mallorca, and had seen a reasonable amount of each island. We'd never go somewhere and just sit on a beach: travelling around a place was something we always did on holiday. I think that set some expectation of what travel should be like.

Years later, after a day trip to Nice with my Dad, he had the idea that if we could to fly to the south of France, explore a little, and get home in the same day then perhaps a little more was possible too. With my sister in tow we eventually returned, hired a car, and drove straight to the Italian town of Ventimiglia.

I only remember two things about this town: walking past a bakery where their cream cakes had ten centimetre deep cream, and someone on the street trying to sell Dad a ladies handbag. We stayed for about an hour before driving to Monte Carlo - the only city in Monaco. We drove some of the Formula 1 circuit, and parked up so we could photograph the famous casino.

The day had been long; but we'd seen a lot. It had been a very different experience; but an enjoyable one. The seeds had been sown for the adventures that would follow.

When I started full-time work things still hadn't changed that much, and if anything I probably did even less outdoors - the days of playing football with friends was mostly behind me. My only regular activity with friends was Judo.

I thought it'd be nice to keep in touch with university friends by going somewhere. I'm not the sort to party, so it wouldn't be to the typical places that students tend to go. There was only one place I could think of: a place I'd read about, had seen in films, and had studied in school. Of course, it was Egypt.

Everyone knows something about Egypt, even if it's only that they built some pyramids. There's a lot more to see for someone interested in their ancient history: not just the Valley of the Kings, but places like Karnak and Abu Simbel.

For a few weeks I bounced ideas back and forth with Andy, one of the friends I'd made at university. I wanted to see everything; but Andy seemed to prefer relaxing holidays. We compromised on visiting Cairo in the first week, and then flying to Alexandria for a more relaxing second week. I'd never even taken a two week holiday before.

It shows that sometimes plans form unexpectedly, and you find yourself doing things you never thought you would do, in places you never thought you'd go. That is how I came to travel across the seven continents, and to understand things about countries that books don't usually tell you.

I had no idea how anything would work:we'd booked the flights and hotels online, and had bought some currency. Beyond that I didn't know what I was doing;this was all new to me. I considered this to be a one-off trip with no plan for others. This was going to be a trip of a lifetime. Yet people didn't seem to understand why I'd want to go on holiday in Egypt. People I told seemed to think I was crazy.

I bought my first suitcase, and a small backpack I could use for hand luggage on the plane. I'd thought ahead and made sure it'd got multiple pockets inside for my camera, and side pouches for holding water bottles. Water bottles would be important in a desert, right?

Once I'd bought a wide-angle lens, although I was new to DSLR photography, it felt I was ready for my first adventure.

2: Egypt

Arriving in Cairo was quite the culture shock. From the moment we left the airport I was wondering what I'd let myself in for. The exit was crowded with a cacophony of noise, and people wanting every passerby to use their taxis. Thankfully I'd pre-booked one that was holding up a sign with my name.

I was used to the relative organisation of England, not the chaotic nature of Cairo's roads. There were more cars side-by-side than there were lanes, and most were weaving about. It was nothing like I'd pictured. I'd imagined it'd be like Stargate or Indiana Jones.

During this journey, one of the two Egyptians that were driving us to the hotel turned around to ask, "why have you come at this time of year?"

I didn't understand. We were visiting in June, surely the weather must be okay? It was already warm. Back home it'd be reasonable to say it'd be sunny, and little chance of rain. He then went on to tell us we'd arrived just after a massive sandstorm, and they were now experiencing temperatures in the high fifties. In Celsius. Apparently they generally don't get tourists at this time of year due to the heat. Oops.

That was my first mistake: we should have checked the average weather for different times of the year before booking. With it being around midnight we didn't yet realise just what this meant.

From then until the moment we arrived at the hotel compound we were taught a little Arabic to help us get by. In the little planning I'd done I'd not thought about language, and had a sudden realisation that street signs would not be using characters I could recognise. At least with European languages you can make an educated guess. Such an obvious thing; but you can forget about these things.

The hotel was just outside Giza, so to get into Cairo in the morning we used the complimentary shuttle bus. Travelling around wasn't something we'd figured out beforehand, so this was a stroke of luck.

On the drive into Cairo we passed the pyramids for the first time. They were incredible, and it was shocking how close we had to pass them to get from our hotel to the city centre. When you see the pyramids on television and in film you don't get a sense of how close Cairo has been built up to them. Any doubts I had about visiting were at least temporarily washed away.

We passed many residential buildings along the way too. There were many that looked incomplete, and some seemed to be built from whatever materials they could find. Despite the splendour of ancient Egypt, it seemed that a lot of the population was now living in poverty.

The shuttle bus dropped us off in a car park

overlooked by an overpass that led to the 6th October Bridge. As I stepped off the bus someone was there to greet us.

"Welcome! Follow me this way," an Egyptian man joyfully announced as he waved us in the direction he wanted us to go.

We thought it odd that there'd be someone there to greet us, after all the hotel hadn't mentioned their shuttle service would take us to someone who would show us around. He seemed friendly enough.

This apparent guide led us to a papyrus shop and ushered us through the door. He introduced us to the owner who went on to show us how they make papyrus, and used previously prepared samples of the paper at different stages of production. He left us to look around at the finished products. I spent more than I should have, probably a little overwhelmed by it all.

The guide took us across town to another shop on the second floor of a building; this time one that sold 'essence', their term for perfumes. Instead of waiting, he disappeared - never to be seen by us again.

It was here we started to realise what was going on. This stranger we'd presumed to be a guide was from the previous shop we'd been to, and had been waiting for some naive tourists to come along, and fall for their scheme. Even if it wasn't a deliberate deception, he took advantage of our naivety, and we learnt a lesson in him doing so.

Neither of us wanted to buy anything, but we were finding it difficult to politely excuse ourselves to leave. Being out of our depth, and not knowing the local language; we didn't want to offend anyone.

Having failed to sell us anything the owner of this shop then led us to another which was inside a courtyard elsewhere. This time we managed to excuse ourselves within seconds, and left to make our own way around the city.

Over the next hour we were pestered constantly by locals wanting to 'show us their business'. To each, we politely replied with 'la shukran'. It's a useful phrase we'd learnt meaning 'no thank you'.

There was one more thing we hadn't thought of: where to buy water from. The guidebook indicated that it wouldn't be safe to drink the water sold by street vendors as they're often bottles that have been refilled from a tap. We took this to be true; but couldn't see anywhere else to get water from. We were starting to dehydrate, and had to find somewhere.

Our search for water took us across a four lane road with curb stones almost half a metre above the road surface. When you see how they drive, having high curbs is understandable. Crossing the road is tricky: you have to step out into the traffic, then hope for the best as you weave in and out of the moving cars.

We found a cosy souvenir shop in a deserted shopping mall, and asked if they knew where we could get water from. The owner helpfully sent his assistant off in search of some, and asked us to sit on the couch: a fairly common part of their hospitality from what we'd seen so far. He brought us two glasses of a red-coloured herbal drink which I understood to be Karkadé - a juice made from dried hibiscus flowers. It tasted foul, but we were thirsty, and I didn't want to seem impolite so drank it.

An hour passed, and after buying more souvenirs there was no sign of any water. We felt we couldn't wait any longer so thanked the owner for his hospitality, and headed to the neighbouring hotel's restaurant for food, and some water.

A day later we took another ride into Cairo: this time better prepared with water bought from the hotel: you can't say we didn't learn from our mistakes.

The road leading to the Egyptian Museum of Antiquities is barricaded on either side with armed tourist police patrolling the perimeter. I watched as they stopped people from passing and I thought maybe something had happened. Weren't we going to be able to visit? Knowing I wouldn't get to visit the Valley of the Kings, the museum was one of only two sights I absolutely had to see during this trip.

It dawned on me that the people they were questioning before allowing them to pass was based upon the colour of their skin. In this surprising case of racism, they were allowing anyone with white skin to pass by unchecked.It felt almost uncomfortable to see: why should we be treated any differently?

Photography is not allowed inside; but the exhibits were amazing just to see. There was one piece that was better than everything else no matter how amazing some of the other pieces were. It was a piece that had captured the imagination of the world when it was first discovered during Howard Carter's dig in 1923. It was of course the burial mask of the boy Pharaoh Tutankhamun, a ruler during the first dynasty of Egypt's New Kingdom. Seeing it was a moment of absolute wonder. I never thought I'd get to see something I'd read so much about. Perhaps travel wasn't so bad after all.

The heat outside the museum was so oppressive that we sat on the steps of the museum eating ice cream. That in itself is totally uninteresting: why wouldn't we eat ice cream on vacation? What we witnessed though was a street vendor from around the corner carrying empty water bottles into the grounds, and was filling them up from a tap normally used for watering the grass. It acted as a reminder to check the seal on every bottle of water we bought.

I'd not made a list of sights, so we found ourselves wandering around Zamalek: the more affluent part of the city. It also happened to be the area that Andy's cousin was staying in on business, and when we met up he decided he'd take us on a Nile dinner cruise. As we ate we watched belly dancers, traditional Tanoura dancing, and some Egyptian singing.

We arrived back ashore after dark, and our experiences so far had tainted our belief that it would be safe to wait for a bus back to the hotel. Instead we found ourselves booking a taxi from the nearest hotel, even though in reality it would have been okay. Our lack of prior experience, and our negative attitude towards the city so far had affected our decisions. I think in this case, the words of Charlie Chaplin were appropriate: we think too much, and feel too little. By that I mean we paid attention to the prejudices we see in the papers and all around us back home, and found confirmation bias in the experiences we'd had. The actions of a few do not represent a majority. We had after all seen kindness too.

When the time came to see the pyramids of Giza, I'd started to feel ill with a stomach ache; but couldn't let this stop our plans. We'd not booked any tours, so we asked at the concierge desk how we could go about seeing them, and that we'd like to ride camels if possible. They called a taxi for us which took us to a small establishment in Giza, not far away from the entrance to the pyramids.

We waited inside a small, dark room as the driver told the gentleman behind the dimly lit wooden desk what we were after. Looking around the room the only light source was the doorway we were standing in, and a very narrow window just below the ceiling. I could see a few other locals sitting around doing nothing except smoking, and one leaning against the breeze block wall besides us. This wasn't the sort of place I was used to; but after the last few days who knew what was normal?

We paid to hire a guide and two camels. Riding a camel is quite different to riding a horse: as it gets up it rises onto its knees first which makes you lean forwards. It is for this reason why it's a good idea to lean backwards as the camel gets up so you don't fall flat on your face.

We were led by camel around the plateau, stopping for photographs along the way until our guide disappeared to get tickets for us to go inside the pyramid of Khafre. Whilst we could take pictures outside, we couldn't inside: it was forbidden to take cameras or bags inside due to the cramped passageway that leads to the burial chamber.

Back outside the pyramid we stood around and took our time taking photographs. Andy suggested we lose the guide, and carry on by ourselves so we could see more. I found myself agreeing, though the guide found us first and led us to the worker's tombs: an area totally fenced off with barbed wire.

A lone tourist policeman sat guarding the fence, and once our guide was certain he wasn't looking in our direction he pushed the fence down and told us to step over.

Any sane person would have alarm bells ringing in their heads at this point. As far as we knew, traipsing over barbed wire isn't something you'd normally do on a sightseeing holiday; but there we were: doing as we'd been asked as we felt we couldn't question it. This is crazy!

The workers tombs, at that time, were not open to the public as they were not safe for visitors - I believe they were still being excavated. The deep holes in the floors of darkened rooms were just one example of why we shouldn't have been there. It may have seemed dangerous, though I think we were also very lucky to see inside.

Before leaving, the guide stopped us whilst out of sight of anyone else, and demanded that we paid him more money before we could leave the tombs. We thought how much he was demanding seemed too much and we insisted we didn't have that much on us. This wasn't an entrance fee, it was a 'tip'.

Eventually we settled on an amount, having felt that

we had to. Perhaps we shouldn't have; but we'd just wandered around somewhere that not many people would have yet had the chance to, and we didn't want to risk trouble. We were incredibly inexperienced in travelling around developing countries.

Our tour of Giza ended with a stop to see the largest Sphinx known to exist. We'd seen far smaller ones already in the museum; but this is the one we all know. The closest we could get to the Sphinx was from a viewing platform due to work on repairing weather damage.

Eventually we rode the camels back to where we'd collected them from, though they tried to charge us a second time. Suddenly we realised the importance of getting a receipt when paying.

Over the days that followed I started to feel worse, and didn't know what to do. I'd never been ill abroad before. Eventually I sent a message to my Dad. I wanted to be at home; but instead all I could do was to call for a Doctor. I was prescribed a number of tablets, one of which was larger than a two pence piece. It wasn't pleasant; but it taught me a valuable lesson. From that point on I was more cautious about what I would eat and drink. I figured that the cause of this was the water used in either the Karkadé, or the 'homemade' ice cream from the hotel. It wasn't a mistake I'd be making again anytime soon.

In the second week we moved on to Alexandria, though I'd not improved that much. I couldn't let the opportunity for sightseeing pass me by so each day I struggled out a little bit further to see what we could. At first I couldn't make it much further than the adjacent street covered in rubble and rubbish. With how 'rough' this looked to my naive eyes, it seemed like what you'd expect of a war-torn country.

I eventually made it a little further, to look around the Montazah Palace gardens - a residence of the Egyptian President. This gave us confidence that I'd be able to manage half a day wandering around the city.

One of the sights was Pompey's Pillar, though as we were struggling to find it we decided to catch a rickshaw. This was a time when having maps on a mobile phone was unheard of so local knowledge came in useful.

It was pretty much deserted except for one tourism policeman standing guard. Underneath the pillar is the Serapeum which is where rituals to the Egyptian god Serapis were carried out. Again, tourists at this time wouldn't get to go down there as it was being excavated: it only had temporary lighting put up whilst they were working.

Originally people believed that standing atop the pillar was a statue of Pompey; hence the name that persisted. The pillar was actually erected in 293 CE for Diocletian: a name I wouldn't encounter again until many years later when visiting Croatia.

We'd visited an ancient Roman amphitheatre on the way to the pillar, and there they'd been strict about no video recording and were watching me when I used my camera. Here, in what seemed like a change in our luck, the tourism policeman standing guard here asked if we'd like to look around the excavations below. There wasn't really anything to see; but whilst underground the generator died plunging us into darkness. Okay, our luck hadn't changed that much then.

When the lights didn't come back on I started to feel for the wall - I knew that if we could find that then we'd find our way back out. Of course we had to find the wall first; but how hard could that be?

I had the idea of using my camera flash to help us get our bearings, and then stepped forwards slowly towards the wall until my fingers were resting against it. From there we were able to follow the wall back out until we could see the light of the surface.

To finish, we visited the catacombs of Kom El Shoqafa. For these we couldn't take cameras inside and there was nowhere to leave our bags so we decided to take it in turns going down. Once again we were the only tourists there.

This necropolis was completely different to what I was expecting. In some ways it felt Norse-like, or rather, more like something out of The Lord of the Rings; but with carved reliefs of the Egyptian gods. There were bits that could not be visited due to them being submerged; though I felt this just added to the wonder of them.

This certainly hadn't been a holiday in the traditional sense. There'd been many lessons to be learnt, and many experiences. In some strange way I did enjoy it though. I got to see the Giza plateau, and the burial mask of King Tut. Perhaps if I was to travel anywhere else some of these lessons could come in useful.

3: Peru

Egypt had felt like an arduous experience which I was in no rush to repeat. It wasn't until speaking to another university friend, James, about the experience that it became apparent he wished he'd gone on the trip as well. He suggested we should go to Peru the following year with tours booked through a tourism company. Surely it had to go better than Egypt had.

I didn't know as much about Machu Picchu and Peru as I did about Egypt. A lot of what I knew I'd learnt when I was younger: from school, and watching an animated series set in 1532 - a time of Spanish conquest. When I was little it'd been one of my favourite cartoons.

Peru was my first experience of a long haul flight, the first time I'd had connecting flights, and my first time in the Americas. Already, my 'continents visited' count was up to three of seven. Not bad going for someone with no plans to go anywhere.

We started with Lima, the capital city divided into forty-two districts. Whilst Miraflores and San Isidro are the more 'up market' districts where tourists would normally stay, up on the hills you could see the poorest ones.

As luck would have it, our arrival in Peru coincided with their Corpus Christii festival. In Plaza de Armas we could see part of this taking place where monks and nuns from every brotherhood and sisterhood were celebrating. On the floor they'd laid out flower petals and spices to create large images.

In the square, as well as in and under the Iglesias de San Francisco we could see Spanish-influenced Catholicism. I'd photographed a lot of places of worship over the years; but human remains arranged in geometric patterns was a new one to me.

The remainder of the day was used to drive us five hundred kilometres into the desert to Nazca. By the time we arrived night had fallen, and our first full day in the country was over.

We'd been advised to eat a light breakfast as our flight over the Nazca lines and geoglyphs could be rough. Sure enough one of the other passengers on this light aircraft didn't pay attention to this and threw up. It didn't distract from the wonder of seeing these famous lines that have survived for hundreds of years.

The flight was in a 6-seat Cessna Skywagon - a craft a little bigger than the Piper I once got to fly in the UK. This particular Cessna, OB-1808, only got a couple more years of operation after our own trip. In 2010, fuel mismanagement caused the aircraft to crash and killed everyone on board. The pilot had been drinking, the ground crew had been arguing, and their checks were rushed. This wasn't something I could have imagined at the time we flew over the lines - it'd been a good experience, and was nice to see a landmark I'd only just seen in Indiana Jones. I'd actually been tempted to get a fedora for this trip.

Our overnight stay on our way to Pisco was in a hotel compound in Ica. This was one of those places where there seemed to be a strong suggestion that you don't wander around outside the compound by yourself. It was new to James, but to me the armed guards reminded me of Cairo. We passed the time by playing mini golf, and exploring the grounds a little.

Pisco was the earthquake-devastated town where we took boats to the Ballestas Islands. If we'd planned this trip ourselves it's likely we wouldn't have known about these islands; this is where tour companies come in handy.

We saw sea lions on the rocks alongside Humboldt penguins. Nazca boobies were flying around the islands, and some were perched on old equipment that had been used for collecting guano. What an overpowering smell!

Once back ashore we stopped by the Paracas National Reserve on our way back to Lima. Apparently they used to get flamingoes; but the earthquake that had killed so many, and had caused so much destruction in this area had also scared them off. A year had passed since, and still they were feeling the effects.

The following day brought with it a change of scenery - we flew up into the Andean mountain range to the city of Cusco, the former capital of the Inca empire. Of all the places we saw in Peru, this one best demonstrated the amalgamation of Spanish and Inca architecture. At first glance the city is most definitely Spanish, but as you look closer at places such as Qurikancha you can see how the invaders also incorporated stonework from existing buildings into the European style.

When the Spaniards arrived they wanted to convert the population to Catholicism so they destroyed most of the Temple of the Sun, and created a cathedral in its place. They thought conversion of existing places of worship would make this new religion more palatable. The same had happened in Britain when Christianity slowly replaced the different pagan beliefs.

Whilst I was photographing the courtyard of Qurikancha I glanced over my shoulder to see where James was. He was crouching down, and wasn't looking too well. His vision had in his words 'shrunk to a point' as the altitude had already started to take its toll on him. All we could do was to take him back to the minibus to let him recover.

By some stroke of luck, it seemed that the fitness I'd gained from cycling to and from work on a daily basis was enough to mean I wasn't affected by the altitude. I could carry on the tour higher into the Andean mountains around Cusco; much to the dismay of my friend. I was now seeing facing illness abroad from the other side, and had an idea of how he must be feeling.

The tour took us on to Sacsayhuamán and Tambomachay. The former had been an Inca citadel with stones that stood over nine metres high, weighing around 250 tonnes. Despite their size, these stones fit together perfectly; but many had been taken by the Spaniards between 1560 and 1664 to build a cathedral in the Plaza de Armas.

This cathedral was one we saw at the end of this tour. Inside it has replicas of famous paintings, each recreated by Inca artists with small differences to set them apart.

That evening our guide recommended eating at Tenupa, a buffet restaurant that only served traditional Peruvian foods. As we ate we were entertained by a cultural show of different Andean dances, with each one wearing the traditional dress of the regional tribe the dance was from. This trip was already so different to my experience of Egypt - I was loving almost every minute of it. Every day was different, and we'd always got something new to see. I was starting to understand just how good travel could be.

A little after dawn we found ourselves descending into the sacred Urubamba Valley that stretches from Pisac to Ollantaytambo. Our first stop was Qalla Q'asa; a citadel which overlooks a large number of terraces in the valley that produce micro-climates for growing crops. As we walked from the mini-bus to the citadel I could hear the sound of panpipes being carried by the wind and amplified by the mountains. It was very atmospheric and made it feel like we were in an episode of that animated series in search of the cities of gold.

I could have stopped there much longer, but a

problem with organised tours is that you can't always spend the time you want where you want it. Instead, we had to move on to Pisac to visit a Peruvian marketplace. Vendors there sold tapestries, ornaments, jewellery, and much more; everything seemingly hand-crafted.

I may not have been that interested in shopping, but the market itself was worth a few photographs with the pisonay tree in the centre. Sadly, five years after this visit, the tree that had stood there for centuries was destroyed in a thunderstorm. Places like this though are preserved in our memories and in the photographs we take.

One of the things about travel is getting to try the local cuisine. We'd already tried some in Tenupa, but whilst in the sacred valley we got to try a local pie made from pork, peppers, and banana. It may sound unusual, but it tasted good. New experiences really do give you new perspectives.

The final stop of the day was Ollantaytambo: a former ceremonial city, and royal estate of Emperor Pachacuti at 2,792 metres above sea level. For this day James had coped with the altitude okay; probably because we were lower than Cusco. Instead of taking the Inca trail from there to Machu Picchu, we were instead ascending back to Cusco.

Before the sun had risen we boarded a train bound for Aguas Calientes: a small town at the base of Machu Picchu - the mountain with the world famous ruins. Most people think of the ruins as being Machu Picchu, but it's actually the name of the mountain they were built on. The mountain peak you see behind it in most photos is named

Huayna Picchu, and can be climbed by tourists. I hadn't known until this trip that my friend wasn't too keen on heights. Climbing the bigger peak would be one to miss.

Our starting point was the guard house: a great place for taking photographs of most of the ruins. By midday our guide had left us to explore by ourselves, and we took this chance to see some of the lesser visited parts such as the 'Inca Bridge'.

It was a bridge in the same way that two or three sheets of paper are a novel. This bridge was a couple of planks of wood stretched across a chasm, and could only be reached by walking along a path that was less than a metre wide in places. We'd made the effort to get there, but we had no intention of crossing it - in part as it didn't seem worthwhile. It didn't seem to lead anywhere, so what was the point wasting precious time?

We'd missed out on lunch as we hadn't thought about taking food with us, but once back in Aguas Calientes we ate in one of the few restaurants that wasn't a pizzeria. There I tried an alpaca steak: it tasted a little like beef but sweeter. It was also served with rice and fries which seem to be served at every meal. Carbohydrates and protein were plentiful with barely a vegetable in sight. Not that I knew it back then; but it was a marathoners dream.

Next morning we set off at 04:30 to get to the top of Machu Picchu before sunrise. Despite the reluctance in getting up early, it seemed like a good plan: we hoped to capture the rising sun illuminating the ruins. Things didn't quite go to plan as clouds lingered below us, hiding the ruins.

By the time the clouds started to part, the sun had already risen. Our guide, who James now referred to as 'the rock lady', was with us again and growing impatient as she wanted to show us the rest.

That afternoon we took the train back to Cusco, and with it brought an end to our tour. It felt a shame to eventually leave those ruins behind as it was unlikely I'd ever see them again. It's not the sort of place people go back to year after year. We now had a few days without any plans; but the return to altitude also meant that James was feeling ill once more.

On the first evening back in Cusco I was sitting in the hotel when I heard a lot of noise coming from outside. My first thought was that a fight had broken out so I went over to the window; but struggled to see what was going on.

Loud bangs were getting closer and closer. My mind flashed back to seeing police carrying assault rifles around the square earlier. Is it gunfire?

As a crowd of people started to move passed the hotel my mind jumped to thinking it was a riot with music. Music? This was no riot. I realised the noise was from firecrackers being thrown around a marching band. My best guess was that it related in some way to the Corpus Christii celebration.

The days that followed felt long, and for much of them I felt bored as we'd very little left to see or do. In all honesty I think James would have struggled to do anything had we got anything booked. He'd confined himself to the hotel for most of that time.

It was a lesson though: to make sure ahead of time that there would be enough to see for the amount of time in a place.

Eventually we were back on the road to begin the tour of Lake Titicaca. For me, the most interesting stop along the way was the pre-Inca settlement of Raqch'i. The large free-standing walls are impressive, and these are complemented by quite a few granaries in various states of repair. The Inca came along later and improved it, including the construction of a temple to Wiracocha: their creation god.

When we reached Abras la Raya we were 4,335 metres above sea level. Somehow, in a group that included a USAF fighter pilot, I found myself being the only one unaffected by the altitude. That left me confused.

In Puno there was the general feeling on the minibus that the area looked a little rough. This influenced our own attitude towards exploring the town, and convinced us to not leave the hotel at night. Looking back, I think that was a mistake. Why go somewhere if you're not going to explore?

In the morning we headed out onto Lake Titicaca, the highest navigable lake in the world at 3,820 metres above sea level. Our destination was the Islas Flotantes Uros: the floating islands made from totora reeds.

Landfall on these islands required a degree of care to make sure we didn't fall into the icy waters. The locals taught us about their culture, and how they use the tall totora reeds to maintain the island and to craft everything they need including boats. Life there isn't just different to back home, but different to the mainland as well.

On some islands they don't like tourists, but on the ones that do they use the money from tourists to pay for medicine and anything they need from the mainland. The Peruvian government don't consider these islands as part of the community so they get no financial aid - they are completely independent.

It was quite a strange feeling to be walking around on an island that was dry, yet still allows your feet to sink into it. Each of these islands are anchored in place to ensure that they don't float away.

In addition to the floating islands are some 'real' islands such as Isla Taquile. The island is surrounded by crystal clear water as algae doesn't grow in these cold temperatures.

The inhabitants of this island greeted us and cooked us a meal of potatoes and some fish they'd caught that morning. I don't really eat fish; but I tried my best to eat what I could out of politeness. After food they then demonstrated how their culture works, and performed one of their traditional dances.

The following day was our long return back to Lima, though instead of driving all the way back to Cusco we used a local airport. The day after this we awoke in Lima to a minor earthquake. It did no damage, but coming from a country where they are very rare it came as a bit of a surprise.

Before flying home we had time for one last bit of

tourism: the Gold Museum. Most of what we could see was from the Sicán era. It also told the story of how gold was abundant in Inca culture, and how one tribe would cover the body of a priest in gold; leading to the legend of El Dorado, 'the golden one'.

I'd arrived in Peru not knowing that much more than what the animated Mysterious Cities of Gold series had taught me, and now here we were finishing the trip with the inspiration for that story.

Something had changed too: I was now eager to carry on seeing more of the world, and had already started to think about where to visit next. If it hadn't been for the success of Peru, I may not have continued travelling. Maybe I could visit a new country every year…

4: Berlin

James was keen to visit Australia and New Zealand. I thought I wouldn't mind going too; but it would be another year before we could go. A big difference when you travel on a yearly basis instead of doing it all in one go is that you've got more time to plan, and to adapt from experiences.

We thought it a good idea to go somewhere in Europe first. It'd be cheaper, and perhaps could be good practice for booking everything ourselves. I wanted to visit Rome to see old buildings, but James had already been there. We compromised by turning it into a multi-city trip across three countries. The first of these was Berlin, and we knew on this adventure we'd be relying on a lot going right; especially with some tight connections.

Things never go the way you want them to though. The week before this journey began I injured my hand at a judo training session where my fingers had bent back almost ninety degrees in the wrong direction. This had left them severely bruised, and unable to hold any weight. Lifting my suitcase wouldn't be easy. It seems there's always some sort of challenge to a trip.

My first impression of Berlin was that the trains were cheaper than back home, and ran on time. At Alexanderplatz station we couldn't really understand where to go, so we asked at a kiosk. Not knowing German ourselves made it difficult, but we were able to convey our meaning through pointing.

Once on the next train we realised that the lady in the kiosk had kept our map that had everything marked on it. We'd now be exploring Berlin without really knowing where we were going.

We got off at the Bülowstraße station, checked-in to the hotel, and went looking for somewhere to eat. We wanted to start the trip off with some of the local cuisine, but found all the restaurants around us only served food from other nationalities.

Whilst looking for somewhere to eat, we came across the Kaiser-Wilhelm Memorial Church. It looked like it had been through a war; which it had actually. The original building was constructed in the 1890's; but during the Battle of Berlin in 1943 it was badly damaged by the Allied forces leaving it in a severe state of disrepair.

It's a reminder that it's not just lives that are lost in war, but also pieces of history. When people lose their connections to the past, they can lose part of their identity in the process. We should have known this would be a common theme in Berlin. I guess in some ways it was at least lucky that it was a relatively recent building at the time it was damaged. The loss of a building hundreds of years old, would have been a shame.

Our hotel didn't serve breakfast, so in the morning

we had to go in search of somewhere to eat again. We were fortunate to find a nice café not far from the hotel with numerous types of coffee beans lining it's walls, and a nice selection of croissants to choose from. In some ways this was better than sleepily arriving at breakfast in a hotel. We made this our go-to place for our entire stay in this city.

The guidebook had warned us that ticket machines in Berlin are not as reliable as the trains. It wasn't joking either: the machine wouldn't accept our money until just moments before the train pulled into the station.

Our destination was Eberswalderstraße, a place which Google Maps at the time claimed was the site of a Berlin Wall memorial. We walked for about an hour with the sun beating down on us; but we just couldn't find any of the Berlin Wall there. My research had failed us. We decided we'd be better off finding a piece of the wall another day.

It took a further hour to walk to the Fernsehturm tower at Alexanderplatz where we tried our first German Brätwurst whilst waiting for our allotted time to visit the top. There's some great views of the city from up there, and we could see just how far we'd walked: three kilometres.

Our goal for the afternoon was to find three iconic parts of the city: Checkpoint Charlie, the Reichstag, and the Brandenburg Gate. Whilst looking for these we passed other sights we hadn't known about beforehand. It seemed nothing we intended to see was signposted which was making it challenging. We had to go so far as to ask for directions from a souvenir shop. If only we'd had a back-up map.

Checkpoint Charlie is a wooden hut with costumed actors you can have your photo taken with for a fee. A tourist trap now, but once it had much more significance: it was built at the end of the second world war after Germany had been divided up into zones controlled mainly by the US, UK, France, and Russia.

The Soviet Zone later became the Deutsche Demokratische Republik, known colloquially as East Germany, and the three remaining Allied zones became the Bundesrepublik Deutschland, or West Germany.

Although Berlin is located entirely in what was the Soviet Zone, its importance meant that it too was divided up into zones. Where east met west a wall had been built to separate them, and Checkpoint Charlie was one of the few crossing points in the wall. This particular checkpoint had famously been the place where during the Cold War, American and Russian tanks faced each other in a stand-off.

We left one reminder of war behind to stumble across another: the holocaust memorial. It consists of many stone blocks which represent Jewish lives that were brutally and callously taken during the war. In some ways it feels more like a graveyard: you can't help to think of the three million lives that were needlessly taken by a fascist regime. This is what happens when hate and distrust is allowed to fester, and be used for political gain.

From the memorial we finally spotted the Brandenburg Gate. This gate was once one of the entrances into the city of Berlin but is now the only one left standing. Once we'd taken some photographs we continued on to the Reichstag - the seat of the German Bundestag. We didn't get to look around inside however as you have to register your planned visit ahead of time, similar to visiting the White House. Instead we photographed the building from the outside on passing, and headed through Tiergarten to the tall golden statue called the Siegessäule: erected to commemorate the Prussian victory over the Danish in 1864.

We'd walked over fifteen kilometres by this point, and it was now becoming uncomfortable to continue even though it was another two miles back to the hotel. The best motivation to keep walking was knowing I could sit down at the end of it.

Our second day in Berlin was another attempt at getting to see the infamous wall. We'd asked about it at the hotel reception, so now knew to head over to the East Side Gallery. In my head I'd imagined that they'd dug up part of the wall and were now displaying it in an art gallery as some sort of exhibit.

We had no idea what to expect so when we got there we looked for signposts. There was nothing along this dual carriageway we were walking down other than a few unremarkable buildings on one side, and an old damaged wall full of graffiti that was between us and the River Spree.

Then it dawned on us: this was the Berlin Wall. The symbol of oppression and mistrust during the Cold War was crumbling into disrepair.

Further along the wall we found a portion of it had been restored with a fresh coat of plaster, and an artist painting new artwork onto it. It felt wrong that they were doing this. The graffiti had in part been an outlet for their frustrations; but now they'd whitewashed some of their history and brought new order to the art.

We continued on to the Charlottenburg Palace but found the visit brief due to restoration work. My blistered feet were far from happy with all the walking so our pace was slowed: wearing new shoes had not been a great idea.

Further along the line we went looking for the botanical gardens. These were trickier to find, but a sign saying 'Botanischer Garten' looked promising. Maybe in Egypt signposts were impossible to follow; but here we could at least guess.

The gate next to this sign was locked; but just as we turned to leave in disappointment, someone in uniform arrived and opened the gate.

"Are the gardens open?" we asked, our hope having been reignited.

The guard looked at us, and after a pause asked, "Are you students?"

As we were both looking a little lost, and carrying backpacks, we may have looked a little like students on a field-trip. We explained we were tourists and he directed us to a visitors entrance further down the road.

Once into the garden the first thing that hits you is the vastness of the place and the diversity of the plants that they have there. In the summer months, such as when we were there, they also seem to get a reasonable amount of wildlife.

We had wasted so much time in trying to find the entrance to the gardens that we didn't actually have much time to look around. Again, the lack of a map had caused us problems. We moved quickly and tried to cover as much ground as we could. There was a lot there wasn't time for: we had needed a whole afternoon but made the most of the time we had.

This had been a quick sightseeing visit covering a lot of what there was to see in just one city. If I was ever to go back I'd have a list of a few places still to see; but would likely want to see more of Germany at the same time. There had to be more to the country than what we'd seen in Berlin.

So far, so good with our planning. It would soon be time to move on to the next city.

5: Italy

We took the train to the airport in Berlin, and flew to Naples to begin the Italian part of our adventure. As we'd struggled to find places in Berlin after the loss of our map, we decided we'd ask on our way out of the airport for directions. The lady pointed at the bus we should take, and told us to take it to the end of the line. Sounded simple enough to find the last stop.

Getting on this bus was like boarding the London Underground: people flooded on until it seemed there was no more room. When people stopped boarding the bus, the driver got out and started to herd more people on. Now I knew what tinned sardines felt like.

At times the bus would pass no more than millimetres from building walls and other vehicles, yet somehow got through unscathed. The first stop for the bus was at the 'Piazza Garibaldi' train station. I thought that was odd as I knew our hotel was next to a train station, and had Garibaldi in the hotel name. The tourist information desk had told us to stay on the bus until the end of the line, so we trusted her, and ignored this amazing coincidence.

Time passed and the bus stopped outside a castle. Whilst there I spotted a sign that had the name of the hotel chain on it. James had a piece of paper with the hotel name on, and gave it to the driver whilst pointing at the paper then the hotel sign. The driver enthusiastically confirmed it was correct.

It seemed strange as after only a couple of stops it couldn't possibly be the end of the line, but we figured that maybe the bus would get closer to the hotel after winding around the streets to stop elsewhere first. We thanked the driver, got off the bus, and weaved through the roadworks.

The hotel reception confirmed it was the right chain, but the wrong hotel. The tourist information desk, and the bus driver seemed to have both misunderstood us as the correct hotel was back near the train station we'd passed earlier. I should have checked the location of the hotel in relation to the airport before we'd arrived.

One taxi ride later we arrived at a very rundown looking hotel. After check-in we remembered the guidebooks comment that crime rate is high here, so we held on tightly to our cameras as we walked back to the castle. We never had any trouble during our time in Naples, just bad directions. One lesson that could be learned here is that people often say places are dangerous or have high crime rates; but then it's probably said about your hometown too. There's a reasonable chance you'll never encounter it.

For once we were lucky that our sense of direction was okay: we arrived at Castel Nuovo just before it closed. The first thing we saw inside the castle was its huge courtyard, and this was surrounded by fairly modern looking rooms. It looks similar to British castles, but still has a European feel to it with a grand staircase on the side leading up to the higher floors, and the ramparts.

There's a lot of religious iconography inside the rooms of this castle, but it's something you'd expect from historical Italian buildings. The most peculiar part of the castle though is that it has a courtroom. Up until 2006 this castle was the seat of power for Napoli - this was their equivalent to Westminster Palace in England.

Inside one of the ground floor rooms is a reinforced glass floor which allows you to see the half-buried skeletons of those who were considered to be traitors. I guess politics is bloody wherever you go.

To finish the day we stopped by a pizzeria where we saw some of the Italian military eating. We thought if they were eating there it was probably okay. The pizza I ordered was unlike any I'd seen before or since. Instead of a tomato base over the crust it had a few cherry tomatoes cut in half with melted cheese over them. I'd never had a pizza like that before or again since. It wasn't great.

I wanted an early start to the next day, but when you're travelling with friends there has to be some compromise and so we headed to the train station later than I'd hoped. Getting tickets for Pompeii was easy, but finding our way to the correct platform wasn't so much.

For quite some time we couldn't find anyone that spoke English, and we couldn't speak Italian. Eventually we found someone who pointed us in the direction of some underground platforms, and there a passer-by was able to translate a guard's directions for us. He advised we needed to jump down off the platform, cross the rails, and climb back up the other side. It seemed crazy, so we checked again, and sure enough that was what we needed to do.

The train we boarded was so run-down and empty we wondered if we'd somehow boarded the wrong train. After a few stops we were confident that we were at least headed in the right direction along the coastline.

We got off the train at Pompeii station, and started looking for the ruins but couldn't find any signs for directing tourists. We found a tourist information building, but it was closed. Things weren't looking good.

Eventually we got lucky and found the Piazza Anfiteatro entrance. It seemed odd at the time that it took so long to find. Isn't this one of the big attractions in this area?

When buying our ticket we chose the one that would be valid for Herculaneum as well. The necropolis by the entrance was empty, but as we reached the Forum, and Via dell'Abbondanza we found the rest of the ruins to be crowded with tourists.

We stayed long enough to also sit and have our packed lunch just outside the Amphitheatre. It's not a bad place to spend several hours; but there was little shade from the ever-present sun.

We eventually left via the Porta Marina exit and quickly found a different train station for the Circumvesuviana train. It confirmed our suspicions: we had taken the wrong train, and that is why we'd had a hard time finding the ruins. Maybe we'd gone wrong, but we'd still found what we were after and saw some of the local town as a result. Nothing like getting lost to add some adventure.

On the way back we got off the train at Ercolano Scavi, and very quickly found 'Vesuvio's Express' that sold bus trips up to Mount Vesuvius. We got there just in time to take the last bus of the day.

The winding bus journey up the side of the volcano reminded me a little of the coach ride up to Machu Picchu from Aguas Calientes, but this one was considerably safer: it had safety barriers. The bus stopped not far from the top, and we were given a bit of time to reach the summit by ourselves, and to get back.

To stay at the summit as long as we could, we decided we'd run back down the side of the volcano. Running kicked up a lot of dust, particularly when sliding on the corners of the switchbacks. I think some of the other tourists thought we were crazy.

The minibus took us back into town, and eventually we headed back on the train to Naples after having found our tickets in fact didn't cover Herculaneum as we'd asked.

The searing summer sun beating down on the train carriages was making them uncomfortably warm. Some of the passengers had opened the doors which is something you wouldn't be able to do on a British train: they're locked for safety. Here people were hanging out the door of the speeding train, and with nowhere to sit I wasn't that keen on standing near the door with nothing to hold onto either. So, I sat on the floor and watched

Italy pass by.

In Naples we decided we'd eat at a restaurant near to the hotel, but it's the one time in all my years travelling that I've been served chicken cooked medium-rare. Even if this pink chicken had been cooked properly, it was still floating atop a pool of grease. It wasn't edible, and was the second disappointing meal of the trip.

Instead of flying to the next city, we took a train to Rome. This one was a far better experience than in Naples. Once there we asked in the train station for directions, and once again found them to be less than accurate. What we hadn't realised though was that if a bus stops at multiple places on the same road then they still count it as a single stop.

We had no map, no internet, and only an idea of where we needed to be. Road after road we hauled our luggage along during the start of a heatwave that had just hit Italy. My injured hand wasn't making it easy so was thankful when eventually we found the right road. The hotel was only distinguishable by the initials of the hotel name printed on one of the windows. It didn't even look like a hotel from the outside.

That evening we were fortunate enough to find a local family-run restaurant that served us our first good meal in Italy. It was a four course meal accompanied by a gourd of water, and a bottle of the house wine. In Italy it's traditional to have a vegetable course, a pasta course, and then a meat course before the dessert. After the meals we'd had in Europe so far, this was what we'd needed.

We awoke to brilliant sunshine, and decided the best use of the day would be to visit the Vatican and churches. At the hotel reception we asked for directions, but soon found we'd been given directions that were in the opposite direction to where we needed to be going. Typical.

Even with how early we arrived at the Vatican Museum, the queue was already incredibly long. It wasn't even 09:00; but it was already 24°C. It took an hour of standing with no shade before we could finally go inside.

Most places inside the Vatican do not allow flash photography even though you're likely to see others trying to get away with it. Behaviour like that will eventually result in cameras being banned inside altogether. I find it a real shame when a complete ban is in place.

We slowly made our way to the Sistine Chapel. Everyone says that Michelangelo's masterpiece is amazing, but to me it was just another ceiling - it didn't seem any better than some modern artists would do. Maybe I was missing the point.

Within two hours of entering the Vatican Museum we had seen everything that was open, so headed out into the 41°C heat to find some lunch. The café we got food from was a really peculiar place-you had to pay a set amount and then decide what it was you wanted in that price range; however barely any of their food was priced up correctly which just made ordering near impossible. I really don't understand the logic behind this method.

Saint Peter's Basilica in contrast to the Vatican museum is incredible:it feels cavernous and incredibly ornate. To me this was better than the Sistine Chapel by far. The current Basilica took approximately 120 years to build, and has the largest interior of any Christian church anywhere in the world. During the 1500's it had fallen into such disrepair that unfortunately the Pope ordered for stones to be used from the Colosseum in its repair.

It seems we may have been locationally challenged on our return to the hotel as in our search for the bus stop we found ourselves at the Colosseum instead. On one side there is a busy road, yet on the other it's peaceful and has a large green area. We decided that as we were already there we'd look around whilst it was quiet. I'm not sure it took much longer to look around than it did to queue to get in.

When we left we got lost again; but this time we found a tourist information building, and got a free map. One lesson learnt from this trip was to be better prepared with maps before travelling.

Our second day in Rome was a day we'd anticipated would be filled with walking. We started at Nicola Savi's Fontana di Trevi, and from there visited the Roman Pantheon: a large domed building which was once used for worship. A shaft of light shone through the oculus inside the Pantheon to illuminate the walls. The Romans really knew how to make an impressive building. Before leaving, I also made sure I saw the tomb of Raffaello Sanzio, more commonly known as Raphael: one of the great renaissance architects, and namesake of one of the Ninja Turtles.

We continued on and found ourselves in Piazza

Navona where there are three more fountains worth seeing. The grandest of these is one by Bernini: Fontana dei Quattro Fiumi. This fountain reminded me of one in Berlin as it featured figures that represented major rivers from different continents: the Nile in Africa, the Ganges in Asia, the Danube in Europe, and the Rio della Plata in South America. It was nice to be able to see a link between two countries on this trip.

When we reached the Piazza del Popolo, a square historically used for public executions, we were finding the summer heat to be too much for us. The water bottle I'd been carrying was now so warm it was a shame I didn't have tea bags with me.

Our final day in Rome was a quieter one. We started with the Roman Forum, and followed this with a film that was set in Rome. It seemed like the right thing to do.

In watching the film we realised that the Santa Maria della Vittoria church was worth visiting to see Bernini's 'The Ecstasy of Saint Teresa'. When we got there we saw a priest sitting on a chair in front of the church.

As we got closer to the church the priest stood up, clutched his cross, and walked towards us as he held it in front of him. He was either trying to say "you're not allowed here" or thought we were were demons. Either way, we weren't getting in. It seemed our sightseeing was at an end.

The Roma Termini is a busy station. We sat waiting for the train, seeing the departures board update frequently with many delays of thirty minutes or more. Our train was late, but apparently for some others it would give them a platform number, and then either change it or remove it. As James said, "The board giveth, and the board taketh away".

The journey was a chance to read, though I looked out of the window frequently. Hours later the approach to Venice by rail was amazing. I looked up from my book, and watched as the Venetian Lagoon approached quickly. The ground seemed to just drop away from below us as we rocketed across the bridge to the islands of Venezia.

We left the train swiftly, and got straight onto a motoscafo. It was expensive compared to other forms of transport we'd used, but it took us straight to the small island of Lido where we'd be staying.

As we arrived on Lido I saw a bus pulling up that had the name of the road we wanted displayed on its sign, so without thinking we ran over and boarded it. Running with my suitcase still wasn't good for my injured fingers.

We started to get suspicious as the direction we were travelling in seemed wrong. We soon reached the end of the line: there was nothing there except for a ferry crossing, and we couldn't see anybody about either. There was a sudden realisation that the bus had started on the road we'd wanted. I'd made an unfortunate mistake.

Our bus ticket had now expired, and with nowhere to buy one from we spoke to the driver. After explaining the circumstances he agreed to take us back to where we'd boarded the bus for no extra fare: an extremely kind gesture. Sometimes double checking where you're going and where you are isn't a bad idea.

We found the hotel very quickly when we arrived back. During check-in I noticed how expensive their internet access was; but it was one of the few times I'd seen it available during the trip. This was a time when internet access whilst travelling wasn't that easy to find even though I'd used it briefly in Egypt from an Internet cafe.

We needed to know how early the boats started running from the island as on our last morning we'd have an early start. Our concern was that if they didn't run early enough we'd have to sleep in the train station overnight. Fortunately the reception confirmed they run twenty-four hours a day.

One day to look around Venice made it seem like we'd be struggling for time. To give us the best opportunity to see everything we got over to the main island as early as we could manage. Even then the humidity was high. In fact, it was so hot that Saint Mark's Square was almost deserted.

We started with the Doge's Palace where they don't allow photography. This same ticket also gave us access to Museum Corro which is full of artwork, sculptures, and armoury. They serve food; but charge extra if you want to sit down. Rather than pay extra, we sat on some steps in the shade around the square instead even though this isn't really permitted.

I was keen to see inside Saint Mark's Cathedral, but as we were short on time we instead went looking for the Rialto bridge. We found many dead ends that meant backtracking to find other bridges until eventually we found it.

The bridge is fairly short; but is wide and lined with souvenir shops. I guess in someways it was similar to what London Bridge had once been; but on a smaller scale.

Our final stop of the day was the Venetian Arsenal: a shipyard that has been used by the Venetian military for hundreds of years. Unfortunately it's still used by their navy so we couldn't go in to look around. Apparently it is opened up to the public for some special occasions however.

That evening we returned to Lido for the last time to have pizza and gelato. It felt like the right sort of meal to have as the sun set on our last day in Italy.

6: Athens

The sun had not yet risen when we prepared ourselves to leave Venice. We took a water taxi at 04:00, and then a train back across the bridge to the mainland towards Milano Centrale. We arrived in Milan on time; but still had to run across the station to catch the airport shuttle that was about to leave. Short connections meant stressful times; but we made our flight.

We'd so far caught three modes of transportation - any of which if missed would have spelt disaster for our flight. Upon arrival in Athens we were no longer on a tight schedule; but still had a lot of travelling to go. We took another bus to the metro station, and from there got most of the way into the city before we had to leave the metro due to maintenance on the line. It was another ten minutes of walking to reach the hotel.

The area looked like it had been in the middle of a war zone. The buildings all around seemed to be under construction, and there was the constant sound of pneumatic drills pounding holes into the road.

The balcony from the hotel room had an impressive view of the Acropolis, though the room itself seemed unfinished: there was a gaping hole in the bathroom wall. Having read a lot about ancient Greece, I'd expected so much more from the modern day country.

The noise of construction continued long into the night, and started again in the early hours of the morning. It didn't help that our room was below the rooftop restaurant either. I could hear talking, and chairs being dragged across the floor for much of the night. I wish I'd read the reviews of the hotel before booking.

Breakfast wasn't any better than the room. The only food on offer was a sponge-like loaf, and some rubber that looked like cheese. We ate a little, drank something that may once have been orange juice in a former life, and headed to the Acropolis.

Greece is another of those countries that is filled with amazing ancient history, and plenty of buildings that I wanted to see. Even though we were sticking to Athens, we weren't short on sights. The Parthenon, despite the damage due to war and theft, is an impressive building that is a brilliant example of the ancient world. It was just a shame that it was surrounded by scaffolding.

Next to this and the temple of Nike had been a museum; but it closed two years earlier. The new one to replace it was not yet open either, which meant there were artefacts we couldn't see.

We were herded like cattle around the site by their staff so that no one place was overly congested with tourists. When we left we continued on to Hadrian's Arch, and the Temple of the Olympian Zeus which we'd seen from the Acropolis. The archway was named after the same Roman Emperor as Hadrian's Wall in England. So whilst one was to keep the Picts and early Britons out, the other was technically for letting people in.

An 'agora' is a Greek marketplace, and in Athens there are two historical ones. The first of these is the Ancient Agora which we found by pure luck: our sense of direction, or lack thereof, did not help in finding it at all. At one end there is a small museum with examples of pottery, and other artefacts found at this site. They do actually allow you to photograph inside there as long as you do not use a flash. At the other end, raised above what was once a bustling marketplace, is the Temple of Hephaestus: the Greek God of technology, blacksmiths, craftsmen, artisans, and volcanoes.

The next marketplace is the Roman Agora, though it seemed like very little remained so we carried on walking straight passed it to Hadrian's Library. Unfortunately there's very little of the library left as well; but we thought it worth a few photographs.

To end the day we took a few trains to get to the port of Piraeus to visit the naval museum. On the last of these trains, James felt a hand reaching into his pocket. He slammed his hand down, and looked around but couldn't see who had tried to pick his pocket on this busy train. It's fortunate we both keep money in concealed zip pockets.

We had no map of this area, and could only wander around in search of the museum. It seemed likely a naval museum would be along the coastline, and maybe in a former dry-dock if they'd got boats. It was getting late and eventually we had to give up. The journey had been a waste of time.

Back in Athens we ate in a restaurant near to the Acropolis. James ordered a side-serving of salad with his meal, though this never arrived. This didn't stop them from trying to charge him for it.

"You've charged me for a salad"

"You ordered salad, no?"

"Yes, but I never got it!"

The exchange continued for awhile until the waiter disappeared. When he returned he admitted his mistake, and changed the bill accordingly. It felt like this trip was harder work than it should have been.

That night I went onto the roof of the hotel with my camera, and sat trying to get some nighttime shots of the city and the Acropolis. I hadn't thought to take a tripod with me though so it was difficult, and resulted in some terrible photos; but it was nice to see the Parthenon lit up.

Our final day of travelling around Europe had arrived. We still had no map to direct us; but we found our way to the Athens Military Museum. The entry was free, and they even allowed photography inside as long as we didn't use a flash.

Each floor covered a different era of Greek warfare with exhibits we could linger over with an unusual abundance of time. After two weeks of dashing from one sight to the next it seemed unheard of.

This trip had covered eight cities, and spanned three countries. The experience made us appreciate the value of a single currency: we did not have to worry about changing currencies as we changed countries, we could just continue using what we had. Moving between the countries in the EU was easy as well. Of course, it also helped us to appreciate the need for maps.

Perhaps these experiences of Europe would help in our plan to see Australia.

7: Australia

Over a year of planning, and we were finally on our way to the other side of the world: the land down under. Despite all this planning we hadn't known about the need for an Australian visa; but was able to pay for it at the airport in the UK when checking in for our flight. This sort of surprise would have been avoidable by having gone to the Government website to check travel advice whilst making the plans.

There was no option for us to fly from England to Australia direct: we had to stop somewhere for the plane to at least refuel. Our first flight was to Hong Kong, and during this I found amusement in being asked which of the two meal options I'd like when there was only one option they still had - it seemed pointless asking. It's just one of those strange things about air travel.

Upon arrival in Hong Kong we had to go through temperature checks along with the usual procedures. This test was to ensure no passengers were infected with the H1N1 virus that had been a pandemic and at this time was only just starting to die out.

I don't know why; but security and checks like this

always make me think "what if I get stopped?". Of course there'd be no reason for this though. I think it's one of those things every traveller wonders at some point; particularly when going through airport security. This would lead into a story for another time though.

The only memorable moment in this airport was when the owner of the Fook Ming Tong Tea Shop 'told me off' for photographing their sign.

On the second flight we encountered some extreme turbulence as we approached a thunderstorm near Melbourne. The timing was unfortunate as we'd only just been served food. As the seatbelt lights came on there was a sudden jolt. My tray leapt up into the air and landed on James' table, whilst his leapt up and was heading towards the aisle. He caught it just in time. The storm delayed our landing by fifty minutes, and left stomachs unsettled.

In Australia, biosecurity is a big deal: they have sniffer dogs looking for food, and they'll ask questions about what food you have on you. I'd got some sealed food I'd not eaten during the flight in my pocket, and decided I should bin it before reaching security. Better to be safe than sorry.

On the way out of the Melbourne airport one of the employees asked where we were staying, and their response was to say "It's haunted there, have a nice time". Thanks for that!

It's a good job I don't believe in the supernatural. I later heard that the place was once a hospital which was why locals had attached ghost stories to it.

The taxi driver wasn't the best either, not because

his driving was erratic; but because he had no idea where the road for our hotel was, and tried to convince us we'd gotten the address wrong. I'd lost count of how many hours I'd been awake for, but I knew it was over twenty four: I really didn't need for us to be arguing with a taxi driver on whether or not our hotel existed. We eventually got him to believe us, but when we got there we had to help him check the numbers on the buildings.

In the hotel they handed us the key cards for the twin room, but we found they didn't work. It took two trips to reception before we could finally get in, but the bad luck didn't stop there: one of the blinds in the room fell down whilst I was closing it, and we had to be moved to a different room. All I wanted was to sleep. Was this entire trip going to be filled with more challenges?

Six hours of sleep later, I was awoken by heavy rain. I gazed out of the window at the houses that surrounded the hotel and realised it looked very much like England. The rain probably helped. Had settlers missed their home this much?

A few blocks away from the hotel, we took a train to Flinders Street station in the centre of Melbourne. From a hotel near to the station we joined a tour group that were on their way to see little penguins on Phillip Island.

The first stop on this tour was the Australian Garden: one of the three places that make up the Royal Botanical Gardens in Melbourne. It was designed by an artist to symbolise Australia and I think that is why I didn't enjoy it: this was more of a concept and less about nature.

We travelled farther along George Bass Road onto Phillip Island; first visiting a chocolate factory, and then a koala sanctuary where they have boardwalks high in the trees for tourists to get closer to the wildlife. Of everywhere I'd been to up until this point, I found getting to photograph koalas up close to be one of the best wildlife photography experiences. Of course though, I'd not yet been on a safari.

Our final destination was The Nobbies: a part of the Phillip Island coast which overlooks the Bass Strait. Although it's home to one of their largest seal colonies we were there to see the little penguins. They're quite elusive birds: hiding under boardwalks, and in man-made burrows.

As night fell, we finished with what is coined as 'the penguin parade'. It's a place where little penguins march ashore in rafts to go inland to their burrows. All photography during this event is forbidden due to people having ignored the rule of no flash photography in previous years.

We opted for the 'plus' option for this tour as it'd get us closer to the penguins. It's true we hadn't realised at the time we wouldn't be able to use our cameras; but it was still nice to be closer to them.

As we watched the penguins waddle ashore we were treated to a light show from a thunderstorm out at sea. It was cooling the air off, and that was probably the only thing that stopped me from falling asleep before making it back to the hotel.

The second day was drier; but we had no idea what to do so hopped on a free tourism bus that took us around the sights. Once we'd seen what we could of the city and had been up to a viewpoint, we collected our luggage on our way to the airport for the red-eye flight to Darwin.

Even after a few years of travel I'd not yet mastered the art of sleeping on aircraft. I was annoyingly awake for the entire journey, and was exhausted when we arrived at the hotel. As we couldn't check-in until 05:00 we thought it'd be a good idea to wander around outside to find somewhere for breakfast.

We had two hours until sunrise, yet the humidity was unbelievable. It wasn't a good sign of how warm it'd be by midday. Breakfast however was not an option: the hotel was in the middle of a new development with most buildings still empty.

To save money and time we'd planned for our flights to be mostly overnight: fewer hotels would be needed. It wasn't the best of ideas.

The first stop of the day was Fogg Dam; a place named after John Fogg. It was built by the Americans in a failed attempt at growing rice; but in more recent years it has become a nature reserve.

We were told a rogue crocodile had been spotted in the rice field recently, and we would have to be cautious of where we walked in case the croc was nearby. It seemed they weren't just saying that for the tourists either -there were in fact a number of traps set amongst the tall grass and lotus flowers. Seeing us getting close to the lotus flowers and the swampy area made the guide incredibly nervous. I guess he feared they'd get a bad review if anyone went home missing an arm or a leg.

On our way to the Adelaide River we stopped very briefly when we passed a small, black snake. Apparently it's quite a venomous one so we weren't allowed off the coach to see it closer. Not even in the country for a week and we'd seen our first dangerous animal. I guess our luck isn't all that bad.

At the Adelaide River we went on what they call the 'Jumping Crocodile' tour: a boat ride along the river in search of crocodiles. Bogart was the only male crocodile we saw, and this section of the river was his territory. The others here were females, and were teased out of the water in impressive jumps with the offer of an easy meal from the guides. To be clear, the guides weren't offering up the tourists: we had to keep arms inside the boat whilst bits of fresh meat were dangled overboard.

After lunch we headed into Litchfield Park to see the waterfalls. The first of these was Wangi Falls where usually it's possible to swim. This time it wasn't safe for swimmers due to the recent rains - they couldn't be sure if flood waters had brought crocodiles into the area. So, lots of rain is good for pictures of waterfalls; but not so good for swimming.

In the trees there were many bats sleeping, undisturbed by the roaring water and chattering tourists. Golden orb-weaver spiders were spinning their webs between branches. Maybe we couldn't swim here, but there was plenty to see by taking the time to look.

At Florence Falls where we were finally allowed to swim in the crystal clear waters. A towel wasn't really necessary as the hot, humid air soon dried me off when it was time to move on.

Back in Darwin we finally checked into the hotel and found what we'd booked was a two-bedroom apartment with en-suite and main bathrooms, a lounge, and a kitchen. Cooking our own food here could have been an option; but we were too tired and jet-lagged to do so.

We thought that at 20:00 it'd be cooler, but the humidity was still over ninety percent. It felt like walking through a steam room until we found an air conditioned fast-food place. It was a chain I recognised from back home, but I'd never eaten there before. It seemed like a good idea to ask the lady serving us what some of the dishes were like. That didn't help as it turned out she was a vegan working in a chicken restaurant known for their stock having lived in harsh conditions.

Our original plan for day two in Darwin was to look around the city ourselves. After experiencing the heat we decided it'd be nicer to book a tour in an air-conditioned coach. This tour was actually quite informative as we learnt that the city was briefly named Palmerston, and was heavily bombed during the second world war.

We stopped at the old Gaol which has been closed for many years. The interior of the prison is split into separate buildings which makes it look like the prison camp out of 'The Great Escape'. Or at least in my mind it did.

As we were guided around, we were told a story of

the last people to be hung there, and the chain of events that led to it. The story goes that a couple of Europeans had a road accident that resulted in a death. Instead of reporting it they fled the scene, and committed a murder to steal a taxi and escape. The investigating officer concluded the initial offence was an accident and they would have been let off for it; but because of the events that followed they got the rope.

At the Darwin Museum the main exhibit was 'Sweetheart': a famously big crocodile that died after being given tranquillisers and drowned. Other exhibits included aboriginal art, and a section about cyclone Tracy that devastated Darwin in 1974. We learnt far more about Darwin than we expected.

The final stop of this tour was in the Darwin National Park. It was a warm, sunny day, yet we could see that the free-to-use barbecue sites were all empty. The park was deserted. The cause? A plague of biting and stinging insects that would feast on anyone who dared go there; such as unwitting tourists. It's one of those places where local knowledge goes a long way.

Back in the city the sun had already started to set by the time we'd found somewhere to eat. The service in this pub was so bad that the bill arrived after thirty minutes, and before our food. The waitress was shocked we hadn't yet eaten, but then told us steak takes thirty-five minutes to cook so we should be patient. We'd not even asked!

Another thirty minutes passed and our meals finally arrived. My steak was the oddest one I'd ever seen. On the top it was like charcoal, but was only lukewarm. On the underside it was rare and cold.

That night we didn't have a hotel booked as we thought we could sleep on the plane to Cairns. We'd got some time until we needed to be at the airport so we thought that perhaps booking the room for another night to ensure some sleep wouldn't be a bad idea. Sadly the New Zealand 'All Blacks' rugby team had just arrived and fully booked the hotel.

Accepting we'd likely get no sleep, we got to the airport early and took two-hour shifts to keep an eye on the luggage whilst the other attempted to nap.

We arrived in Cairns in the early hours of the morning, had breakfast, and headed to the Skyrail: a series of cable cars that would take us through the rainforest to Kuranda. On the way there are two stations with boardwalks. Most of the support poles for the boardwalk had orb-weaver spiders spinning giant webs. I decided it'd be good to get some close-ups of these spiders so I hung over the railings of the boardwalk to get closer. Of course, I was careful that my camera was secure and wouldn't become a victim of the long drop below.

Whilst I worked on photographing them James asked a ranger if these spiders were dangerous. He told us they weren't: a relief; but then after a dramatic pause he told us that they give a really painful bite. It seems a lot of animals in Australia will hurt, maim, or kill.

Once in Kuranda there were two main things to see: a koala sanctuary, and a bird sanctuary where a single ticket can be used for both. Whilst there we came across the opportunity to hold a koala, and no longer being one to miss an experience I thought I may as well. Their fur is incredibly soft, yet their claws are very sharp; perfect for climbing trees.

For the return to Cairns we used the Scenic Railway which passes Barron Falls. With our return to the city we encountered intermittent torrential downpours. The tropical heat, even that late in the afternoon, quickly dried us off after each shower.

Next morning was our first day with a scuba diving school. This was something I'd never considered doing before I'd started to travel. I'd never been anywhere where it'd felt it could be useful or a necessity. Being so close to the Great Barrier Reef is what we felt made it worthwhile. Neither of us had any idea what to expect; but at least it would be a few days without another flight.

The lessons started with a video, and a number of quizzes. We were told how fun scuba is; but also how dangerous it can be - decompression sickness being a particular example. We learnt about a diver named 'Claudio' who'd been overly confident about his diving ability and wouldn't listen to Scuba Steve, our instructor. Between the mask squeeze and the other calamities I found it difficult to believe it was a real person, but it was entertaining and educational.

Another of his students had suffered from nitrogen narcosis: an intoxicated-like effect caused by nitrogen under pressure; usually when diving below around one hundred feet. We were told how he'd been taking her out on a lesson and she'd taken the regulator from her mouth, and started waving it through the water. Baffled by her behaviour he'd taken the regulator from her hand, and put it back in her mouth. A few minutes later she did it again, and he decided to end the dive.

Back on the surface he asked her, "what were you doing?!"

"It looked like the fishes couldn't breathe"

Nitrogen narcosis impedes rational thought which is why it can be so dangerous:it's something we needed to recognise the symptoms of. This actually sounds dangerous!

We then proceeded to the swimming pool to continue the lessons, and to prove we could swim. The lessons went well for the most part. Though I wondered how I'd cope on the open water as I found I had problems equalising ear pressure on the descent.

After our first day of lessons we paid to attend a talk about the barrier reef. It covered things like how the different animals behave, and which ones are venomous. At the talk we were also told there was only a 10% chance we would be going out on the boat due to an inbound cyclone. Many tours were already being cancelled. It was frustrating to say the least.

On the second day of lessons we worked on some of the harder skills, and finished with a final exam. We were now ready for the reef; weather permitting.

That evening we decided to cook our own meal using what we'd bought from the supermarket a couple of days before. There was just one problem: the kitchen only had a microwave - there was no oven. If you've ever tried to boil vegetables in a low-powered microwave, or tried to cook chicken in one then you'll know how this ended.

It failed. Paying attention to what kitchen facilities are available really does help.

Scuba Steve was wide-eyed, awake, and lively when he collected us in the early hours of the morning. It seemed like he was permanently suffering from nitrogen narcosis, or must really love scuba diving.

Onboard the boat, we were briefed by the crew. Part of this message was that in order to conserve water we could only use the cold showers once per day, and for no more than three minutes. Cold showers? Sure, quick is a good thing!

We were then assigned to living quarters. When I say living quarters, what I actually mean is a room below deck that was not much bigger than the size of a bunk bed. The room was that small there wasn't even enough space for the door to fully open into it. Each room had a two person occupancy, but I don't think it was possible for two people to stand in the room at the same time. It was basically a large cupboard for keeping people in.

Three hours later we arrived at the Great Barrier Reef. Due to the cyclone we were one of only a few boats that had risked going out. Were we crazy? Maybe.

James said he's usually fine on boats, but had taken seasickness tablets just in case. They hadn't helped in this chop, and he was suffering: he spent most of the day leaning over the side of the boat. He couldn't risk diving like that.

When I entered the water for my first dive the waves were crashing around me. I'd never swam in the open water like this before, and unintentionally swallowed seawater. It was foul, and was making it difficult to swallow for equalising pressure in my ears on the descent. Unable to equalise I had to resurface and abandon the dive.

Missing this dive meant I couldn't join in on any of the other dives and had lost my chance to become PADI certified. James, still feeling ill, didn't make the dive either so was in the same boat, so to speak. Things on this trip really weren't going to plan.

In the afternoon after this failure I returned to the water wearing just the stinger suit so I could go snorkelling by myself. Well, almost by myself: there were jellyfish, a shark, and a shoal of fish around me. The stinger suit was there to offer some protection from the deadly irukandji.

Next day, the boat rocked even more intensely by waves crashing against it. It was fortunate that anything not in use on the boat was tied down. Though with the ferocity of the waves, some things were still shaken loose during the navigation back to land.

That night I slept on land without the sound of water against a hull, or the rocking of a boat. It almost seemed strange; but was peaceful.

We had one last morning in Cairns before we'd need to move on once more. We'd heard about a wildlife dome above the casino so we thought we'd check it out. This was just a short walk along the Esplanade to get there - you can't walk on the actual beach due to saltwater crocodiles in the area.

I stopped to take a picture on our way there and

suddenly felt a pain in my leg. I looked down and found a green ant had crawled up my leg and had sunk its pincers into my calf. The Esplanade decking was covered in them. It's unbelievable what fauna Australia has.

In the afternoon we flew to Sydney where once again we found a taxi driver didn't believe us when we told him our destination. He checked his satnav, and sure enough it agreed with us that the road existed. He also charged us an extra AU$12.50 for a toll road we could see cost him less than AU$5. We didn't feel like questioning this, even though it's something to watch out for, so let it be.

To start off our exploration of Sydney we had another organised tour. This one took us through the city, and over the harbour bridge. Organised tours were starting to feel laborious - it felt like we were spending the most time in what to us were the wrong places.

Most of the group didn't see the point in stopping in the small town of Leura. It had been founded by British settlers wanting to escape the heat of Sydney. It is known as the 'Garden Village' as when the settlers arrived they also brought with them a lot of English flora which is evident as you look around. It seemed like this stop was just to delay our arrival at Katoomba for some food.

Their all-you-can-eat buffet lunch was on a revolving platform which made it a bit disorientating when going to and from the buffet: your seat and table wouldn't be where you'd left them. It did mean that diners each took it in turns to be closest to the window with the view though.

From the restaurant we took a 'mine cart' down a steep track whilst the Raiders of the Lost Ark overture played in the background. It was overly commercialised, but at the end of this track was a viewing platform for the 'Three Sisters' rock formation. They accompanied this with a folktale: their way of adding interest to a landmark to make a living.

Instead of returning direct to the city afterwards, we were taken to a ferry crossing where a catamaran was waiting to take us the rest of the way. It took us under the harbour bridge, and stopped in Circular Quay next to the opera house. From there we walked around the market at The Rocks, and looked for a restaurant that would serve a decent steak.

Our second day in Sydney was our day to climb the Sydney Harbour Bridge. Yes, climb it. There was a company we'd booked through to do this. All they required was for us to sign a waiver, be breathalysed, put on a one-size-fits-all overall, and to remove our watches, and everything from our pockets. Those of us with glasses had to have them tied on as well.

Before going out onto the bridge we had to go through a room practicing climbing ladders and crossing walkways whilst attached to the railings with a safety line.

On the actual bridge we started underneath the road and went through an area they call 'the squeeze' which is a narrow passageway where you have to duck and climb to get through the pylon. This takes you onto mesh walkways to the ladders that lead up through the road surface and onto the outer shell of the bridge. Once there it is a steady walk over the arch to the summit.

As you're not allowed to take your own cameras on the bridge, they take your photo at the top so they can sell it to you at the bottom for a hefty fee. It wasn't a very well taken photograph, but I thought it worth the purchase this time.

In the afternoon we visited the Sydney Opera House for one of their guided tours. It felt that a lot of the tour was just pre-produced video. We could see inside a couple of the rooms; but couldn't take photographs due to the copyright of the stage dressings. I actually preferred walking around the adjacent botanical gardens.

Australia hadn't been what we'd expected. It had certainly been an experience with the good outweighing the bad. We'd somehow still managed to see, and do most of what we'd wanted to. Maybe our planning hadn't been as bad as we'd thought.

8: New Zealand

Our flight leaving Sydney was delayed first by two passengers being removed from the flight and having to wait for their luggage to be removed, and then by needing to run calibration tests. Tight connections are one of the most stressful experiences you can have when travelling. It's amazing we hadn't learnt our lesson from travelling around Europe; but here we were again preparing to run across an airport.

Our connecting flight out of Christchurch was a rush, but we made it just in time and arrived safely in Queenstown. In the evening we ate outside at a restaurant, and whilst waiting for our food I spotted a couple of people I recognised from our Philip Island tour in Melbourne almost two weeks ago. It's strange to be in a foreign country and to actually see someone you recognise from another country. It wasn't the last time I'd experience that either. Years later I would bump into a runner in Malawi and Amsterdam that I'd first met in Nepal.

Overnight I could feel the rumbles of a

thunderstorm passing overhead. If I hadn't been so exhausted I would have watched it, and perhaps photographed it; but sleep felt more welcoming.

When morning came we boarded a coach headed for Milford Sound. It's a famous fiord that Rudyard Kipling is attributed to having described as the 'Eighth Wonder of the World'. It sounded worth the long journey which I spent gazing out of the window at the passing countryside. A lot of it could easily have been Wales; there's a lot of sheep farming here too.

After ninety minutes the driver took a phone call, which was followed by an announcement that the trip had been cancelled due to a tree blocking the road to Milford Sound. It seemed crazy that a tree could stop a tour going ahead. We even irrationally thought that with the number of people on the coach we could move it ourselves. Of course though we had no idea what the road or the tree would be like. We were just disappointed we couldn't continue.

We didn't turn around straight away, we carried on to Te Anau. In the visitor centre there they had a sign which read 'Milford Road is' followed by a magnetic sign saying 'closed'. This suggests it happens often enough for them to require these notifications. As there's only one road it felt that it would make sense for them to have a way of quickly maintaining the route to one of the biggest tourist attractions on the south island.

Two hours later we were back in Queenstown, and were told that it would take a few days to clear the road. Too late for us.

Filled with disappointment, we decided on walking

to the Kiwi Wildlife Reserve - maybe the day was still salvageable. The entry fee was a little high, but the price of the ticket goes back into the conservation of kiwis and other endangered birds- so worth it.

Their conservation efforts have allowed the birds to live as though they were still in the wild but with night and day cycles reversed so that these birds can be seen whilst it is day for us. Of all the animals we could have seen in New Zealand, I was glad we'd had the opportunity to see these.

In the morning we had another coach to catch - this time we were a little more hopeful of reaching our destination as we were on the road to Christchurch via Mount Cook. Though we knew it wasn't going to go entirely to plan as we were told from the start we wouldn't get to see the mountain due to the heavy rain. Another plan gone awry. Still, I hoped that maybe the weather would improve by the time we got there. I wasn't ready to give up hope.

After a brief pause at a fruit shop we passed the man-made Lake Dunstan, and the Lindis Pass. The latter of these reminded me of The Lord of the Rings movies: rolling hills which I could picture the Riders of Rohan charging down. If only we'd booked a Lord of the Rings themed tour. I'd actually taken a replica of the One Ring with me, intending to use it for some photography; but never found the right time.

We next stopped in the small village of Omarama. They have an antiques shop that at the time had props from Hercules, Xena, and Cleopatra 2525 - all of which were produced in New Zealand. There wasn't much else other than information about a big sheep called Shrek that hid in caves. Sounds more like an ogre to me.

We stopped briefly at Peter's Lookout to see the milky blue waters of Lake Pukaki. The wind was so strong there that we couldn't really leave the coach for long so drove on to the Hermitage for dinner. This entire section of the journey from the lake to the Hermitage should have been in sight of Mount Cook; but all we could see was cloud.

Whilst in the restaurant we asked one of the waiters if they could point out Mount Cook to us. The waiter pointed out two clouds, asked if we could see them, and then told us Mount Cook was between them: behind the clouds. Another plan had been foiled by the weather.

Our chance to see Mount Cook had passed, and we continued on to Christchurch via Lake Tekapo, and the Church of the Good Shepherd. This final section felt like it lasted forever with nothing much to see but passing fields. In Christchurch we were the last to be dropped off at a hotel, after them attempting to drop us off at the wrong one first.

We had just one morning to explore Christchurch, and that seemed to be all we needed. We walked around the botanical gardens, which could easily have been an English park lifted straight out of a city. A year after this visit the city was devastated by an earthquake that left most of this area cordoned off for several years afterwards. If we were ever to return we could be certain that change would be noticeable.

The flight from Christchurch to Wellington was a turbulent one: a sign that the bad weather we'd experienced thus far was not yet over. We landed with just enough time for us to reach our connecting flight to Taupo as they were boarding.

This plane in contrast was far smaller: a Beach 1990, and capable of seating around twelve people. This aircraft was so small that they moved us around to balance the plane. The cockpit door was left open so the pilot could shout back to us when he needed to.

The airport in Taupo is incredibly small too. There was one single room, smaller than the duty free shop at Heathrow, and used as both arrivals and departures.

We stood around waiting in the airport for our baggage; but there was no sign of it. Eventually we thought we'd wander outside to see if there were any signs of life. All we could see was a trailer that had been left at the side of the building; but there, alone on the trailer, were our suitcases.

One long taxi ride later we arrived at our accommodation for the evening; but found it a struggle to find anywhere to eat. It seemed we were in the middle of a residential area with almost no restaurants or stores other than a bar.

When we returned to the hotel after a meal, we got a call from the adventure company we'd be doing the 'Tongariro Alpine Crossing' with. The call was to convince us that the tour needed to be cancelled due to extreme weather concerns.

After everything we'd missed on the islands we selfishly didn't want our final tour to be cancelled too.

There was a chance though, perhaps with an alternative route, and if the weather improved by breakfast time we might just get to do it.

Next morning we were driven to the Tongariro National Park. It looked like in better weather it would be pleasant, and relatively easy to do any of the walks. They do however say to expect the unexpected, and in our case, New Zealand wanted to throw everything it could at us.

Preparation for the crossing was basic. They checked to make sure we had walking boots, and suitable clothes for keeping us warm and dry. There have been tourists that have died of hypothermia doing this crossing; so this was important. The adventure company would provide a packed lunch for us.

The hike started on boardwalks which kept us off the volcanic, rocky surface. It's scattered with small greenery and trickles of water making it look like moorland. After about three kilometres is the ascent known as the Devil's Staircase: it's supposed to be a slow, two kilometre climb up; but we left our guide behind, and ascended them quicker than he was used to.

As we approached the top of the Devil's Staircase there were groups of people passing us in the opposite direction. They'd decided it was too risky to continue, and had abandoned their attempts to cross. A Channel 3 News reporter spoke to our guide, and recommended we turn back before the weather worsened - it wasn't safe to climb with the approaching weather. The reporter had been up near the south crater, and hadn't been able to proceed any further. It's times like these that it's recommended that you don't risk the crossing. If we ran into any trouble on the mountain there'd be no rescue in these conditions. Our guide turned to look at us, and as the rain started to fall we told him we'd push on if he was happy to.

At the top of the stairs are the final toilets of the trek, we weren't told this at the time; but we used them as shelter to put on our waterproof clothing, gaiters, gloves, and other warm clothes. We'd already started to get damp, so this was an important break to prevent issues later.

When we reached Mount Ngāuruhoe, the mountain that had doubled as Mount Doom in Peter Jackson's Lord of the Rings films, we had a choice to make. Climb this first and risk not getting to climb Mount Tongariro if the conditions worsened, or climb this after if there was time. We decided it best to continue with the crossing.

As we started to climb to the south crater we encountered snow and ice; but this turned to hail at the crater. The view from there wasn't great: we had about five metres of visibility at best. It had become understandable why every other group had turned back at this point: the weather was getting far worse, and the wind was picking up speed.

It's likely that we were crazy to do so; but we decided to continue. We'd come this far and didn't want some 'bad weather' to beat us. After all, there's no such thing as bad weather, right?

More time passed, and we started to trek across a

plateau that didn't seem too bad - the weather had settled a little and was just sleet by this point. It was a bizarre landscape though; it looked like it would have been better placed on an alien world. There was no sign of animal life: just ash, rock, small tufts of grass, and yellow patches that looked to be rich in sulphur.

Some of the climbs were incredibly hard work and precarious. Our guide was the sort who didn't mind taking risks, and going off-trail. At some points on the climb after the south crater the only way across was to stretch out and jump, grabbing on to rocks wherever possible to maintain balance. We knew that if we missed a step we'd slide down the mountainside and likely wouldn't stop before reaching the bottom. It might not sound too bad; but this wasn't a hill, it was a mountain, and sliding down through ash and rock would have a serious conclusion. What am I doing here? I thought to myself. This wasn't the sort of thing I'd usually do. It seemed likely we weren't even taking the normal path up.

As lunchtime approached we descended a little through the snow and ice to a place called the Emerald Lakes. They are the site of explosion craters from volcanic activity, and get their name from the colouration they have from the minerals that have accumulated in them. The most noticeable thing at that moment was the smell of hydrogen sulphide. I could imagine that in good weather they would have looked incredible.

The rain continued but the wind had calmed a little which allowed us to sit inside a tent. It hadn't been put up with pegs and poles, it had just been thrown over us, and we sat on the edges to keep it in place. It was a short reprieve to eat and recover.

When our trek continued, every step we took was opposed by the wind making it difficult to keep our footing. Every dozen or so steps required us to catch the breath the wind was stealing from us.

Eventually we reached the summit. Or at least we thought we had until our guide caught up with us and pointed out there was a little more to do. Clambering over rocks we eventually reached the actual summit of Mount Tongariro. We looked around but couldn't see anything - the clouds were too thick. It felt like an achievement though: we'd reached the top when all others had turned back.

On the way back down our guide said he knew a shortcut; it did however turn out to be a particularly dangerous path. Time after time I was knee high in volcanic ash, and at one point managed to slide down the side of the mountain only to stop myself by grabbing hold of a rock before a long drop off. After I'd regained my footing, James then slipped in the same place I had. He came sliding down the scree the same way I had; but before I could react he came crashing into me - taking my legs out from under me. We recovered quickly and climbed back up to the guide.

Our guide was used to walking on this mountain every day, but visibility was so poor that he occasionally needed to ascend a little to get his bearings. We made it back to the plateau; but we were welcomed by winds exceeding 120 kmph - at least they were according to our guide. He'd encountered winds that were confirmed as around 100 kmph days before, and he'd said this felt far stronger, estimating what he thought it was.

It seemed dubious that it could really be that strong as on the Beaufort scale it'd be rated as 'hurricane force'. Whether I believed it or not, there were times when I planted my feet firmly on the floor to brace for the wind; but was still blown backwards - creating gouges in the soft floor from my feet. Even when the wind wasn't blowing us backwards it was frequently halting progress or slowing us considerably.

It felt like a lifetime had passed whilst crossing that plateau, and I wondered frequently why I was doing it. I'd never been an outdoors-type person, even if I did now enjoy taking photographs of it; but there I was in conditions far worse than I would ever consider going out in. We were walking through what could supposedly be called a hurricane.

At the Devil's Staircase the wind and rain eased off. The last two kilometres of our nineteen kilometre walk gave us the chance to dry off as the cloud cover started to break. We'd missed climbing Mount Ngāuruhoe but we were thankful it was over, and we were in one piece. We'd lived to tell the tale of a partial crossing we should never have asked the guide to do.

Everyone we spoke to had said the conditions were too bad, and should have been impossible to climb; but our guide got us there, and back again. Thinking of how this place had doubled as Mordor, the place described as having an evil that does not sleep, it was like we'd not just awoken it; but called it names, and poked it in it's eye.

In recent years the laws have changed, and this

climb would no longer have taken place. In fact, you're no longer allowed to climb the mountains there either: only the crossing is allowed. Some of these changes are to respect local Māori beliefs, and some for safety.

Somewhere at the bottom of the crossing we came across a souvenir shop where we both bought t-shirts that said 'Tongariro Alpine Crossing - been there, conquered it'. We sure had; though the shop owner didn't believe we'd summited. Who cares though? We did it.

Back in Taupo we couldn't face waiting at the bus station for the next eight hours so checked back into the lodge for a few hours to rest, recover, and to dry hiking clothes. There wasn't time to sleep unfortunately.

Our bus out of Taupo was scheduled to arrive at 01:50 but didn't turn up until thirty-five minutes later. We were worried we'd somehow missed it, or had gone to the wrong place. It wasn't a pleasant wait in the cold night.

Hours passed by on our journey to Manukau City, and the unfortunate truth was that I'd been unable to sleep. By the time we'd taken the shuttle bus to the airport, and got breakfast I'd been awake for over twenty-four hours.

More hours passed, and we had lunch in the airport as well before heading through security for the first of our flights. The wait wasn't over: there had been a delay due to engine problems, and after over two hours had passed they handed out food vouchers to the waiting passengers. Knowing you're on an aircraft that's had engine problems isn't the most inspiring of thoughts.

Fortunately Europe had at least taught us to leave a

long stop-over in Melbourne before our flight to Hong Kong. I was so tired from two days without sleep during the flights that followed that I don't really remember it that well. When I got back home I had less than a week before I'd be off again to do the 'Three Peaks Challenge' over the Easter weekend. At least that would easier than Tongariro.

9: The Three Peaks of Great Britain

In the few short years I'd been travelling so far, I'd learnt to avoid saying "no" when an opportunity for a new experience arises. A colleague decided that for his stag party we'd be doing the Three Peaks challenge; but spread over three days instead of the traditional twenty four hours.

The weekend started with driving 420 miles north to the town of Fort William in Scotland. Our first peak would be the largest in the British Isles: Ben Nevis. We'd heard the weather reports saying that it would be under heavy snow so our first task upon arriving in Fort William was to find somewhere we could hire crampons from.

After visiting a number of places that had run out we were given details for a small company who might still have some left. The problem was that with the amount of snow on the mountain it wasn't really possible without the correct equipment which meant most places had hired all theirs out. This last company fortunately had enough crampons left for the seven of us.

When we got back to the hotel we made sure we had a rough idea how to fit the crampons to our walking boots: of course, the following day when we climbed the mountain we found we'd done it wrong. We'd also hired a guide for the day who met us in the morning.

The other guys had some experience from doing some minor peaks around England, but nothing this high over the previous weeks. Maybe I hadn't been able to join them on their adventures; but I'd had one of my own on Mount Tongariro. I wasn't going to be forgetting that anytime soon.

The start of the climb was easy and could have been done in normal hiking gear. When we reached the start of the snow we fitted the crampons: they're a little strange to walk in at first; but as we reached deeper and deeper snow it became more comfortable.

There were instances where it wasn't clear where the path was, and stepping off it meant I'd suddenly find myself knee-deep in snow. Our guide took this as an opportunity to teach a few basic skills for climbing mountains in the snow. The first one was an avalanche test.

He took his ice pick and dug out a deep square area in the snow. He then put more and more weight onto the snow to see how easily it'd break. If the snow broke easily then there'd be a real chance of an avalanche.

The reason this test works is because when the temperature warms slightly it will start to weaken the bonds between snowflakes on the top layer. As it freezes again it will not be as strong as it was previously so will not take as much weight. When snow falls on this weaker layer of ice it becomes a risk that the weight of the snow, or people walking on it, may then cause the sheet to move.

When our guide tried this, it broke. Easily. He shrugged his shoulders, "I've not seen that happen before". Then continued leading us onwards. Hang on a minute, it broke easily? Shouldn't we-

It hadn't bothered him, so maybe it shouldn't bother us so on we went. When he next stopped we were taught how to stop ourselves if we slipped in the snow. With crampons it's more difficult as you have to be careful they don't suddenly get a grip as that could break your leg from the force of suddenly stopping. It's amazing what you can learn on a trip.

The snow near the top was heavier, and the visibility changed frequently. One minute we were shrouded in an eerie fog, and the next we were squinting from the sun reflecting off the snow.

The climb does get harder near the top and it's wise to stick to the area marked out by chevrons due to the number of gullies that are not easily seen. I apparently almost walked off one of these when our guide got mixed up about where the 'hidden' gully was located. Apparently he'd fallen down it once before, and was saved only by his quick thinking and having an ice pick to stop himself.

Reaching the summit of Ben Nevis felt like an achievement, even though I'd climbed higher in worse conditions. This was a snowy adventure with friends.

We sat and ate snacks, drank some champagne

another group had shared with us, and after a few photographs we were ready to go back. The descent was far quicker; but more dangerous due to the increased likelihood of slipping.

To avoid an icy path we decided to take off the crampons, and slide down part of the mountain on our backs. On one of these slopes I was the first to go, and found myself buried up to the waist in snow. It somehow even made it into my shoes.

We celebrated our first mountain with a pub meal, and drove to Scafell Pike in the English county of Cumbria for our next overnight stay.

It was another cloudy, and damp morning. Before beginning the ascent it was a hike through the countryside, carefully crossing streams along the way.

Snow covered the path sooner than we'd expected. This time we didn't have crampons or a guide. We would have to rely on ourselves to get to the top, and so we decided we'd take the 'easier' trail which is a relatively gentle climb winding around the far side of the mountain. The more direct route through a gully would have been impossible without equipment we didn't have.

Wind and fog added to the deepening snow to make the climb harder and colder than Ben Nevis. There was one map between us all; but our group had drifted into two. With the fog we couldn't get too far ahead, but looking back we could see the murky outlines of the others not too far behind.

Except the outlines we could see were not the others from our group: they were further behind, and these were strangers. When we summited we had another five minutes to wait before the furious second half of the group arrived. They were not happy at all; but I think they realised it was unintentional.

There was a biting wind at the top, and any lengthy stay there would have been a bad idea. The descent was mostly uneventful, though we managed to take a wrong turn somewhere and found ourselves in a farmer's field. It was a slightly longer route, but a pleasant walk.

My feet had gotten wet on Ben Nevis and were now blistered after Scafell. I should have learnt my lesson from Berlin; but now I finally made a mental note to take blister plasters with me on trips with excessive walking planned.

In the afternoon we drove to the Snowdonia mountain range in Wales for our final mountain. It was raining when we arrived, and continued raining into the night.

I awoke to find the rain had not yet stopped. We realised that waterlogged fields would make the ascent of Mount Snowdon more difficult than usual; but went ahead with the attempt. In places the mud was so bad that I found it difficult to lift my feet - it was like the ground wanted to swallow them whole.

The higher we climbed, the stronger the wind got. After a while we thought it'd be a good idea to leave the path in search of some shelter. This was a mistake.

Off the track the wind was worse: it went from being gale force to one that was starting to remind me of the winds on Mount Tongariro. We were struggling to stay on our feet- some were even swept from their feet, and blown across the long grass into a wire fence. The rest of us clambered over the fence, and kept low whilst running for cover behind a rocky outcrop. Why am I doing this again? This isn't me.

In the relative safety of this shelter we discussed what to do next. Someone realised the wind would only get stronger as we continued to ascend. I didn't really want to quit now after braving the elements that long; but the majority of the group wanted to turn around. We had to stick together.

With the wind as it was, there was a severe drop in temperature. None of us wanted to move. It even drove one of our number to consider using the bivouac he'd packed to try and conserve body heat. Surely things weren't getting that serious, were they?

A lull in the wind was our signal to begin our descent. We tried to move; the wind was still strong enough to push us back. We had no choice but to return to shelter. What do we do now?!

It was no longer a question of whether we continued the climb; but a question of how we'd get off the mountain. An option was to take a different route down through a gully that seemed to be sheltered from the wind. We couldn't see from the map where we could go once descending that way - there was no choice but to fight the wind.

One by one we left the cover behind, kept low, and struggled through the wind back to the wire fence. With each step we were checking behind to make sure everyone was safe. Once over the fence we worked our way back down to below the level of the wind. It was a confusing mix of relief, and regret as we left the mountain behind us.

Mount Snowdon was meant to be the easiest of the three. It had however defeated us; but we left with a vow to return.

10: India

Pleasure isn't the only reason for travel; sometimes it's necessary for work also. It's not something I'd ever needed to do; but just months after doing the three peaks I was off on my third adventure of the year.

On the way to Chennai, the city formerly known as Madras, I got a connecting flight through Dubai airport. This was the most amazing airport I'd come across with polished faux marble floors, and expensive-looking furnishings. At least I assumed the marble was fake. Chennai airport on the other hand was the polar opposite: it looked half finished, or at least had seen better days.

I queued with two colleagues to go through immigration in a room that was missing some exterior walls. Whilst waiting, something small caught my eye, scurrying across the floor. It was gone so quickly I couldn't be sure if it was a reptile or a rat. Comparatively, this queue was so slow it would have done England proud.

Maybe slow queues is something we exported when the East India Trading Company invaded this part of what was once known as British India. It's a shame that we, along with other European nations, used to be obsessed on conquering and exploiting other countries.

A pre-booked taxi driver met us outside the airport, and led us through the humid air of monsoon season to an air-conditioned car. The hour-long drive reminded me very much of my arrival in Cairo: some buildings were made from pieces of wood and metal, and were incomplete; whilst others closest to the hotel in the Siruseri district were tall, and expensive-looking.

Everywhere we went we could hear car horns blaring. Apparently they're not used offensively: they're more of a general warning to other drivers that you're coming through. Another thing that was confusing was that they would flash their headlights to let people know they were going through instead of it meaning they were giving way as it would back home.

Rubbish littered the streets whilst cows and goats roamed freely with the traffic swerving to avoid the animals, pedestrians, and other cars. This could easily have been any of the other developing countries I'd visited, though having animals wander across the roads was a new one to me.

It was interesting to see auto-rickshaws on roads in their abundance. In Chennai I think it makes travel easier than a car.

The hotel was another flashback to Cairo: it was like a compound with armed guards and an angled mirror to check under the vehicle for explosives or people clinging to the underside. I imagine we were perfectly safe; but there's something a little unnerving about it the first time you see it.

Our driver was booked for the rest of the day, so after dropping off our bags we headed out to see some of the sights. The driver didn't speak much English so him describing what there was to see wasn't easy.

We stopped at 'The Bank' where they breed crocodiles for export to the rest of the world; but the day we were there was the one day of the week they're closed. Instead we carried on along the coastal road to Mahabalipuram.

This place is filled with temples, a relief called 'The Descent of the Ganges', and a massive boulder called 'Krishna's Butterball'. The relief was created to celebrate the victory of Hinduism over Buddhism and depicts Shiva fighting in the Mahabharata war.

We were of course approached by many people wanting to sell us some of their wares or their services as a guide. One of these decided that even though we'd said "no" to him he'd follow us around anyway, and tried to tell us about some of the places. Of course that meant he'd be demanding payment at some point.

The temples were great examples of the local historic architecture; but I was distracted away from them by my first encounter with a rhesus macaque. Monkeys!

I edged closer slowly whilst crouching, and started taking photo after photo. It was one of my colleagues that then pointed out to me that there were more macaques next to a rock, and one of them was young enough to not yet have grown fur.

When we finished, the driver asked if we'd like to see more, and pointed towards a beach. We were sleep deprived and felt it would be better to head back to the hotel instead of seeing a beach. What we'd not understood until it was too late was that he'd meant there were more impressive temples further along the coast.

Not researching before a trip, even a business trip, and not being able to understand the local language can mean missing out on sights worth seeing. Hopefully I wouldn't make that mistake again.

That evening the company we were in the country to see took us out for a meal. The restaurant was on a beach overlooking the Bay of Bengal, whilst a lightning storm lit up the night sky in the distance. We were told that this beach wasn't safe for swimming due to strong currents, and that the whole area had been devastated by the 2004 Indian ocean tsunami. In the intervening six years they had done a great job in rebuilding.

With the meal I thought the proper thing to do in India would be to have a cup of tea with it, but I hadn't realised that when served with milk it would be boiled instead of being pasteurised. It tasted very different, and I couldn't drink it. The food however was amazing: a mixture of local dishes, which were mostly curry. Some were even too spicy for our hosts.

On our way back to the hotel it started to rain with such ferocity that rain droplets were bouncing back up off the road by at least half a metre. It was like driving through a stream with water showering the car from both directions. As quickly as the rain had started, it passed, at least for a while. It reminded me of 'April Showers' back home. This is what monsoon season was like.

Our first full day in Chennai was the first time we witnessed an accident. With the driving the way it was, it had to happen sooner or later. We sat waiting in the queue for the tollbooth as a truck carrying wooden poles pulled up alongside us. Moments later a bigger truck came crashing into it from behind and shunted it passed the tollbooth window.

That in itself was shocking to us; but what was even more shocking was that nobody reacted to it. The driver of the front vehicle passed some money to a passenger in the back of the truck who handed it over to the attendant and then drove off as if nothing had happened.

It's amazing how different cultures perceive things differently. To me this was crazy; but to them it was everyday life.

Over the days that followed we spent most of our time with the company we were there to meet, and our spare time was taken up by them taking us out for meals. Every day was a different experience, but each day's breakfast was the same. Having curry for breakfast, lunch, and dinner felt excessive, though apparently the reason for spicy food is that it makes them sweat. Sweat helps them to stay cool in the often oppressive heat.

Not all lunches were curry: one day they brought a pizza to the office for us, and on another day we got to eat in the cafeteria with their employees. Other variations in mealtime included one of our hosts asking if they could have their picture taken with me. Apparently, despite wearing a Superman t-shirt, they thought I looked like Peter Parker - the alter-ego of Marvel's Spider-man. It seemed they were referring to Tobey Maguire's Peter Parker.

It was an unusual week, but by the end of it I found myself hoping that I would one day get to return to explore the country in more detail.

11: Ecuador and the Galapagos Islands

When visiting Australia's northern territory, we'd visited the city of Darwin - named after the famous English naturalist. Charles Darwin's contributions to the theory of evolution and our understanding of nature hadn't come from just sitting around the English countryside. His studies had taken him and the HMS Beagle on a voyage bound for the Americas.

They visited a series of geologically new islands which led him to realise that environmental conditions had an effect on the species that lived there. These islands were the Galápagos Islands.

I'd seen David Attenborough talk about these islands in documentaries, and it was somewhere I very much wanted to go one day. We had however heard that they'd further limit the number of tourists allowed each year to protect them. James was keen to visit, and knew his friend Andy would be too. So that was it, our next destination had been decided: it would be our first trip dedicated to seeing wildlife.

The journey to Ecuador was long with many stops:

one of them at Bonaire, a small Dutch principality in the Caribbean. We landed in the middle of the night at an airport which didn't seem big enough for the plane we were on. Everywhere was pitch black except for the aircraft; it looked eerie and completely out of place.

When we eventually arrived in Quito we wondered if we'd be okay at immigration when we saw there was a restriction on what you could bring into the country. Between the three of us we had enough camera and other electrical equipment on us to open a small shop. Of course that isn't what we were doing and fortunately customs were fine with it being for personal use.

The tour company met us at the airport, and took us to the hotel. Along the way we were told that they'd had a lot of rain over the past few days. My first thought was:we're British, we're used to that. We were then told that the rainwater that had washed down the side of the volcano was plentiful enough to have flooded the tunnel we were driving through. Drivers at the time had to abandon their cars, and swim for safety. Okay, that might be a little worse.

Our tour started with the Basilica of the National Vow: the largest neo-Gothic church in all of the Americas. We didn't get the opportunity to look inside; but from the outside I could see that although it looked a lot like British cathedrals, it wasn't like other cathedrals. Where it differed was in the detail.It had gargoyles and grotesques like many others; but the ones here were designed to resemble local animals such as the condor.

Our next stop was at a charity that helps locals learn important skills; but it was closed. Instead we were led back to the coach and driven through some areas of the city our guide described as being unsafe. I wondered if it was true, or some sort of classist prejudice. Back home there'd be areas we'd think of as 'rough'; but are they actually any more dangerous? Or is that white male privilege being able to think they're okay? Our views of the world are often based upon the version of the world we grow up in; trips like these help in learning other perspectives.

As it started to rain we were taken to a church of San Francesco. The interior of this one was amazing, and it reminded me of the Catholic churches we'd visited in Peru. Here they allowed photography inside so I could attempt to capture the amazing detail of the gilded altar.

We were about to visit a Jesuit Church; but our guide quickly changed direction and led us into a nearby library. She told us she'd spotted pickpockets, and wanted to wait until they'd passed.

Our city tour ended with a quick visit to the Presidential Palace. We didn't get to go in, but there was a photo opportunity with the Palace Guards. The way they stood motionless on plinths reminded me of the Grenadier guards in front of Buckingham Palace in England.

That evening we decided to explore a little to see where we could find to eat. We wandered for about an hour and eventually found a Tex-Mex place that seemed reasonable. From the looks of it I would have guessed it was a place for the locals rather than tourists as the people there did not speak any English. We ordered quite a bit of food between us; but even with a generous tip it came to very little.

It rained throughout the night, and was now slowing for our morning drive up into the Andean mountains. It'd been a few years since I'd last been in this range, and was glad to be back. If I'd travelled the world in a single trip then this experience would have been different. I imagined it would have felt like these South American countries were one with memories blurred between them. The way I was visiting them: they were distinct trips, and memorable in their own right; but maybe harder to see some of the more subtle cultural differences.

Getting through the checkpoints out of the city was slow progress as a lot of people were leaving for the Easter weekend. At Guayllabamba we stopped by a roadside fruit stall, and tried a Cherimoya: a fruit with a smooth texture which is full of seeds, and quite messy to eat. Although it originated around the Ecuador and Peru region, it now grows in other countries, and is also known as a custard apple.

The sun came out as we arrived in the village of Cayambe: a place where they have a coloured line to mark where the equator passes through. The tour guide then balanced an egg and said it proved they're on the equatorial line. It doesn't, not even in the slightest; you could balance an egg with equal effort at any latitude.

We also looked around one of the many rose farms. This one had five acres of varying colours, and they demonstrated to us how they create new species and how they deal with disease. They also claimed they provide

Amsterdam with their famous tulips. I doubted this; maybe what they meant was lost in translation.

After a lunch stop the rain had returned for our drive to Otavalo. The market there was a place we were encouraged to haggle. Doing so is almost impossible without thinking of Monty Python's 'Life of Brian'. Though it also feels wrong to when we can afford their prices; especially if they're already reasonable.

The day ended at Cotacachi, one of Ecuador's many volcanoes. We walked to the Cuicocha crater which now has an acidic lake with two small islands in the middle. Apparently the acidity of the water is great enough that you wouldn't want to swim there. I was happy to accept their advice without question.

Our time in Ecuador was already at an end. We flew to Isla Baltra, one of the Galápagos Islands, and met up with Byron who would be our guide. Once the rest of the group arrived we were taken on a ferry over to Isla Santa Cruz, and by truck to Puerto Ayora.

On the way to the port we were taken onto private land to see our first Galápagos tortoise. As Byron started to tell us about the rain on the island an incredibly strong downpour started on cue, which made us run for shelter. Does he have a remote control for the rain?

The Galápagos Voyager, also known as the El Gran Poseidon, was anchored in the port and waiting for us. In small groups we transferred to the yacht by panga whilst our luggage was loaded onto another. The pangas are very stable fibreglass boats with inflatable sides, and powered by an outboard motor.

Onboard the ship we were assigned our cabins, and after a quick lunch we headed back ashore. Our guide flagged down a few taxis to take us less than a kilometre to the Darwin Research Centre. Why we couldn't have walked that, I have no idea.

At the entrance to the centre we watched marine iguanas sunbathing next to a jetty, and numerous birds on the surrounding trees. One of these trees was a poison apple tree which giant tortoises find good for their digestive systems.

Inside the breeding centre we saw giant tortoises of various ages divided into different enclosures. We kept an eye out for Lonesome George: the famous giant tortoise from Isla Pinta who had been the last of his sub-species. We thought we hadn't seen him as he wasn't in his enclosure; but when reviewing the photos after the trip we found that one roaming free in the centre had actually been him. A few years later he died, and with him his sub-species was now extinct.

Each day onboard the ship we'd be up no later than 06:00 for breakfast so we could beat the midday sun. Our first full day started with a trip over to Plaza Sur where we made landfall on a concrete jetty.

We were greeted by sea lions, marine iguanas, and land iguanas. We had to be careful not to get too close: during our briefing we'd been told that the park rules are such that you can't get within two metres of the animals.

At times it wasn't easy to stay away. We couldn't leave the trails either and sometimes where animals were sitting on the path we'd need to get close to them in order to pass. Animals would sometimes come to us as well.

There are so many different species on this island - it's the perfect place to be for any wildlife enthusiast. The early morning sun was beating down on us, and insects were wanting to bite too. If this was what it was like early morning, what would it be like by the afternoon?

As Byron was an employee of the national park he had an incredible wealth of knowledge about the animals, and the habitats. He spent a lot of time talking, and although he sometimes repeated himself, it was giving me more time for photography.

In the afternoon we got to enjoy some snorkelling around Isla Santa Fe. The water felt cool; but nowhere near a cool as it'd be back in England. I really did enjoy this: not only did I see plenty of fish species I'd not seen before; but also blue-footed boobies on the rocks.

In Australia I'd used my underwater camera for the first time: here I practiced more at letting the current move me into place for photographs whilst holding it steady.

The day ended with an excursion to Isla Santa Fe; we had to wade through the water onto a sandy beach full of sea lions. I'd chosen to use this excursion to observe only, and had left my camera behind on the ship. A few from our group spotted a snake; but by the time I got there it was gone.

Our second day on the islands started with a rough panga ride through high waves to Isla Española. The sun was even warmer than the day before; it felt oppressive as we passed more sea lions, and begun a three kilometre walk around the island. This hike took us passed nesting albatrosses and a Galápagos hawk. It was seeming that every species here had Galápagos in its name.

Although we'd seen a reasonable amount of vegetation on this island, it was clear that this, one of the oldest of the islands of the archipelago, was becoming barren and slowly dying. It's one of the interesting things about the Galápagos Islands-you can see volcanic islands in various geological stages, and we'd already seen two in our first two days.

We saw marine iguanas nesting: some were digging holes, and there was the occasional territorial fight break out as well. It was like watching a David Attenborough documentary but without his hushed narration. Instead we had Byron talking loudly about their habits. Oh well.

Between the hike and an afternoon deep-water snorkel it'd been a very active day. When night fell I relaxed on the deck of the ship, gazing at the night sky. We were so far from civilisation that I could see the stars without light pollution. I'd never seen them with such clarity before. This is what it was like to truly be in the wild.

Before breakfast we arrived at Kicker Rocks - remnants of an old lava cone. Nesting atop these high rocks we could see magnificent frigate birds nesting. As we ate, the ship navigated to Isla San Cristóbal - a larger island which was the first one Charles Darwin landed on in 1835. It felt like a wasted morning in the Interpretation Center; but not all days are exciting and filled with adventure, and this was one of those days.

If only we'd known that things were about to change.

We had become accustomed to hearing the ships engines, and the way the boat would move through the water as we made our way from island to island. Something was different when we awoke this morning. It seemed… quieter.

Sleepily looking out of the cabin window I could see we were moving very slowly, and something didn't seem right. We were being towed by the two pangas, and the deck reeked of diesel fumes spewing from the open hatch to the engine room.

During the night the ships engines had died, and these small craft were now our only method of transportation. The pangas running flat-out were capable of towing the ship at a speed of approximately one mile per hour; but we weren't going to reach Isla Santa Cruz. Byron hoped the National Park would let us visit North Seymour instead as we could get there in an hour.

As we waited, the sun disappeared behind clouds and torrential rain began to fall. Waves crashed against the ship and slowed the pangas even further. It wasn't looking good at all.

The crew began siphoning fuel from the ship so the pangas could run for longer. It was now becoming a question of what would give out first: the waves pushing us back, or the fuel driving the pangas forward.

James and myself were lucky though, whilst Andy and the rest of the passengers had to wait we'd got a morning of scuba diving booked through another company. We'd both got our diving qualifications after returning from Australia. For us to make this excursion one of the two pangas took us to the rendezvous point, leaving the crippled ship behind.

We arrived at the dive boat late due to the issues the ship faced. This turned it into the quickest dive preparation we've ever experienced with the dive masters helping us. Just as we prepared to enter the water, the valve blew on my tank.

The sudden release of air was deafening; but they quickly sorted it so I could roll backwards into the water. We never got to perform buddy or buoyancy checks - we just had to demonstrate a couple of basic skills such as mask clearing to 'prove' we were qualified.

This first dive lasted for thirty minutes, and was the most incredible dive I'd experienced. I saw a large group of eagle rays swimming by overhead, partially silhouetted by the light shining through the water. There were a few small manta rays, white-tipped sharks, and octopuses making this a dive I could never forget.

James started to get low on air, and indicated to a dive master he had fifty bars left. To explain what went on in these dives, you need to realise that an octopus in diving terms is also the name given to a secondary release valve with a spare regulator. This allows for buddy breathing if your dive buddy experiences issues with their own tank. This is because sharing a single regulator can cause panic, so a secondary is safer.

The dive master passed James his octopus and they began their ascent to the safety stop. This had been my deepest dive to date at only 17.9 metres; but on what we'd been told was a fifteen metre shelf. I wasn't quite sure how that works.

I felt seasick though, and wasn't sure if I could dive any more. To take my mind off it I went for a snorkel, whilst the others ate lunch. As it happened, this was enough to make me go for the second dive.

I took it slowly, and at one point crouched on the seabed as a white-tipped shark brushed passed me. I could have stretched out my arm and stroked it. To me, these are the experiences that scuba diving is all about.

As the dive went on we encountered a large snake, and another octopus. I couldn't take pictures though as it seemed my battery had died between dives. I was tiring, and the extra exertion used up my air quicker than normal. James' was even worse so again he signalled to the dive master.

You would expect them to begin their ascent at that point but they continued the underwater tour until his own tank was running low. A minute into their safety stop the DMs tank ran out of air. There was no choice but to risk cutting the stop short, and to get to the surface to manually inflate his BCD. This is a scenario a qualified diver should never find themselves in.

It could certainly have been worse; but his actions were still dangerous. This second dive had also been deeper than the first: something you wouldn't normally do as this is what's known as a reverse profile dive. Both dives were deeper than our insurance covered us for as we were not yet advanced divers. It was lucky nothing had gone wrong. In our lack of knowledge about multi-level dives we were concerned decompression was required;

though after several hours decided it was okay. So much for the PADI motto of 'plan your dive, dive your plan'. Maybe the end of this dive wasn't as planned, but it had still been an incredible experience.

We caught up to the El Gran Poseidon - it hadn't moved much since we left it as both pangas had left to fetch supplies from the nearest port. After three attempts at lining the boats up, we eventually jumped from the bow of the diving boat onto the stern.

I dried off, and checked my camera. Something didn't seem quite right. I opened the housing, and found it had leaked: the camera was ruined. It was probably still in a better state than the ship's engines though - the crew wouldn't tell anyone what the situation was, or how long it would take to fix.

Patience on the ship was wearing thin. That evening Byron held the daily briefing with some good news: they'd got a new part for the engine and after midnight we'd continue our voyage. The bad news was that due to the delay we'd no longer visit Isla Genovesa - the only place we could see red-footed boobies.

I awoke next morning, wondering where we'd be. When I looked out of the cabin window, my stomach sank. We hadn't moved at all.

At breakfast I could see passengers faces were filled with anger. Byron had disappeared instead of providing an update, and this just made things worse. Eventually he found the courage to face us, and tell us the bad news: when they started the engines up they had started to spew smoke and failed again. It'd be another day with an altered itinerary.

He didn't have an answer for what we'd be doing - he needed to wait for the National Park Authority to tell him what would be permitted. It felt like a mutiny could happen any minute. Some of the older passengers demanded to see the Captain. I wasn't sure what they thought that would achieve; but I kept quiet.

The Captain didn't speak English, so all communication had to be done via Byron. The Captain spoke for minutes at a time; but Byron's translation was far shorter - I think he was summarising the conversation. They promised us that a speedboat with two motors would arrive to take us to Bachas Beach in an hour. The situation can't have been good for the crew; but they could have handled the communication with passengers better.

An hour passed and there was no sign of another boat. We waited and waited until a boat arrived with a single motor. This is why it'd taken far longer than expected.

Bachas beach is an amazing sandy beach with some of the softest sand I've come across. Protruding up out of these sands were pieces of rust-covered metal from barges that had mostly corroded away after the second world war. The local pronunciation of 'barges' is how the beach came to be known as Bachas.

After passing a nearby lagoon with flamingos and their strange upside-down beaks, we headed for Black Turtle Cove. The name conjured images of pirates, but there were no pirates here. There were dense forests of mangroves that concealed baby sharks, and rays. It was like a natural nursery for sea life. To get around we had to use oars instead of engines. In the shallower waters we could see turtles surfacing for air.

On our way back to the ship, we saw the flamingos leave the island as the sun set. We'd been very lucky to see them, and more luck awaited us on the ship. The repairs were almost complete, and we'd soon be heading towards the volcanic Isla Bartolomé.

In the early hours of the morning I was shaken awake as the ships engines kicked to life. They'd finally got them working. What a relief!

Although it was several years later I heard about it, there was allegedly an incident the following year when it was on its way to Guayaquil for maintenance. A collision along the way caused major hull damage which caused this ill-fated ship to sink. This being the second mode of transportation I'd been on that crashed within a year of using it was an unfortunate coincidence. For now though, our journey aboard the Galapagos Voyager was continuing.

Our first stop were the barren, uneroded black lava flows of Sullivan Bay on Isla Santiago - one of the newest islands in the archipelago. We got to snorkel in the crystal-clear waters with penguins; though with their speed I couldn't keep up. They were truly at home here.

In the afternoon we moved further around the island to where some of 'Master and Commander' was filmed. Our excursion was along a boardwalk with 370 steps up to a viewpoint.

We could see the island in full: from the submerged

volcanic cone to the jagged edges of Pinnacle Rock. The sun setting on the landscape before us was the last we'd see on these islands. Our time in the Galápagos was at an end.

Early in the morning we took a panga to the shore, and passed the sinkholes of Los Gemelos on the way to the airport. The airport was chaotic with manual bag searches due to a faulty x-ray machine. With the tin roof being baked in the sun, it was overly warm, and not somewhere I wanted to be for long.

In Quito we met up with our final guide: she told us that as an apology for the boat issues we'd be taken for a meal in the evening. Awfully kind of them; but before food we needed to find a pharmacy for some antibiotics.

Andy had injured his leg on a rock whilst we'd been on Isla Santiago. The crew couldn't help him, and by the time we'd arrived back on land it had become swollen and warm to the touch. We'd soon be heading to the cloud forest, so something needed sorting first.

None of us had slept much when the time came to head to the Bellavista Cloud Forest. Andy had been kept awake by his leg, and had even called for a doctor. Hopefully he'd be okay.

It was an hour bus ride into the mountains to reach the forest with nothing but our backpacks. Within minutes of arriving we saw hummingbirds flying around the nectar feeders outside 'The Dome' - a building that houses a mess hall, and storage room.

At the start of our first hike the guide pulled a

flower from a plant called 'the Incas Earring'. She said they tasted like apple, but to me it tasted like I was eating a leaf. The rest of this hike was pretty uneventful: it may have been incredibly scenic; but it was completely devoid of animal life.

As we got towards the end of the hike we saw a large tarantula web; but I couldn't see any sign of the spider. I also found my stomach was starting to feel unsettled, but tried my best to ignore it.

There was a second hike where we finally got to see some wildlife: a solitary toucan seen through binoculars from a distance. At least when we returned to the dome there were plenty more birds to see.

Our room was a wooden construction in a tree - a little like a treehouse. There were gaps in the walls where the wooden panels didn't quite fit together right; but this room did have electricity, running water, and one of the most amazing views over the canopy. Well, for most of the time it had the modern conveniences. In the evening the electricity cut out leaving us in complete darkness so we could sleep amongst the treetops.

Our penultimate hike was a shorter one before breakfast. It was hoped that in going out before it got warm we'd see animals that would be hiding later in the day. We didn't though - even the morning chorus seemed bereft of life.

Following a quick breakfast we headed back out. The guide planned on wading through waist-high water at a waterfall; but none of us were prepared for that. Instead, we were climbing waterfalls, jumping from rock to rock, and walking through streams. It was amazing we stayed mostly dry.

It had only been a couple of weeks since the guide last took this path, but already she was needing to use a machete to take the path the forest had reclaimed. By midday our hiking was over - good timing as I was starting to feel even worse. The subsequent journey back to Quito felt like it was never going to end. It seemed likely I'd got food poisoning.

After a sleepless night, we were finally on our way home. Having long haul flights when feeling that ill is an experience I'd rather never experience again. It didn't help that the flight from Bonaire to Schipol was delayed. It was however a long enough flight that by the time I arrived back in England I was starting to feel better.

It had been a rough journey home; but the trip to Ecuador and the Galápagos Islands was both worthwhile and unforgettable. The diversity of the wildlife, and the experience of the diving there was second to none. It was going to be difficult for another trip to beat this.

12: Iceland

On Christmas Day I got a message from James - his sister was going to Iceland, and having seen the pictures himself he was trying to organise a trip. Plans moved quickly and before New Years day we'd booked a couple of tours with the goal of seeing the Aurora Borealis - more commonly known as the Northern Lights.

Time was a luxury we didn't have - we had to prepare quickly, and buy all the cold-weather gear we'd need for a winter trip to Iceland. I bought a carbon fibre tripod, and then borrowed a suitable 50mm lens from my Dad. James had more to prepare: he'd just bought his very first DSLR so I helped him get used to this during a snowy day at Warwick Castle. I didn't do a very good job of explaining it, but he learnt quickly, and would go on to teach himself how to use it properly.

A delay in our outbound flight meant we arrived in Keflavik at 02:00 onto a snowy runway. The flight had been an eventful one when they requested that any medical doctors made themselves known as one of the passengers was having an allergic reaction. I guess this isn't limited to movies after all.

A few hours after arriving, and on very little sleep, we took a bus to do what they call the 'Golden Circle' tour. With a name like that our hopes were high that we'd get plenty of photographic opportunities. There was however a lot of fog and snow.

Our first stop was the brilliant white Skálholt cathedral - almost invisible against the snow except for stained-glass windows by Gerður Helgadóttir. The interior was filled with the sound of an organ, and accompanying vocals from a choir. It felt peaceful.

This area is an important part of the Church of Iceland, and although it was only built for the Millennium celebrations there had been previous churches that have stood there since the Icelanders converted to Catholicism in the 10th Century. They haven't however forgotten their roots: the Æsir and Vanir clans of gods those Scandinavian settlers would have worshipped.

The closer we got to Gullfoss, the heavier the snow fell. By the time we reached the most impressive falls in Iceland, the snow was making it almost impossible to use cameras. The falls on the Hvítá River are made up of three stages with a total height of about sixty-four metres. With the snow as it was we couldn't get too close due to the frozen staircase. Maybe it'd be easier to take photographs in the next place.

Rather than waste time in a restaurant, we had fast-food whilst visiting Geysir Verslun. It gave us more time to view the geysers there; but even though it didn't seem possible before - the snowfall increased in intensity. It was likely the heaviest snowfall I'd ever seen at that point. I know people say that there's no such thing as bad weather, just incorrect clothing; but the snow was getting ridiculous.

We wandered around in the snow long enough to get pictures of Great Geysir bubbling away with a steady flow of steam, and watched Strokkur erupt a couple of times. It sure was nice to be back in the warm coach afterwards.

On the way back to Reykjavik we stopped first at Þingvellir where the Eurasian and North American tectonic plates meet to form the mid-Atlantic ridge. This was the first time I'd seen a fault between the plates of Earth's crust, and here it was a fissure filled with water. Some of these are apparently good for scuba diving, though my trip here was too short to be able to try it. Short trips like this could be good for inspiring future trips.

This was also the site the National Parliament, the oldest parliament in the world, formed in 930 CE. To get an idea of how old this is - it was a few years after King Æthelstan had kicked the Norsemen out of York to finally rule over all of England for the first time in Anglo-Saxon history.

For once, the drama that followed was not our own. We came across a bus that had broken down in the snow so took on the passengers of that one too for the remaining journey.

When we got back into Reykjavik we were told the evening tour to see the Aurora Borealis was cancelled: there were still too many clouds about even though it'd stopped snowing. The upside to this was being able to finally get some sleep.

The second day in Iceland brought warm sunshine with it. It made photographing places such as Eyjafjallajökull far easier, and it helps we were taught how to pronounce these names. This particular place was infamous for the 2010 eruption that disrupted European air traffic. It had showered the surrounding farmland with ash, and farmers feared they'd never be able to farm this land again. After the ash had blown away they found the minerals left behind made this land more fertile than ever.

At the Mýrdalsjökull glacier we dropped off people that were going to do an ice walk, and the rest of us got to see the glaciers up close. The size of the blocks of ice on the glacier were almost indescribable. There were places where it was possible to crouch underneath the ice, knowing that there were tonnes of ice and snow above. In other places it was precarious where snow was hiding thin ice. Wherever the ice broke underfoot it meant plunging your foot into the cold water below.

Our next stop was the farthest point: the impressive basalt columns of Halsanefshellir at Reynisfjara. Powerful waves broke along the beach that was dark with ash. It was like looking at an alien world. The sea here was far too rough for fishing ports or harbours to be feasible: it was devoid of life.

On the return journey we stopped in Vík í Mýrdal for dinner. It was cheap, but there was little choice. The food swam in pools of grease, and service was slow due to the large number of people. The 'fast-food' took forty minutes to get a barbecue burger which left us very little time for exploring.

In Skógar we stopped at the Skógasafn folk museum which is run by Þórður Tómasson, and his daughter. They were both enthusiastic about Icelandic history which made the tour a lot of fun.

They have a large Pétursey fishing boat, many books and furniture, and a number of turf houses that have been relocated from elsewhere on the island. There's also a church which is made from parts of other churches - the interior mostly coming from the Kálfholt church built in 1879.

It seems strange to think a building can be moved to preserve it; but the difference is that in the UK buildings we want to preserve have continued to be in use, and are made of more permanent materials. Here they were mostly made from wood.

The waterfalls we saw after this, Skógafoss and Seljalandsfoss, were both easier to photograph than when we'd seen Gullfoss. As we stood and watched tonnes of water come crashing over the precipice a fine spray blew across the river below. Where the sun shone through the water droplets in the air we could see the arc of a rainbow making it even more picturesque.

As the sun set on our journey back to Reykjavik we got confirmation that our Northern Lights tour would be going ahead despite the cloud. Back at the hotel we quickly prepared our cameras for a night of photography.

We left Reykjavik far enough behind to avoid the worst of the light pollution. During the drive the guide explained that people should not bother using flashlights or camera flashes as it will not make any difference when trying to take a picture. It might seem like an obvious thing; but you may be surprised at how many people would still try this.

The guide pointed out the Northern Lights to us; but all I could see were wisps of cloud. I couldn't see the colourful, cascading waves of light I expected. However, apparently the wisps of cloud were in fact the lights, just lacking visible colour.

I set-up my camera, and started to experiment. This was a photography excursion so you'd expect people to be weary of what they're doing; but sadly it didn't stop people walking in front of my lens during some of the long exposures.

Through the camera I could see green hues, created by particles from the sun colliding with oxygen atoms in the atmosphere. This was more like what I expected. Had television caused me to expect different to reality? Or were we just unlucky?

It was a cold evening; but I was fortunate I'd gone prepared with hand warmers. I didn't know they took thirty minutes to warm up though, so it was another lesson learned for any other cold trips in future. Would I really want to experience this cold again though?

When the aurora activity came to an end the coach immediately turned on its lights and signalled for people to board. By the time we got to the hotel we had less than six hours to pack, sleep, and get to the airport. Who needs sleep anyway?

It hadn't been a trip that had gone entirely to plan. We both felt we needed another attempt at seeing the lights; but it'd have to be another year. Perhaps we'd needed more time for this visit. We already had a trip to China booked, and it wouldn't be long before we'd be on our way.

13: China

After visiting Peru I decided I had to one day visit China, another country with amazing history. It had become part of a list that had started to grow, and now included Antarctica as a place I'd like to one day visit. It was an expensive and almost unobtainable dream; but perhaps one day I'd make it there. For now I had a different adventure.

As the Olympics made their way to London, I met up with James once more to visit the location of the previous games: Beijing. It was handy having a friend who enjoys travel too. The visa for this trip required a similar level of detail to visiting India; but for this we had a tour company arrange everything.

When we arrived in China, it'd been a long and tiring journey so we started with a visit to a coffee shop before starting a tour by rickshaw. This took us to a hutong - an old style of neighbourhood that is common in Beijing. During the Ming dynasty hutongs formed concentric circles with the Forbidden City at the centre. The higher the social status meant the closer to the centre you were allowed to live.

At the end of the Qing Dynasty the era of feudal China was coming to an end. With this, hutongs were now built haphazardly with seemingly no planning at all. During the thirty seven years of the Republic of China, the condition of these deteriorated. After the formation of the People's Republic of China they then started to disappear - over ninety-five percent had been demolished in the lead-up to the 2008 Olympic Games.

We stopped at the entrance to one of these residences and our guide began to explain what could be determined from an entranceway. During the reign of Emperors, commoners could only have black doors. Red, the colour symbolising luck, was reserved for the Emperor and his family.

The beams above the door were also an indication of status: there would be none, two or four. If the door had stone drums either side then it was the house of a General, and if it had stone squares it was the house of a civil servant. The majority of doors would also have a barrier to step over as well as the Chinese believed that evil spirits could not lift their legs so that would stop them from entering. It's also traditional to step over them with a particular leg first depending on gender.

Inside this one we met the people that lived there - one was the son of one of the last Emperors chefs. He welcomed us into his kitchen, with a photograph of Chairman Mao Zedong above a table, and made us a cup of tea. The older generations seem to have great respect for Mao. Though, if this connection to the last Emperor was genuine then could showing support for Mao have been a way to stay safe rather than reverence? On the other hand, if that was the case, then surely he didn't need to continue showing support? Maybe he genuinely did believe in Communism.

The following morning we visited the Temple of Heaven. It dates back to the Ming dynasty; but the colours are still vibrant as it was recently refurbished. If Chairman Mao destroyed much of China's heritage, how much of this was the original? It's a question I asked myself time, and again on this trip.

We also visited the nearby tea house where Miss Tea, a pseudonym I'm sure, taught us the tea traditions of China. As we were taught how they taste and drink tea, I was surprised (or should that be horrified) by the amount of tea that would be spilled onto trays.

"Would you like to buy some tea?" Miss tea asked me afterwards.

"No, thank you" although it'd have been nice to take some tea home, the prices were higher than I was willing to pay.

"You break my heart"

"Sorry," I carried on walking back to the coach, unwilling to partake in peddling mind games.

I was sure there'd be more chances to buy souvenirs to take home. Though I had to admit I didn't realise just how many. For now, we were instead heading to the infamous Tiananmen Square. The name may mean 'Gate of Heavenly Peace'; however in 1989 it was anything but that when the army shot thousands of protesting civilians.

The square is now surrounded by low railings and

can only be entered through guard posts manned by both the police and military. Apparently they also have undercover police wandering around. Although irrational, I found this instilled some paranoia: I was extra careful of what I was photographing in case any took offence.

On one side of the square is the mausoleum of Chairman Mao, and opposite this is the Forbidden City. Before entering the city properly we had to pass through two outer courtyards.

The Imperial Palace in its current location began construction in 1406 by Zhu Di, and took fifteen years, and over a million workers to see it to completion. Since then the Forbidden City was the seat of the Chinese Empire until the end of the Qing dynasty. I felt this to be one of the most iconic structures in their history.

After the abdication of Puyi, the Last Emperor, the outer courts were opened to the new Republic of China. In 1924 Puyi was forced out of the city, and the palace turned into a national museum.

It was a struggle to work our way through the crowds: we tried to move patiently with the crowd; but found local tourists would raise their elbows and push their way passed us to get through first. I thought it very rude; but it's a different culture, and this seemed to be the normal for them so we couldn't really be too judgemental about it.

As dusk approached, we left the city through the Gate of Divine Might. We'd packed masks to protect our lungs from the smog; but had found in the perfect blue skies they hadn't been needed.

In the evening we went to a Peking Opera show. The performance covered a few themes; but the 'singing' part is probably an acquired taste. If anything, it'd probably help remove wax from your ears.

In the morning we visited Yi He Yuan: gardens built by Emperor Wan Yanliang of the Jin Dynasty in the year 1153. Years later Empress Dowager Ci'Xi, a former consort of the Emperor Xianfeng of the Manchu Qing dynasty, was able to appropriate funds intended for the Imperial Navy and rebuild these gardens. It was because of the Empress that they were later nicknamed 'the summer palace'.

The grounds of the palace include a large man-made lake: Kunming. Sitting on this lake at the end of a long corridor, Cháng Láng, is a boat made from marble. We however took a more traditional boat, one shaped like a dragon, to reach our coach on the far side.

I didn't realise it at the time, but the jade shop we visited next would be the first of many compulsory factory shops that tour companies have to make - apparently as part of an agreement for operating in this country. It was explained that there are different types of jade; but it's possible to tell which ones are real based upon how light shines through it.

One food stop later we were wandering through market stalls, reminiscent of Aguas Calientes, that led to a cable car onto the Great Wall of China. Upon disembarking the cable car we started to run. We were slow, weighed down by our cameras and backpacks; but we wanted to get far enough along the wall to take photographs clear of tourists.

At the farthest point there was an incredibly steep climb onto one of the towers which required hands like a ladder. From the top we could see through the polluted haze that surrounded us, and beyond the Mutianyu section of the wall we were on. I could see small settlements along the Chinese side of the wall, and cherry blossom heavily scattered all over.

Our return along the wall was leisurely, and it gave us time to haggle in the markets as well. It's one of those fun things to do; but I didn't want to try too hard. Rosemary, our guide for the full trip, had advised us to be careful of t-shirts as the cheapest ones would be what she called 'three generation shirts' - they shrink after each wash.

A new day, and a new city as a morning flight got us into Xi'an in time for lunch. This city has a wall surrounding much of it with openings for the traffic. At one of these openings we we were greeted by a lady who gave everyone a key, and thus started the Imperial Welcome Ceremony filled with performances and singing.

Even with the wait at the entrance, we somehow managed to arrive at the hotel ahead of our luggage. Our luggage had been put on a van; but unfortunately it'd broken down. Whilst we waited we all checked into our rooms, though unfortunately the non-smoking ones still smelt of smoke. The first room was so bad we got Rosemary to have us moved, though this required a long debate with six of their employees.

Our luggage in the meantime had been delayed

further. The replacement van that had gone to collect it had itself been in an accident. Apparently the accident was bad enough to involve the police; but as far as we knew no one was injured. So they sent another van. Third time lucky I guess.

With nothing better to do we paid for an optional excursion to the Tang Dynasty Opera. This wasn't really an opera: it's a culture show with cabaret-style tables. Filled with light and colour, it was incredibly rich with both Chinese culture and the external influences it's had over the years. It was actually very enjoyable.

Instead of going straight to the Terracotta Army of Emperor Qin Shi Huang, we used some of the next morning to visit the Shanxi Provincial History Museum. It was interesting; but I rushed more than I should have: I was eager to see the warriors. It was delayed even further by a visit to another factory shop where they produce replicas. I just want to see the real thing!

Finally we made it. This famous army had been discovered by local farmers in 1974 when digging for water. They'd been discovered in pieces; but we'd be seeing the result of extensive repairs. Evidence suggests they were once under a roof of wood and reed; but they were crushed when it collapsed during a fire.

Not all warriors have been repaired, but now they're all protected inside what looks like an aircraft hanger where flash photography and tripods are banned. It was fine by me, I didn't need a flash - I just wanted to use my long lens. One of the guards was unhappy with me as he thought I was trying to photograph the archaeologists with it so I had to stop.

It was a very worthwhile trip, and I'm sure I could have spent another hour there had it been possible to get close to the warriors. There wouldn't really have been time though as we needed to be back in Xi'an for our evening meal at a dumpling restaurant.

I also needed to get some more of the local currency. I'd been advised to take US dollars with me as it'd be easier to change into yuan. What I hadn't been told was that the notes have to be pristine: they cannot even have the slightest pencil mark on them. It was something to bear in mind for future trips involving local currency exchanges.

At the dumpling restaurant we were each served an incredible seventeen different types of dumpling. Some were savoury and contained spicy chicken, or vegetables, and some were sweet such as ones containing walnut and chocolate. This was our only meal without rice, but they did serve noodles.

We'd become accustomed to long days. On the first day, Rosemary had said "it's like a marathon - you'll be exhausted by the end of it". I had no context for what that is like. Already it did seem tiring though.

We visited a calligraphy museum in Xi'an where we got to practice writing in Hanji, and also the Small Wild Goose Pagoda: a library of Buddhist scrolls dating back to the Tang Dynasty. If you wanted to ring the bell then there'd be a fee. Everything comes at a cost: they really have embraced capitalist ethos.

After lunch we were taken to the Great Mosque;

but tourists aren't allowed inside. We took photos of the exterior and wandered around the surrounding area until it was time to head to the airport.

We were in need of an evening meal; but there was very little choice at the airport. Our flight was delayed by twenty-five minutes, and then by a further forty-five minutes. It seemed our hopes of getting food in Guilin were pretty slim.

By the time we'd collected our luggage in Guilin there were only a couple of hours left in the day. My luggage was the second casualty of the trip: they'd broken the handle, and lost my tags. At least mine wasn't the one with the destroyed zip. When we reached the hotel and checked in we knew food would not be an option.

In the morning we were all eager for breakfast as none of us had eaten for almost twenty hours. We had to be quick though as we needed to get to the Lijang River for a cruise: the entire reason for being in Guilin.

At the riverbank a number of boats were moored together, and our group was assigned to one of them with a couple of other tour groups. We had to wait for the other boats to fill as they always leave out together.

The river is flanked by limestone karst formations, and various small settlements. Towards the end of this tour we also got to see fishermen using cormorants tied to their boats.

A couple of hours in they served food; but it was so cold I was convinced it'd have been warmer if they'd left it out in the sun to cook. The cruise should have lasted a little over four hours; but as the water was unusually high they decided to go faster so we reached Yangshuo ahead of schedule.

It felt like everything was a constant rush to be somewhere. Sure we got to see a lot; but it meant we also got extra time where we didn't need it such as around the market stalls in Yangshuo. Our drive to Guilin did include an unscheduled stop though: the driver was good enough pull over so we could watch people working in the rice fields.

Being in another city did of course mean another factory shop visit. This one sold pearls, and had no educational value. I was bored out of my mind with the exception of finding amusement from a map that had two North Atlantic oceans and no Pacific ocean.

I did get some free time afterwards, and spent most of this photographing modern pagodas until sunset and our lift to the airport arrived.

Our arrival at the hotel in Chengdu had been in the early hours of the morning. Over breakfast I found there'd been yet another luggage casualty from our latest flight: they'd need to be taken to buy a new suitcase. What is it with suitcases in China?

The rest of us were taken to Jin Li Street; a place which since ancient times has been used for shopping. Oh joy.

I might not be a fan of shopping; but I did enjoy looking at the old timber buildings, and the black swans swimming on the stream that ran through the street. At least that was the case when I wasn't dodging the crowds that occupied this street.

As we were now in the Sichuan province, an area famed for its spice, it meant there'd be a greater variety in the food we'd have here. Our lunch was actually quite mild though as Rosemary had phoned ahead under the assumption that would be what the group wanted. I'd have been happy with spices! In fact, I'd have probably tried anything the locals eat regularly as long as it wasn't seafood.

Our afternoon was spent at the Giant Panda Breeding Research Centre. The first giant panda we saw was asleep on a wooden platform inside an enclosure. As you can imagine I took many photographs as we passed, just in case we couldn't see any more. We did though: there was another enclosure where they were feeding young cubs as well. It was as we'd come to expect though - crowded with tourists pushing and shoving to take photographs; some holding iPads up in the air.

We felt there was no sense in joining the crowds so we moved on to the smaller pens. These were little more than cages where the pandas are kept when they're not on show. Rather than hang around there, we moved on to the red panda enclosures.

They're much smaller than their giant cousins, and a lot quicker. They may look like some sort of cute fox; but they're actually quite vicious: they'd chase each other around the pen to fight, and one had bitten the tail clean off a rival.

That evening we went to the Sichuan Opera. The operas we'd seen so far had been indoors; but this one was out in the open air of a tea house. The acts consisted of mask changing, music, shadow puppets, and a comedyit was more like a cultural variety show.

At this show they were serving tea; delivered to people via what looked like a watering can with an incredibly long spout that reached out across the audience. It's an amusing yet effective way of serving a crowd. I'm surprised it's not made its way to theatres in other countries. Just imagine sitting in the cinema, and being served a cup of tea on demand.

From Chengdu we had a five hour journey to Chongqing to catch a boat. It was a tight schedule, but we knew we'd have one stop along the way at Dazu for the Buddhist carvings. Surprisingly they did allow us to stop briefly to watch a farmer, knee deep in mud and water, using a water buffalo to plow a field as well. It must be so much harder than using a tractor. It's things like this that make us appreciate how lucky we are in one of the richest economies in the world.

In Dazu the sun was so warm we decided we couldn't stand around listening to detailed explanations about each carving. We made our own way around, and picked up what information we could.

The rock carvings spanned the Tang, Ming and Qing dynasties starting from around 650 CE, and cover Taoism, Confucianism and Buddhism. The place we saw was actually just one of around seventy-five different sites that vary in age and dedication; but between them all there are over 50,000 carvings. Even in the one we saw they varied greatly in complexity and size. The massive 'Sakyamuni Entering Nirvana' carving is phenomenal.

Zhao Zhifeng started these carvings during the Song

Dynasty and spent seventy years of his life working on them. It was incredibly lucky their remoteness protected them from the destruction of the Chinese cultural revolution.

Meanwhile, our guide had got carried away with the carvings and was running an hour late. Time was now against us, even more so when we reached the traffic of Chongqing. Fortunately the ship was waiting for us.

The best way to describe this ship is as a floating hotel. Each cabin, not much smaller than a hotel room, has its own private balcony. In the main lobby they even have a glass elevator and a chandelier.

Upon arrival we were told our tour to Fengdu would not be going ahead, and we'd now be going to Shibaozhai Pagoda instead. It was a shame as it'd been described as a place filled with historical buildings, and the Snow Jade Caves - one of China's youngest and most beautiful caves. We were never given an explanation for this change.

There was optional tai chi before breakfast, and the occasional excursion between meals; but no chai tea. For hours at a time we'd be travelling along the Yangtze River with nothing to do. It didn't help that the meals were sometimes questionable - one was simply described as 'fish'.

"What sort of fish is this?" James asked the server.
"It is fish"
"Yes, but what type of fish?"
"Fish!"
It wasn't the answer he'd expected, and we were

unsure if he hadn't understood the question, or simply didn't know what type.

Our first excursion was the afternoon of the first day: the Shibaozhai Pagoda. Upon stepping foot onto the shore many market stalls suddenly came to life. The guide ushered us passed all these stalls to reach a suspension bridge that swayed as we walked across.

Since the building of the Three Gorges Dam, the water levels in the area have been so high that this is the only way to now reach the pagoda which itself is protected by a high wall that was constructed around the grounds.

The pagoda is built against the side of a cliff face, and has nine stories that you must climb up through before reaching a series of temple buildings on the summit. The steps inside the pagoda are a little steep, and rickety; but they are safe to climb. The pagoda was originally built as the only way of climbing the mountain safely.

Since then some stairs had been constructed on the opposite side of the temples, and we took those to head back to the boat as heavy rain started to fall.

That evening there was cabaret for entertainment, though after all the shows we'd been too already I found this one to be cringe-worthy. When the crew started singing 'YMCA' some of the passengers stood up to dance. I stood up too; but walked straight out the door and went to get some sleep.

Our next excursion was an optional one to Baidicheng - the White Emperor City of General

Gongsun Shu. During the Han dynasty he rebelled, and created his own state in Shu. Due to the white fog that he believed looked like a dragon, he declared himself as the White Emperor.

Leaving for the shore was chaos. Nobody knew what was happening, or where we needed to be. I asked guide after guide until I found one that spoke English, and she told me to join her group on the coach. It stopped at the 'Wind and Rain' bridge: another post-dam construction that would let us reach the partially submerged city.

Sometimes it can get annoying when a guide repeats themselves and never stops talking; but this one didn't talk at all. She lost half of our group without even wondering where they'd gone. She moved so slowly that by the time we got back to the coach park she said it'd left without us. I could see it hadn't though: I'd made a note of the number plate when we got off the coach, and that one was still there in front of us.

This part of the trip was getting frustrating, and the ship was due to leave shortly. The guide ushered us onto a different coach, and for the entire journey we were nervously clock-watching - worried the ship may have left. Fifteen minutes after it'd been scheduled to leave, we found ourselves to be lucky: it was still there.

An atmospheric cruise through the fog of the Qutang Gorge got us to Wu Gorge. The boat stopped at the head of the narrow Shennong stream where a smaller ferry was waiting for us. This took us downstream for an hour to where a floating platform had even smaller boats moored up. These smaller boats were wooden and rickety, and had no actual floor: just a plank of wood to stop your feet from getting wet. They didn't feel entirely stable - I wasn't confident I'd be staying dry.

These long boats sat two by two in four rows with a three-person rowing team, someone navigating, and a local guide telling us about the area, and how the government dam project had affected the communities that live there. They may not have dared to say so; but there was the feeling that they were not happy with it.

Eventually we returned to the floating platform, and the ferry took us back to the ship. Over an inedible evening meal of bone, gristle and fat, we heard that the dam had been closed, and so we wouldn't be passing through the lock gates as expected. We'd need to disembark at Maoping in the early hours of the morning, and continue by coach. It felt like our group was cursed.

Our cruise ended as the group watched nervously at the luggage being loaded onto the coach. Hopefully they'd all arrive safely.

The coach took us to the Three Gorges Dam, and after a basic security check we were allowed onto Jar Hill where we could look down at the gates. An hour later we reached Yicheng, and another coach that would take us the rest of the way to a museum.

As the museum guide was having lunch, we were first taken to see the embroidery work of a local minority group. The work there was incredible, and deserving of the high price tags. The museum however was largely uninteresting; but it was selling a large number of authentic items that were eighty or more years old. They were doing this to raise money to expand; but the oldest on sale would not be allowed to leave the country due to the law. I wondered how often a tourist would buy one, and then have it confiscated at the airport.

Our next stop was at a bonsai garden, or more accurately, a penzai garden. Bonsai is a Japanese term for the cultivation of small trees, but apparently the Chinese equivalent predates it. Though considering their rivalry I couldn't be sure how true it was.

It was a fairly interesting place to walk around; but most of my attention was focused on the very large paper wasp that was flying around. I had to get a photograph of it, and with some patience I did.

Following some afternoon tea in a hotel, we made it to the airport and through security just fifteen minutes before the scheduled boarding time. We'd cut it closer than I'd like; but as it happened the aircraft we needed to board was still in Shanghai. In fact, the passengers for the previous flight to Shanghai were still here as well. Something wasn't right.

Hour after hour passed with no update on what was happening. Rumours started to circulate that a joint military exercise between Russia and China had grounded over two hundred planes in Shanghai. I'm not sure what their source was. How do people find these things out?

The terminal was becoming chaotic by the time Rosemary received a call from our Shanghai guide. She'd been told our flight would be leaving at 21:40 and everything would be okay. When our updated flight time came, and went we were told it'd been delayed by another eighty minutes.

At least now we were getting updates; but that flight time came and went also. It was 23:15 when we finally boarded, and this delay meant we didn't arrive at the hotel on the Bund in Shanghai until 02:30 the next morning.

Six hours after arriving we had to be back on the road for a day of tours. Despite the delays, the tour company refused to be flexible with the schedule. It was okay - I think. Sometimes it's good to battle through tiredness to see more.

At the Jade Buddha Temple we saw Buddhist monks wandering around, and various statues of Buddha. Those made from jade we could not photograph. They believe that jade is the only non-living thing that can hold a soul, and that taking a photo steals some of it. Sometimes it'd be nice to find out where these beliefs come from to better understand the culture.

Not far from this was our final factory shop visit. They demonstrated how they produce silk starting with the lifecycle of the silkworm. Whilst there I needed to retrace my steps, and found that the workshops we'd seen people in were now empty.

When I rejoined the group, Rosemary explained that these workshops are just for show when tourists visit. Most of their products are produced elsewhere in very different conditions. I'd been given the impression that a lot of what we'd seen in China was manufactured for appearances. I found myself wondering how would our view of the country have changed if we'd stayed there for months instead.

No matter how much had been rebuilt or faked, it'd been a trip rich with culture and history. I had however learnt that it can be a good idea to have some snacks packed for the trip if you're a fussy eater.

14: Scotland

You don't have to go overseas to have an adventure. Living in the United Kingdom means we've got four countries that function as one, with many experiences to be had. Though it seems I'd done little to explore them.

That finally changed when my frequent travelling friend James organised a road trip around Scotland to celebrate a birthday milestone. We flew from London to Edinburgh, and hired a car at the airport. They tried to up-sell as is normal; but as they didn't have any of the car class we'd booked we got the upgrade for free anyway.

Our plan for this trip was detailed down to the day with lists of what we wanted to see. This started with a brief diversion south of the border into England to see Alnwick Castle. It'd been used as a double for Hogwarts School for Witchcraft and Wizardry so we felt we should see it whilst we were this far north.

The castle is in pretty good condition as it's still lived in, and the gardens are impressive. Running up through the middle is a large cascade with water jets firing. Off to either side and at the top there are various sorts of garden. One of the more interesting ones can only be viewed as part of a guided tour - the poison garden. There they grow plants such as Belladonna, these days more commonly known as deadly nightshade.

Back in Edinburgh we started our tour of Scotland with Calton Hill to get panoramic shots of the city - it's probably the easiest place to do so. Finding Edinburgh Castle from there was fairly easy, but our time would be extremely limited.

We stood in a long queue at the ticket office, thinking that we might not have enough time - we needed to be on the road to Glasgow to catch the last tour of the day at the Auchentoshan Distillery. Apparently a tour of the castle can last three hours; but we believed we could do it in half that. If we could get in quickly.

Technology can be a brilliant thing, and in the last couple of years it had gotten to the point where it was now common to have internet access on a smart phone. I had the idea of buying tickets on their website as this meant we could switch to a far shorter queue and walk almost straight in.

It's thought that Castle Rock, upon which the castle sits, was settled upon at least as far back as 2 CE. It wasn't always a castle of course; but there's been one there at least as far back as King David the First, who had occupied Alnwick Castle for a time.

Even taking our time in places, we were able to see everything in the castle in just under seventy minutes. We rushed back to the car, drove to Glasgow, and found our way to the distillery despite the satnav leading us wrong due to the postcode.

This tour lasted an hour, showing the entire process of producing Scottish whisky, and ending with a tasting session. It seemed like the thing to do in Scotland.

We were told one story about a group of international visitors who had bought one of their bottles that cost more than £2,000 along with some hip flasks for the coach ride back to Glasgow. Their wives didn't allow them to drink, and this was their chance to try some whisky on the sly.

"Did you throw the hip flasks in for free?" someone on the tour asked.

"Did we heck?!"

"Oh yeah, Scottish" they sniggered in reply.

I guess they were reinforcing the stereotype of Scots being thrifty, even though that's far from the truth.

We'd spent so much time driving it felt like we hadn't seen much so far, yet this was already our second day coming to an end. There was just enough time left to see the Kibble Palace botanic garden, Saint Mungo's Cathedral, and the Necropolis.

To get to the Necropolis we had to cross a footbridge over the road into the Victorian-era 'city of the dead'. The hill is filled with tombs, gravestones, and mausoleums. It was a good chance to practice with exposure bracketing - a photography technique good for high dynamic range lighting.

It was now time to move on from Glasgow, and through the Highlands to Fort William and the Glenfinnan viaduct. The entire area is so picturesque that you could spend a lot of time in the area, and not just the day that we had.

The viaduct had been used in the Harry Potter films, and so as a fan it was something I had to see. A steam train only crosses it twice a day so our entire day was to a schedule: we had to be there in time for when it was due for its second pass. Our first job was to find somewhere suitable to set up our tripods, and then to wait patiently.

Behind us, bathed in sunlight, was the Glenfinnan Monument. Although we didn't get to see it closer, this monument was created in memory of those that died fighting for the Jacobite cause: a movement which had hoped to restore the exiled King James VII to the British throne.

Over the next few hours we drove back to Fort William and then on to the Isle of Skye. This had to be done without the satnav as it didn't seem to know about the existence of the Skye Bridge that would make the journey shorter. I guess it's a good idea to make sure maps are up-to-date before travelling.

Once over the high, curved bridge onto the Isle of Skye we made a few short stops. Each was a good viewpoint; but the midges in the air made it unpleasant. We could either suffer, or hope that we'd get another chance. For that reason, we made no attempts to get photographs in Portree as the sun set on a day that had been mostly driving.

We awoke to torrential rain, and wind so bad that it threatened to close the bridge. If this happened then a backup plan was to take the ferry; but this would add many hours to the journey and also stops running in bad weather. There was a chance we wouldn't be leaving the island.

Instead of letting this halt us in our tracks, we continued on with our plans. We drove to The Storr: a rock formation overlooking Portree. The rain was still heavy, and fog had descended; yet for some reason we started to climb. It didn't take long to be covered in mud and our waterproofs were next to useless.

I wondered what the point was - when we got there we couldn't really use our cameras. It felt like we were surrounded by rain, mud, and trees that had been chopped down. We never made it to the top, falling metres short of our goal in favour of getting back to the warm, dry car.

The rain somehow got heavier, and so at the 'fairy pools' stop in the Cullen Hills we decided to not leave the car. Nine miles walking in this weather wasn't appealing. Instead, we headed to the Skye Bridge passing a waterfall that had grown from a trickle to a raging torrent of water blasting off the hillside. Nature can be an incredible sight to behold: never underestimate the power of water. The way flowing water can change like this is also a good reminder not to camp too close to a river if ever we were to do so.

As luck would have it, the bridge was open so we were able to stop at Castle Eilean Donan for lunch. It was built on the site of where a church of Saint Donnán of Eigg once stood.

Prior to the current castle, there had been one built by clan Mackenzie which was destroyed during the

Jacobite rebellion. This new one had been built after the first world war by the McRae family.

Three hours later we reached a guest house near Loch Ness, and the rain had finally stopped. We dropped off our bags, and headed to a nearby pub for a warm meal. Whilst there we took the opportunity to book a tour of the Loch that was being advertised. By the time we left the pub, the last of the light was leaving the sky so watched the waves of Loch Ness crash on the pebble beach as it got dark.

The morning sun was shining when the time came to drive to Dochgarroch Lock. We sat and waited in the carpark at this lock for a boat to arrive, though there was nobody around. Then we spotted a sign:

"For the foreseeable future all tours will be leaving from Clansmen Lock"

We drove there as quickly as the roads would allow. At the ticket office they handed us our tickets, and then told us we'd not got long to get to Dochgarroch Lock. Apparently the sign we'd seen was incorrect. When we arrived there was now a queue of people waiting to board the boat that was just arriving.

It was a fairly short tour: it took us down to Urquhart Castle, dropped a few people off, and then returned along the loch. From there we drove on to the largest settlement in the Scottish Highlands: Inverness.

It was a brief visit, and soon I was back behind the wheel for the long drive to Edinburgh and our last guesthouse of the trip. With all the places we'd looked at whilst planning, I'd made a note of the wrong one so turned up somewhere we weren't expected. I had to continue on closer to the city to the correct guest house, opposite the Edinburgh Zoo. I guess it'd be another lesson for future trips.

For our final day in Scotland we walked from a bus stop near Princes Street Gardens to the Real Mary King's Close where we'd got a tour booked. With some time to spare we decided we'd look around the Royal Mile first, and found The Elephant House - a cafe famous for being where J.K. Rowling wrote at least some of the first Harry Potter book.

The close does not allow photography; but it's still interesting. From the entrance you are led downstairs to what is like an underground city that runs beneath the Royal Mile. Each close used to be at surface level, and would be where a lot of the population lived. They told us about the conditions, and about the plague. It was well worth the visit.

With a few minor stops after this, it brought our swift road trip around Scotland to an end. Maybe it'd not been massively exciting as far as trips go; but it proved we could explore on our own doorstep.

15: Norway

As another winter approached we looked at what possibilities there were for getting another look at the Aurora Borealis. We found a guide, Alister, who runs trips aimed at photographers, and had worked as a cameraman for the BBC, National Geographic, and Discovery Channels. It seemed like a good choice.

What hadn't sunk in was that for the time of year we wanted to go, and how far north we wanted to travel it was going to be cold. Very cold. This trip would take us over three hundred miles into the Arctic Circle, and was predicted to be somewhere between -20 and -40°C. What sort of sane person choses this?!

Little by little, the things I thought I'd never choose to do were becoming things that I'd walk into willingly, and sometimes even eagerly. This was just cold weather, surely it can't be that bad.

The cold can take hold quickly and cause frostbite or worse. We had to pack sensibly, and try to minimise exposure to the elements. I'd seen on television what it could do - Sir Ranulph Fiennes lost parts of his fingers, cutting them off himself after getting frostbite.

I needed more cold weather gear than I'd bought for Iceland. I bought a winter buff, balaclava, ski goggles designed to fit over glasses, and would be renting mittens and snow boots from Tromsø. I had no intention of losing appendages if I could help it.

People in the UK often complain about the country grinding to a halt in the snow. In Norway, they get so much of it that they invest in infrastructure to keep the country running. The flight from Oslo to Tromsø required the aircraft to be sprayed with what I assumed to be antifreeze before taking off.

The days were short too: when we arrived at midday the sun was already setting. Alister was there waiting for us with the rest of the group so we could travel by minibus to the hotel. There was one further member of our party who would be driving himself and boxes of Arri-loaned Alexa equipment by car.

The hotel check-in for a group of our size took some time, particularly because they seemed to have lost the booking. This is the point you start to worry.

Once it'd been sorted it gave us chance to head into town through the incredibly long system of tunnels through the base of a mountain. It felt like a James Bond villain's base; but they are in fact remnants of Nazi-occupied Norway. During the Cold War they had also been used for nuclear storage.

That evening we all ate together and was briefed for the week ahead. Food was expensive - even a burger and fries cost 211 NOK, the equivalent at the time of £21. It's a wealthy country.

After food we drove north out of the city for fifteen minutes so we'd be away from the majority of light pollution. We setup our tripods, and waited for a chance to see the aurora. It was uneventful, just like Iceland.

The morning was our last chance for a warm shower until the end of the trip. Ravnastua, a lodge not far from Karasjok in the Finnmark region, is without plumbing or heating. It'd be simpler than I'd ever experienced.

After two hours we crossed from Norway into Finland. There was a customs hut but they waved us straight through. For hours there was nothing but wilderness: trees, reindeer, and snow.

Before we reached our destination, the car following behind almost hit an oncoming car, and then skidded into the snowbank as his wheels locked. He was uninjured, and the car undamaged; but he'd need to be more careful as it got darker.

The temperature was dropping quickly, and the last I saw was -22°C when darkness fell. We'd already travelled 540 kilometres, and could no longer travel by road. Oskar, our host for the week, was waiting on the roadside with snow scooters and sledges.

As we moved suitcases from the minibus onto the sledges, the car arrived. This time the driver managed to ground it as he pulled off the road. Alister was not impressed: he felt the driver was already becoming a burden on the group.

We unloaded the Arri equipment from the car to

make it lighter and then we pushed it the rest of the way off the road into a parking space.

I couldn't be sure if the temperature had dropped any further after nightfall; but when travelling at 60mph across frozen lakes the wind chill makes it feel twenty degrees cooler anyway. To try and stay warm, most of us were underneath reindeer furs.

Time was immeasurable for this journey. With darkness all around, all we could see was what was illuminated by the headlights of the scooter - trees flashing by. It felt surreal, and not something I could ever have imagined. It was like being in the Blair Witch Project.

The cabins we were heading to were first built around 1890; but were burned down by the Nazis. These were just some of a large network stretching across Norway, which are all about a days trek apart.

We unloaded the luggage into these cabins whilst Alister got a fire burning. The hut we were using had a few rooms with bunk beds, and a wood burning stove.

The cloud cover meant it was warmer than it could have been, but also meant that we wouldn't be seeing the northern lights. We waited patiently in the communal hut until our evening meal was ready: reindeer soup with carrots and potato, and accompanied by glasses of meltwater from a nearby stream.

The temperature in the sleeping cabin was -2°C - far warmer than outdoors; but cool enough to sleep fully clothed.

Overnight the stove had gone out, and the

temperature dropped further. Sleeping in the cold is not easy; but it's not helped when a roommate snores loudly, and had an alarm set for 02:00. There was a lesson to be learned here: always travel with earplugs.

It wasn't possible to shower in the morning, and even using the washroom facilities was a chore. What we had was a frozen trough outdoors, sign-posted as the 'pissoar'. As bathroom breaks required full cold-weather gear it needed a degree of planning. There was also an out-building which had a polystyrene seat over a hole as it'd still be cold there. It was there primarily for any females; but us males could use it when we needed to be sitting.

Breakfast was in the warmer communal hut - a table spread of goats cheese, jam, dried reindeer, fish eggs, smoked salmon, and bread. The cheese was brown and chocolate looking; but tasted like a strong cheddar. Remember: don't let looks put you off.

In daylight we could now see just how far from civilisation we were. There was nothing around. You'd think that like some parts of the UK, there'd be no signal here in the Arctic Circle. You'd be wrong though; due to a Norwegian safety law, all of the country has coverage.

With nothing better to do, we took snow scooters north of the tree line so we'd have space to practice driving them. Sadly, I didn't get my chance before the sun started to set and we had to be back at Ravnastua for lunch.

Lunch was similar to breakfast, but with leftover reindeer soup. Whilst the group ate, Alister looked up the forecast for the day. Unfortunately neither the weather, nor the solar activity was looking promising. Looking out the window I could see that it had already started snowing again, and by sunset the clouds were thicker than ever.

Hours later a small break in the clouds appeared. It was like a call to arms as everyone rushed to prepare their camera equipment to deploy outside the cabin. It was then a waiting game to see if there'd be activity. There wasn't.

This evening meal was one where I ate just carrots and potatoes whilst the rest had halibut. I don't really eat fish so was glad when we found there'd be dessert - blueberry mousse. As we finished eating, Oskar headed to Karasjok to pick up two backpackers that would be helping him for the next couple of days.

Stuart, an avid storm-chaser, put his beer down in the snow outside for a moment whilst he checked his camera. When he picked it back up it was mostly frozen. It was so cold we could see water molecules from the air being frozen and falling as a fine dust.

Some of us stayed up talking until midnight, partly because it was warmer in the communal hut than in the sleeping hut. I was able to get almost an hour of sleep before we got an alert that the aurora had been sighted. I leapt off the bunk bed, and got kitted up as quickly as I could manage. Unfortunately by the time I was outside with my camera there was only cloud. I didn't give up though - I stayed out in the cold.

My patience was eventually rewarded with the faintly glowing arc of the aurora reaching out across the sky. By 03:00 the aurora was once again hidden by clouds, and sleep beckoned.

The night had been long, and our sleepy start to the day took us by snow scooter to a frozen lake. Oskar used an ice auger to start boring into the ice to demonstrate ice fishing. The ice here was too thick however - the ice extended all the way down to the silt.

Since our initial arrival at Ravnastua over two metres of snow had fallen, and the lake we'd crossed previously was no longer safe for the snow scooters. We could have gone farther to have another go at ice fishing, but we risked the snow scooters getting stuck and us being stranded in a dangerous situation.

That being said, one of the scooters got stuck in the snow when turning around. Fortunately we were able to help push it out so we could get back to camp where to pass the time I wandered around until lunch - being careful to avoid the places where the snow was beyond waist deep.

A lack of activities is a good time to talk though. Alister and Stuart told us about their adventures chasing storms, and horror stories of upturned buildings. It felt like they were living inside the movie 'Twister'; but these were their real experiences. It sounds dangerous, but I was intrigued - they made it sound like it could be fun to try.

As it was a night without solar activity we made use of the sauna. I changed into swimming shorts, put on my snow boots and a coat, and headed from the sleeping hut to the sauna. Inside there were two shelves so you could roast at different temperatures.

The idea was to sweat in there until you can't stand the heat, and to then run out into the snow and roll around in it. The first time diving into the snow is a bit of a shock, and some of the group ran back into the sauna screaming. I laughed, and was determined not to react in the same way. For the three people that had decided to go 'au naturale' I imagine diving into the snow was risky business.

The sauna was also a chance to wash, and feel clean again. The first time in days. By the time I was done I'd repeated the cycle of 'fire and ice' four times, and was the second to last person to leave. At the time I left the sauna the temperature had risen to 80°C in there.

The advantage of this sauna meant it raised our core body temperatures. I could wander around outside in just swimming trunks and not feel the cold for some time. By midnight I'd started to cool off, just in time for another cold night in the sleeping hut.

When the sun rose, it was the first time we'd seen it through the clouds. It gave us hope of finally seeing a good aurora display. After breakfast I spoke to one of the backpackers, and was handed an axe to have a go at chopping firewood. This was cut short when the opportunity arose for a snow scooter lesson, and a chance to drive it by myself. They're good fun once you get the hang of them.

Lunch was in Oskar's lavvu - a kind of tent that looks like a Native American tepee with a hole in the top to let out the smoke from a fire used for cooking. We sat on reindeer furs, and cooked reindeer meat on sticks over the fire. Embers glowed around the edges of the meat as it cooked - it felt like the sort of wilderness experience you'd see on television, or in a movie.

On our way back to the communal hut, a husky dog team arrived and moved into a couple of the spare rooms in the sleeping hut. They kept to themselves, and we ate in the communal hut and played cards whilst hoping the cloud cover would eventually break. It did not.

In the morning it was time for us to return to Tromsø. We had been relatively unsuccessful in our quest for the northern lights. It was like Iceland all over again; but this time we'd experienced truly cold weather.

The vehicles we'd left parked up were now buried in snow; but not quite as bad as we expected. We were handed shovels so we could dig the minibus out of the snow, and then helped to push it off the ice that had formed.

The car had a flat battery, and even thirty minutes of trying to get it going didn't help. Alister's frustration at the driver had been growing over the last few days and could take no more. He decided this was a hopeless case, and left him waiting for the breakdown services. The rest of us continued our journey up to Alta, along the coast, and passed some impressive fjords.

There was one stop we made of particular note - it was a fjord where during the second world war, the supposedly unsinkable German Bismarck-class battleship Tirpitz was severely damaged before eventually being sunk. This was on the 12th November 1942 when Allied forces performed a bombing run using Lancaster bombers equipped with 'earthquake' bombs, more formerly known as the Tallboy bomb. To look at the area now, we'd never have guessed.

We stopped for fuel in a picturesque coastal village called Talvik where most buildings are painted in different colours. They stand out against the white canvas of snow, and bring life to a town that otherwise seems desolate. Due to time we'd lost with the car troubles, we couldn't afford any further stops; we had to make it to Olderdalen in time for the ferry crossing.

In Olderdalen we saw cars still boarding the ferry, and rolled onboard just minutes before they raised the ramp. On the other side, in Lyngen, we had forty minutes to cross the island to catch the ferry to Svensby and the road to Tromsø. It seemed everyone else on the ferry had the same plan, but we got there in time. Twenty-five minutes later we'd crossed and was ready for the final hour of driving.

It's amazing how much you can miss modern conveniences when you've been away. A warm shower felt amazing. The relaxing didn't last long though as we needed to be quick in order to go out in search of the Aurora Borealis one last time.

We set-up our tripods on a lakeside far from most of the light pollution of the city. Above us we could see the lights already dancing across the sky - we were in for a show. At last!

As the night went on it got colder. The aurora kept improving in waves and then fading, so we persevered through the cold. It was an amazing sight watching arcs, and wisps of green light weave across the night sky, and through the camera we were picking up reds and yellows on the fringes of the lights.

These extra colours in the lights were a strong indicator of higher solar activity as it meant solar particles were also colliding with oxygen particles in the atmosphere which are far less numerous at that altitude.

By the time we'd done there had been incredibly bright displays, double arcs of light, and I'd seen my first ever 'shooting star'.

At 23:45 we called it a night and headed back to the hotel even though we knew it was likely to get better. The cold was getting too much for some of our group, and you have to draw a line somewhere.

In the morning we had a little free time to explore Tromsø. The architecture of the cathedral there is magnificent. In some ways the angular roof reminded me of the Sydney Opera House. The best view of this is from the other side of the water; but without my cold weather gear this was a chilling walk.

On the other side, whilst looking for a good spot to take photos, we spotted an Indian Submarine moored up - the INS Sindhurakshak. This was a former Russian submarine that would soon be on its way to Mumbai. We did however learn that on its return it caught fire, and sank. My photos from this day got used on many news reports without my permission which led to me eventually adding watermarks to my images.

For the little time remaining, we continued looking around the town and came across a statue of Roald

Amundsen, an Antarctic explorer who was the first to reach the south pole. If only it was somewhere we could see too. Norway was perfect practice for it.

Another adventure had come to an end, and although we'd only visited Norway for the aurora it had been an experience unlike any other we'd had. In just a couple of weeks time we'd be on our way to Africa.

16: Kenya

After returning from the chilling temperatures of Norway; Kenya would be around 60°C warmer. It's almost unimaginable to think that such a difference is possible.

As I'd be flying from Kenya to Tanzania I needed a yellow fever vaccination in addition to taking anti-malarial tablets. When it comes to tablets there are a few different ones available depending on your situation and travel plans - I went with malarone as it seemed the best choice for me.

The only other preparation for this trip was buying a second camera body - I knew the savanna grasslands would be dusty and didn't really want to be changing camera lenses.

Fifteen minutes after leaving the airport in Nairobi we were at the hotel and ready for a late breakfast. I'd have said it's not every day you're offered wine and champagne with breakfast, but in Africa I'd eventually find it to be normal.

Although tired from the flight, we had a city tour scheduled for the afternoon. We visited the Nairobi National Museum and snake pit, and the rest of the sights were pointed out from the minibus.

As we turned down a road where people filled the streets, the driver asked us to close the windows and lock the doors. He then mounted the curb and started driving down the pavement. It doesn't feel like this should be normal behaviour, yet the pedestrians didn't seem bothered by the car forcing its way passed them.

A strange day then ended with food at the infamous Carnivore Restaurant. As we entered we could see them cooking food on spits over a large fire. At least it's a sign the food was cooked fresh.

They shown us to our seats and served a bowl of leek soup. One by one, waiters then arrived at our table with spits of different meat. We were told that once we'd had enough we should remove the flag from our table to show we'd surrendered.

By the time we were done we'd had chicken, chicken wings, chicken leg, pork ribs, lamb, beef, pork sausage, beef sausage, crocodile, ostrich meatballs, fried chicken gizzards, and ox testicle. There are meats there that you just don't expect to eat, but I tried them all to avoid missing any of the African experience.

For our first full day in the country we joined the rest of the tour group to be driven to the Aberdares country club. Along the way we passed a convict chain gang working on the roadside. I'd never seen such a sight before - surely these were things you only see in movies?

Shortly after we were stopped by an officer carrying an assault rifle.

Apparently these armed stops are just for asking about vehicle condition, and the frequency of which they use this road. They obviously take their road planning very seriously here.

Our lunch was at Aberdares; between this and our scheduled nature walk was just enough time for me to swim a little in their pool. Although a warm day, the only other occupant was a peacock.

Now the nature walk was something I'd been looking forward to. We walked along a dirt track passing the occasional warthog. Hakuna matata! I thought to myself, even though there wasn't a meerkat in sight.

We saw zebra and impala mostly running away from us, and at the end of the trail was a clearing occupied by small family of giraffes. I edged closer to them slowly, careful not to startle them, until I was as close as our guide would allow. From there I crouched and watched them interacting whilst enthusiastically taking photographs. At last our safari had truly begun.

After breakfast we were on the road once more. We crossed the equator twice, and paused to see Mount Kenya before reaching Samburu.

As our driver left us at the gates to the Buffalo Springs Reserve to pay the entrance fee, the locals descended on us like vultures. Each of them had different items they were trying to sell and were quite persistent. Maybe it made some of the group feel uneasy; but it's what the locals have to do to survive.

The road into the reserve was bumpy, and kicked up clouds of dust and stones. At the end of this road is the tented camp we'd be staying in; surrounded by black-faced vervet monkeys. Each 'tent' has a large wooden frame with material covers for each wall. It's hard to call it a tent though when it's got a working indoor shower.

Surrounding this camp was an electric fence to deter the wildlife. Of course it doesn't stop monkeys jumping over; but the camp has a catapult-wielding naturalist to keep them away from the dining area.

It seems wrong to hit them; but I can understand why they do it - they don't want wildlife to become lazy and dependent on human food. Finding food in the wild is a skill they shouldn't lose in this delicate ecosystem. I guess you could call it 'tough love'.

After lunch we reconvened for tea and biscuits, something that felt so British, before heading out on our first game drive. Almost immediately we saw an elephant feeding on a bush, and as we drove along the dried-up riverbed we saw a whole herd amongst the trees.

We saw gazelle and impala grazing - two of many similar species we'd encounter. By the end of the week we were referring to them as 'DLCs': deer-like-creatures. It really was proving to be a great game drive; but it would have been nice if the driver had been more willing to pause for some of the smaller birds and not just the most popular of the animals.

It shouldn't have been a surprise that we were covered in dust when we got back to camp at dusk. Unfortunately the hot tap of the shower felt cold, and the cold tap felt chilled. I guess during the day it could be refreshing to have that; but in the cool evening it encourages a sense of urgency to use less water. Maybe that was the point.

When food was served, the staff were all wearing traditional garments from Samburu tribes. One of them played music using a woodwind instrument capable of only two notes. It was a nice surprise to get this unexpected entertainment and cultural lesson.

Back in the tent I realised how amazing the savannah is at night. It comes to life with the sounds of animals that sleep during the searing heat of the day. I could hear bullfrogs croaking, and the flutter of insects swarming around the lights. The tent had retained most of its heat so I left it open with the mosquito net in place.

I opened my eyes to the sun illuminating the sprawling savannah. The sun had risen early, and with it we needed to be on our way to the pre-breakfast game drive in hope of seeing our first big cat.

We were driven along trails, following the tracks of a lioness. The driver hoped to find us a leopard; but neither could be found. All we saw was a solitary giraffe, and a silver-backed jackal.

We saw more wildlife than that whilst eating breakfast: a troop of baboons passed through the camp whilst monkeys stole food from the plate of a fellow tourist. I was sure it'd taken a rasher of bacon; I guess it'd caught the naturalist off-guard.

Once fed we were back out on the road on our way to visit a local village. As luck would have it we saw a lioness along the way. It looked like this top predator had fallen on hard times - she was ragged and looked malnourished. We really needed that David Attenborough commentary here.

A few minutes later we stopped again when we spotted a crèche of fifteen ostrich young being protected by an adult male and female. This is something which is fairly common amongst ostriches - in this case a female was leading the way as a male guarded their rear.

Eventually we made it to the village with a US$30 entry fee we'd not been told about. With most of my money back at the camp it meant I wouldn't be able to buy any souvenirs from them; but at least this little money would go towards the needs of the entire tribe.

The chieftain had elongated earlobes from various ear piercings. He welcomed us in, and asked us to join them for the 'lion dance'. The women and children would form a semi-circle, whilst the men took it in turns to jump their highest into the air.

He told us about their way of life, and shown us inside one of their huts. It had two mattresses, though they weren't what we'd consider to be one in the western world. They were made from the leather of cattle skins, and just rested on the soil alongside a small fire they used for cooking maize and beans. This was a very simple life.

The food we could see cooking was only for the women, children, and elderly though. It's considered shameful for an adult male to eat here - they have to eat outside the village.

The tour concluded with a demonstration of how to make fire using sticks, and donkey excrement. I'm sure it's a useful skill to have; but I have to say it's not a skill

I've yet needed to use.

Lunch was back in the camp, and just happened to be timed with the arrival of some elephants bathing in the river. Considering what another elephant was doing further along, I don't think it was the cleanest of water.

After a final Samburu game drive, and amidst the various times the power generator cut out, it was time to pack ready to move on.

In the morning we drove back to Aberdares as a place to leave our luggage before continuing on to an overnight stay at the Ark. We stopped in Nanyuki along the way as this is where the country crosses the equator. So of course this meant a demonstration of the Coriolis effect.

The driveway to the Ark was a good place for spotting African cape buffalo, and mantled guereza. At the end of this drive there are stairs leading onto a boardwalk through the trees to the Ark itself.

The Ark has viewing platforms on each floor, and a hide at ground level with views of the watering hole. African elephants were drinking from it, and licking salt from the ground.

Each room had a buzzer which would sound if there were any sightings of note. The more buzzes there were, the rarer the animal, or the chance of an impending kill. Everything here is all about witnessing nature.

There were activities in the afternoon such as bird-watching; but once night fell I was in the hide: waiting and watching. There was a point when hyenas skulked out of the darkness to approach some bush-bucks, but they were startled and ran away. By 22:45 I decided it was time to rest.

Even though we'd be awoken if there were any major sightings, I was awake at 05:45 and sitting in the hide before sunrise. The hours passed by quickly, and soon breakfast was being served before the bus back to Aberdares to collect our luggage.

From there we were driven to Thomson's Falls - a waterfall on the Ewaso Ng'iro River, and named after a famous explorer of Africa. It's also one place where they charge tourists for everything. If you want to sit down on the grass, on a picnic bench, or walk close to the edge of the cliff to see the falls - you'd have to pay for each activity.

We had lunch at Lake Nakura; but had to be quick - we'd been delayed in Nakura by our driver forgetting his smart card, and had to be at Lake Naivasha for an optional boat tour at a specific time. It meant our game drive was quick; but we got to see flamingos in the lake, and a pair of white rhinoceros hiding in the tall grass. Even for a vehicle they're dangerous animals, so we had to keep our distance.

As we left Lake Nakura our itinerary suggested we'd be at Lake Naivasha in an hour. Even with the driver doing an excess of 100 kmph it took us twenty minutes more than that - meaning we only just made it before the last boat of the day left.

We paid the fee, and was directed down to the shore to the small boat equipped with an outboard motor. We saw kingfishers and other birds who call this lake home;

but we also saw the heads of something else poking out of the water: hippopotamus.

Rather than linger, the boat made landfall on Crescent Island - the location where Audrey Hepburn's 'Out of Africa' had been filmed. For the production they'd moved many animals onto this island; but only removed the lions from it after filming. It means there are a lot of difference species to be seen there such as black-faced vervet monkeys, and Masai giraffe. Without predators it means they're braver than they would be on the mainland.

Once we'd finished on the island we took the boat back to where we'd started; but got to photograph a baby hippo on the bank eating grass. Apparently it's quite rare to see them leave the water during the day; though to be fair it was almost sunset.

The sun had set by the time we reached the lodge, so they first briefed us on the rules there. We would not be allowed outside after dark for our own safety as hippos roam freely amongst these trees. If we wanted to venture out, such as to get our evening meal, we'd need to call reception for an armed escort. They're not allowed to shoot the animals, nor should they; but gunfire would be enough to scare them off if the situation arose.

It was time to journey into one of the most iconic parts of Africa: the Masai Mara. As we prepared to leave the lake we watched a large number of Colobus monkeys sitting on the roof of the lodge, and perched in the trees around. It was like Planet of the Apes - they'd taken over during the night and were now watching these strange hairless apes walking upright beneath them. Nature can be fascinating for us to watch, and it seemed we fascinated them too.

When we stopped at a curios shop, we were told we'd got five to ten minutes. Before this time was up our driver, and the vehicle had gone. We'd been left to bake in the sun as other tour groups arrived and left. It seemed we'd been abandoned; but still we waited. Surely the driver would come back for us if we waited long enough. almost an hour had passed when eventually he returned. The driver had been stuck in a queue to get fuel during a fuel shortage in town.

Out of town the paved roads gave way to bumpy dirt tracks that led into the Masai Mara National Reserve. Moments after entering we saw an injured lioness resting underneath a tree. Even injured, she was in better condition than the one we'd seen in Samburu. Yet it was a nice first sighting.

Time became difficult to keep track of as the bumpy trail continued all the way to the tented camp. These tents had less building material than in Samburu, but now included twice the number of mosquito nets, and overlooked the Mara River.

Not long after arriving we headed out on the first of our game drives. As we approached a steep path that led down to the river, James joked that because the driver was on the phone he was probably warning the RAC that he was about to be stuck in a stream. As if that would actually happen!

The driver drove down the steep path, and entered the river. Halfway through the river, the vehicle started sliding sideways instead of moving forwards, so he tried reversing. That was his mistake: by losing his momentum he'd now got it stuck. The driver made several attempts to move; but it wasn't budging. I was imagining us being stuck there for hours and missing the rest of our game drive. Sometimes it's easy to jump to the worst conclusion.

So the driver got out of the vehicle and started forcing small rocks under each of the wheels. It seemed a sound plan - put something solid there to give the wheels more traction. Of course though, it was dependent on getting the wheels to actually roll onto them first, and that wasn't really working.

Three more vehicles turned up, and one ejected its passengers into the wild so it could pull us out of the river. Well that was the plan anyway if it hadn't got stuck itself.

So what do you do when half the vehicles are stuck? You try the exact same tactic with one of the remaining ones! This time it worked better: our vehicle jolted back a metre as the rope went taut. It was just enough to have another go at crossing the river. This time successfully.

Having finally crossed the river once, we crossed it a further two times as the drive went on.

"Oh no!" our driver loudly exclaimed on the latter of these. We'd gotten stuck again.

A putrid smell drifted up from this river, seemingly coming from the hippos upstream that were watching us intently. Fortunately this time the driver was able to free us by himself. If hippos can think the way we do, who knows what they thought of us.

After that much drama, you'd think that'd be the end of it; but, no - there was more excitement to come.

We spotted a male lion that was heading over to two more that were feasting upon a hippo they'd killed the night before. Their faces were smeared with blood as they tore away flesh, and growled at the humans watching them. It felt like living in a wildlife documentary. This wasn't something I could have imagined having witnessed even just a few short years before.

Just moments away from this, a lioness had caught a buffalo she must have managed to separate from the herd. We watched as she attempted to suffocate it - a way of expending the least amount of energy for the kill. As the last vestiges of life left the buffalo, the lioness let out a low growl to let her cubs know that dinner was ready.

So much had happened on one drive. How could anything top this? We headed back to the camp as the sun was setting, and giraffes appeared to be worshipping a windsock. *Strange.* It had however been a perfect day of excitement, and adventure.

Before breakfast we were back out watching wildlife. It had been quiet, so when we saw two lionesses standing in the tall grass we stopped to photograph them just because they were there. I guess it was a strange change in attitude considering how sedate Samburu had been in comparison; but when you've seen so many lions already it doesn't feel like you need to go out of your way to see two more.

When we started to drive away from them, having moved two hundred metres at best, we saw some antelopes bolting across the savannah in the direction of the lionesses-something had spooked them.

As soon as our minds registered what was about to happen we knew they were done for, though our driver hadn't. We urged him to reverse back; but in the blink of an eye one of the antelopes disappeared. Seconds later we could see antelope feet sticking up in the air, as a lioness made short work of the kill.

When we approached them they were already feasting on their kill with some ferocity. Three hyenas approached, and challenged them for the meal with their wails. At least two lionesses would easily see off three hyenas!

The hyenas immediately started pulling at the meal, and the lionesses skulked slowly back into the tall grasses without much of a fight. Unexpectedly, the hyenas had won. More and more hyenas arrived with each passing minute - so this was why the lions had fled.

The kill attracted more hungry animals: waiting nearby, hoping for scraps. I'd never heard anything like the cacophony of noise created when the hyenas started to fight amongst themselves. It was a feeding frenzy with a cheeky silver-backed jackal sneaking away with a tiny morsel. Before we knew it there was nothing left; not bone or skin-the ravenous hyenas had eaten it all.

The rest of the game drive was quiet and ended with a bush breakfast overlooking a hippo pool. As we arrived they gave us champagne, and the rest of the breakfast was buffet style. It felt a little surreal to be sat out in the open at a breakfast table in the middle of the Masai Mara, and to be surrounded by nothing but savannah after what we'd just witnessed.

The following game drive was the complete opposite - so quiet that we were finally allowed to walk around a viewpoint. I could see the grasslands sprawl across the Masai Mara in Kenya, and the Serengeti in Tanzania. This is where we'd soon be.

On our drive back to Nairobi we stopped to look across the Great Rift Valley one last time. Our arrival back in the city coincided with election day, and masses of people queuing for the chance to vote. The increase in security here was obvious.

There were concerns that after the election there may be riots and violence like there had been after the previous one. Last time this happened the police opened fire on the rioters, and this escalated the violence even further. Violence doesn't solve violence.

It was said that one of the opponents of this election was facing charges for encouraging post-election violence again.

Our driver was being very careful to make sure we didn't stop anywhere near where there were masses of people to be on the safe side. There were no reported occurrences of riots that day, and none happened until almost a month after we left.

We were leaving Kenya behind us; but our safari wasn't over. We boarded a 68-seat propeller plane on our way to Tanzania.

17: Tanzania

"Yellow fever card," I was asked, after having crossed the tarmac of the Kilimanjaro airport. For arrivals from Kenya it was necessary to have proof of the vaccination.

I checked my backpack; but it was nowhere to be found. My stomach sank, and my mind was racing; trying to think where I'd put it. "Sorry, I've left it in my checked luggage".

I wasn't sure if it was true; but it was the only place I could think of. I was worried they'd turn me away; but she waved me through, with that being enough 'proof'.

We completed our visa application on arrival, and had our fingerprints taken - something which was becoming more common for immigration. It was pretty easy and quick, and before we knew it we were at the mountain lodge in Arusha exchanging some dollars into shillings. These were a reminder of the past. Both Kenya and Tanzania had used East African shillings until 1966 - a leftover from their British colonial days.

Usually I find the best currency to convert from whilst abroad is US dollars as they're generally accepted in most countries either in shops, or for exchange. China had taught me to make sure the notes were pristine though.

When morning came we joined five others, and divided ourselves between two land cruisers to head to Lake Manyara. One of this group had been a gladiator on the 1990s TV show, Gladiators. As I'd not seen the show, I had no idea who she was.

The shops we visited along the way seemed wealthier than they had done in Kenya - I supposed that perhaps they got more of the tourism on this side of the river. Though equally, the look of it could have been misleading.

We checked into the lodge at Lake Manyara, and after lunch went for our first game drive in this country. We'd seen most of the species before so it felt uneventful. There were some in our group that figured we must be all safari'd out; but our hope was that we'd eventually get to see a cheetah or a leopard.

Maybe we didn't see much wildlife, but during our evening meal we saw our first African thunderstorm. After it had been going on some time, the hotel staff approached and asked us what we'd like to do about the morning bush breakfast if the rain continued. It was kind of them to ask; but surely they should be telling us what we'll be doing? It's not like we knew what the options would be, or what their policy on it is.

By morning the storm had subsided. Champagne was served with breakfast once again, and I was starting to get the impression that alcohol consumption at breakfast is fairly common in this region. Was this tradition? Or maybe they think alcohol is safer than their water supply?

It was already time to move on from Lake Manyara - we drove through the Ngorongoro conservation area, along the edge of the crater, and stopped in a Masai village. They reminded me a lot of the tribe I'd seen in Samburu - their customs and lifestyles were very similar.

We had lunch at Olduvai Gorge on our way to the security checkpoint for the Serengeti National Park. Whilst waiting there I had a wander around, looking for photographic opportunities. On my way back the wind seemed to pick up and I could see dust all around me. A dust devil had formed in the spot I was standing. I moved quickly to protect my camera, and carried on back to the land cruiser.

What followed was supposed to be a game drive; but I struggled to see how driving down a trail at 60 kmph for twenty minutes could count as one.

When we saw a lioness on her back in the tall grass, we begged the driver to stop. He hadn't seen her, and it took three attempts to convince him that she was there. As it happened there were two females, and also one male that was about to mate with both of them. This isn't something tourists often witness; they should have some privacy really.

He did allow one further stop when we saw another lying on some rocks that reminded me of Pride Rock from The Lion King. The driver would not allow any further stops, and put his foot down to get us to camp.

Our expectation for the following morning was that we'd be out early for a balloon ride; but the guide told us he'd collect us at 08:00 for a game drive. It appeared they didn't know we'd got this ride booked, despite them having organised it for us. The troubles didn't stop there.

The timings the tour company then gave us didn't match up with what the ballooning company told us, so we had to pass these details on.

We then found the twin room we'd booked was a double instead. In all the years I'd been travelling with friends across what at that point had been five continents, this was the first time a room had been wrong.

The lodge explained they didn't have any more twin rooms, but in my mind it was tough - we'd booked a twin room, they'd accepted the booking, that's what we should have got. They agreed to sort it by moving another bed into the room, and so we went for dinner.

As they served the soup, they told us some bread rolls for the soup would be along shortly and took our order for drinks. Twenty minutes later we'd finished the starter and moved on to the main course - though it wasn't what we'd ordered. To make matters worse, the meat was mostly fat and bone - just like one of the meals we'd had in China.

Whilst eating we were asked if we'd like a drink with our meal, and by this point James had reached peak sarcasm.

"Yes please, I'd like the ones we ordered fifteen minutes ago"

Instead of bringing the drinks, they brought the bread rolls they'd intended to bring with the soup just as we were finishing our main course.

"Enjoy your meal," they politely told us. I'm sure they were trying their best; but out of all the places we'd stayed on this trip it felt like this was the one place that couldn't cope with tourists.

Back in the room we found their solution had been to squeeze a camping bed into the remaining floor space. At least I'd only need to sleep on it for six hours.

I awoke before dawn to the ringing of the phone at 04:10. It was time to get ready for a balloon ride. This lodge requires security escorts when walking to the main building as there are no electric fences to keep the wildlife out. Some of these guards are armed with AK-47s - a bit extreme just for warning shots. Were they to protect against poachers too? Or just for the odd rowdy tourist?

It seemed the security guard wasn't going to arrive, so cautiously we made our own way. Maybe it wasn't the most sensible thing we'd done; but we felt the chances of encountering a lion would be slim. Better than being late.

At the balloon launch site there were four balloons being prepared whilst we were briefed on safety procedures. The wicker baskets were then turned on their side, and we were prompted to climb in and sit facing upwards like you'd see for a rocket launch. We'd been advised to wear hats as the heat from the burners was incredible. I'd got my baseball cap with me that'd I'd so far worn in every country I'd visited.

As the balloon started to fill in ripples with hot air it tugged at the basket, pulling it upright. Moments later we were leaving the ground, and our journey across the

Serengeti had begun with the sunrise. It wasn't the first time I found myself thinking of the song 'Africa' by Toto.

Captain Nick, an English expatriate, was our pilot for the balloon ride. His nasally voice reminded me a lot of another Nick who'd been a lecturer at University. This Nick told us how the temperature of the ground below would affect control over the balloon in addition to the different thermal layers. He seemed to know as much about balloons as the other knew about Java.

Two thousand feet in the air we drifted passed giraffes and antelopes. Seeing the world from this perspective was jaw-dropping. It's not like anything I could have imagined. It's not the same as when you see the world below from an aircraft.

Our eventual landing was smooth, bouncing once as a fleet of land cruisers raced to greet us. They drove us to a place where they'd set up breakfast tables under a large tree, and handed glasses of champagne around. Again with the breakfast alcohol. French balloonists would often carry champagne with them in case a surprise landing angered or alarmed anyone around. The drink would be a way to appease them. So the tradition stuck.

After breakfast they took us to meet up with the rest of our group, and from then until midday we were on a game drive. We saw a lioness with young cubs, which was nice; but it was a leopard perched up a tree that made it memorable. To avoid disturbing this leopard and her cub we kept our distance.

One packed lunch later we were continuing the drive, albeit with a very stressed driver. There was a moment early on when we started to pass some elephants

- the others in this group had not yet seen any up close. One of them then started making clicking noises at the herd - which seems like an innocent; but strange thing to do. All of a sudden the driver slammed on the breaks, and turned to her.

"What are you doing?! Do you want to die?!" he shouted.

It was a reaction we hadn't expected; what was going on? He went on to explain that the elephants wouldn't recognise the sound, and could attack if they thought it a threat to their calves. When you're travelling there's always so much to learn.

The driver started to pull away again; but it was just as an elephant calf ran in front of us. Instead of stopping again the driver continued to drive on behind it - between the calf and the mother. There was then a loud trumpeting noise from behind us as the mother raised both of her front feet in warning. I thought she was about to charge us; but the elephant calf moved to the side to let us pass, and this calmed the mother. I later wondered if the elephant had actually been telling her young to get out of the way.

It was already an unforgettable day, yet there was more to come. Storm clouds were forming overhead, and the sky went dark. When the rain started to pour it got heavier, and heavier until it seemed like the rain couldn't get any heavier. This was when the thunderstorm started. We couldn't see much further than the front of the land cruiser; but could make out the glow of some tail lights seemingly floating in front.

To avoid the rain, tsetse flies started to swarm the

inside of the vehicle. Knowing that their blood-sucking bite would not be good, we began to swat them. One of them exploded in a bloody mess when struck; but it seemed none of us in this vehicle has been bitten at least.

Back at the safety of the lodge, in the ten metres running between the vehicle and the lobby, I got drenched to the point where I may as well have been standing at the bottom of a lake. I was pretty sure I'd never seen a storm so intense - the lightning bolts almost seemed constant. If I hadn't been so mesmerised by it, perhaps I'd have taken some photographs or video. Sometimes just witnessing the world is enough.

Next morning was another early start as we began the drive back to Ngorongoro. We had one last game drive on the way out as there were reports of a cheetah nearby. Perfect - this was the last of the big cats we wanted to see. Sadly I never got to see more than the outline of one perched on a rock above the grass at what seemed to be half a kilometre away. At least I'd seen it though.

The lodge in Ngorongoro was constructed on the rim of the crater with covered boardwalks between the reception and the block with the rooms in; they gave us an incredible view into the crater. When a thunderstorm arrived we could see it roll up and over the rim of the crater on the far side. It passed through the crater interior with lightning bolts somehow striking with a ferocity that surpassed the one we'd seen in the Serengeti. There was no doubt the rainy season had come early.

It felt like our first afternoon in Ngorongoro was wasted; but in the morning we finally got to go out on a game drive. Here wildebeest passed us by, and we could see a pair of black rhinoceroses in the distance. These are more likely to charge than the ones in Kenya so we needed to stay as far away as possible. Maybe one day I'd get to see a rhino up close.

Some animals we did see in almost touching distance, such as lions that sat around the sides of our vehicle, and birds which would swoop down and take food from your hand. They said not to feed the animals; but in this case they were feeding themselves.

One of our group ignored the signs and was told off for feeding the birds. His excuse though was that the sign said 'Don't feed the animals', and tried to claim that birds aren't animals. Obviously he hadn't got a clue, and with me being my usual self I explained to him that they are animals - the animal kingdom contains a phylum called Chordates that mammals, birds, and other back-boned animals are part of.

The rest of our day was left empty with another thunderstorm approaching. It seemed to build up more and more against the rim until like a bursting dam it pushed over into the crater - now resembling a super cell. It was amazing to watch; but when it reached us, the rainwater flooded the boardwalks. It was nothing short of a miracle that it didn't start flowing into the rooms.

The end had come. The morning after the storm we were driven back to Arusha for our flight home from Kilimanjaro airport. I thought that for the second of two flights, from Nairobi to home, that I'd be able to sleep across three seats of the plane. I was wrong - these seats were broken so the arm rests wouldn't raise. Instead I tried to sleep on the floor in front of these seats; but was awoken by a flight attendant to be told off, and asked to stay in my seat.

I don't think I'd been so tired on a flight since my trip back from New Zealand; but it was worth it. Those wildlife encounters had made this into an adventure, though I knew my next trip would be even more of one - a trip that had been years in the planning.

18: San Diego, CA.

I *knew* that my next trip after my African safari would be Antarctica. For most people it's their last continent; but for me - I'd not yet visited North America. Ideally I needed to go there first, though was in need of a plan.

I'd always assumed that I'd one day get to visit the USA, though an opportunity never arose. That was until a colleague started a one year road trip to cover the contiguous states of America. Before him and a friend left we decided to try for tickets to the popular San Diego Comic Con - usually abbreviated to SDCC.

I've been to conventions in the UK as both an attendee, and as someone helping out so have seen both sides. The ones I'd been to focused on traders; but I knew SDCC would be different, and very Hollywood centric with a focus on 'panels' discussing popular TV shows.

We were lucky to get some tickets before they set off on their journey. As they were now busy it was sometime until we were able to book accommodation - something that fills up quickly around the time of popular events. It was making me nervous.

After extensive searching we were able to book a hostel in the historic Gaslamp Quarter - so we were actually incredibly lucky as it's very close to the convention centre, and the centre of everything. The downside though, was that I needed to be at the airport for my flight at 03:25; but the trains near me stop running for about eight hours overnight. It meant I was in the airport early, and trying to sleep on the floor. I should have planned better.

This was the first time I'd flown by myself; but I was confident that my previous trips had prepared me for this. It's true, I found myself running across Frankfurt airport to reach the gate as they were boarding; but that was due to a tight connection. I could see one day that could go badly.

I met up with Jacko, and his friend, Wes. They'd arrived a few days previously, so already knew some of the places around. I checked into the hostel, secured my luggage, and was ready to experience the convention atmosphere the city had embraced.

People were wandering around dressed as Disney princesses, a bar had been dressed to look like the one from a big sci-fi show, and larger-than-life LEGO models of characters from The Hobbit had been created in front of a life-sized LEGO Hobbit hole. The city had become a celebration of nerd culture. It was fantastic!

We decided to find somewhere to eat. The first place we tried didn't tell us they'd stopped serving food until after we'd ordered drinks; but we found somewhere open that sold slices of pizza. That'd do - even if it was almost midnight.

Sleeping in a hostel was a new experience for me. I found earplugs are a good idea - particularly if after fifty-seven hours you need rest. At the hostel you make breakfast yourself: they provided free pancake mix, maple syrup, and some basic kitchen facilities. It was the first time I'd made pancakes myself so I was very lucky they came out edible, and in one piece.

For the rest of the day we wandered around San Diego, experiencing the 'off-site' aspects of the convention. Hotels had been repurposed as gaming lounges for playing upcoming video games, and prizes were given out for taking part.

We found that in a parking lot they'd created an area for boat races where the fastest time for the day would win a viking shield signed by the cast of a show - it sounded fun, and we thought we'd give it a good go.

Before we could get into one of the viking boats we had to first sign a waiver, and then put on a life vest and helmet. We worked hard though we weren't working in rhythm - making our boat rock considerably. When we finished we found we'd achieved the fourth fastest time of the day.

Having realised this we thought we'd have another go. This time we put everything we had into paddling; but again we didn't row together. What we did do however was to create big enough waves so that the boat we were racing was capsized by them. Hopefully they weren't too angry we'd caused them to get a bit wet.

The downside to convention week though is that every restaurant gets very busy - there's around 130,000 extra people in the city all wanting to be fed. Meal times would mean plenty of waiting, or finding out-of-the-way places. We got lucky and found a sports bar that was fairly quiet, though when we left there a couple of ladies stopped us in our tracks.

The reason for this? We were each wearing Mario hats we'd won from Nintendo, and here during SDCC week everyone is a target for being photographed. After our photo had been taken, we moved on to continue exploring some more.

We got to walk onto a set from an upcoming movie, and look at the props and set dressings. Elsewhere we were asked TV trivia, and again got to win more goodies whilst watching sizzle reels and features for upcoming shows and films. Time during SDCC week really is quite surreal.

Whilst looking for one of the rooms we'd need later in the week, we came across an actress who appeared in a TV show I'd watched. I walked over to her, and waited patiently to ask if I could take a picture; but she was surrounded by her fans wanting autographs. Unfortunately someone arrived to lead her out, and I missed my chance.

Jacko was not feeling well by this point so he headed back to the hostel whilst me and Wes got food.

I'd intended that the first day of the convention would start with me joining the queue for badges as early as possible. These badges are needed for entering the convention itself. However, my alarm never went off.

If asked, most people would say one of two things when asked what the biggest thing about SDCC is: either the queues, or the panels. We were fortunate and managed to get into a panel to listen to the writers behind one of the biggest sitcoms of the time. Not only were the writers there; but so were two of the actors after a funny Star Wars-themed introduction.

The exhibitor hall is where all the traders and other businesses set-up stands. It was bigger than any I'd been to in the UK; but was also overrun with big businesses rather than the private traders I'm used to seeing. Microsoft and Sony were there to give people a chance to try out their latest gaming consoles before release. It felt like this convention was being driven by brand promotion.

It's strange though that you can randomly bump into famous faces whilst wandering around. I saw Patrick Warburton, various actors from Star Trek, and even Kevin Sorbo who had played Hercules in the New Zealand produced TV series.

After the three of us were photographed on a reconstruction of the bridge of the USS Enterprise D, we went our separate ways for the remainder of the afternoon. We each had things we wanted to see; but we met back up in the queue outside Hall H to see the heavy metal band, Metallica.

It was a long wait, and for most of this time someone was walking around with a sign saying that we're all damned, and using a megaphone to preach about Christianity. Apparently we were all damned for attending comic-con. That's nice.

Apparently quite a few people had been in there all day which explained why it's usual to only see panels in there if you've queued up outside overnight. It made me wonder if they should empty the room after the panel to give everyone a fair chance, though it'd also mean the turnaround time between panels would be longer and you wouldn't be able to see two consecutive panels you're interested in.

For my last full day in San Diego I wanted to squeeze every last minute out of the day. My friends were more interested in sleeping. I can understand it; but it felt like wasted time. As it happened this meant most of the morning was then wasted - we arrived in the queue for the panel we wanted to see too late to get in; but queued for most of the morning just in case.

We'd gotten unlucky there, but we got lucky with the queue for Ballroom 20. We got to see panels for numerous shows, one after another. Half of them were for shows I'd not really seen; but the last two were ones I really wanted to see. They were for shows I'd watched every episode of.

With the last of those panels over, I went back to the exhibitor hall one last time before leaving for food. There was a large number of people leaving at the same time we did, and amongst them was a horde of zombies. Not real of course, just lots of people dressed that way, and in make-up because they were fans of a zombie-themed show.

Just before we got back to the hostel I photographed a famous US model named Adrianne Curry who was cosplaying as Mileena, a character introduced in Mortal Kombat 2. She's a well known fan of science fiction and fantasy, and her cosplay is always impressive.

With that done, that was it - SDCC was now over for me; so I finished the day in the most American of ways - with a burger and fries.

Before heading to the airport, I decided I'd walk from the hostel to the USS Midway with my suitcase dragging behind me. I probably didn't take the most direct route there; but as I'd got the whole morning available it really didn't matter.

Sometimes what seems obvious is not always correct. I queued up at a kiosk for tickets to board, and then paid the fee. It wasn't until afterwards I found that they'd sold me a boat tour, and what I actually wanted was another kiosk hidden away elsewhere so had to be refunded.

This tour was pretty good: they let me leave my luggage and backpack at their visitor information point, so I could wander around unencumbered.

It was a little different getting to explore an aircraft carrier - I could go up onto the bridge to look out over the flight deck, and look around below deck. It didn't take long, so I continued walking to the airport for my flight home.

19: The Voyage Begins

For a few years I knew I wanted to visit Antarctica - it would realise the recent ambition of visiting every continent in the world at least once. For some time it looked like it could be prohibitively expensive. I told a few friends and colleagues that I was determined to go there in the next few years. I don't think they really believed I would go.

As the years passed by I visited many countries; but the desire to go there remained. James, who had been on a number of these trips with me, probably wanted to go there even more than I did. We started to look at the options more seriously, even on a budget it would be expensive. To get an idea of how much a trip like this can cost as even a minimum, just know that there are brand new cars you can buy for less. Maybe with a lot of saving, just maybe, we might be able to do it.

We looked at what companies would offer landfall on the continent itself, and looked at where else they'd visit along the way. It took some time to narrow down which company to go with; but eventually we settled on an expedition that sounded like it'd be the best in our stretched price range.

Antarctica is on average the coldest, driest and windiest continent in the world - yet we'd be visiting during its summer. This was not to say it would be warm; it's likely it would still get very cold. Our previous trips to Iceland and Norway went some way to prepare us.

The journey to Antarctica was a long one, and it started with an evening flight from London to Madrid just a few days after Christmas. When we arrived there, although only in transit, we had to pass through security. On the other side we found the options for an evening meal very limited - the best we could find was a baguette for €13 that could be heated in their microwave.

From Madrid we were flying on to Buenos Aires; but our flight was delayed at first by an hour and then two hours. Flight delays are nothing unusual; but it's less than helpful when it pushes your flight time into the early hours of the morning.

We arrived in Buenos Aires two hours late, and met with Julieta - our guide for the day. She took us to our hotel, and left us for a couple of hours to find somewhere to eat before she'd start our tour.

We decided on a restaurant opposite the hotel for convenience, though found the service wasn't great. Anyone who arrived after us took priority just because they could speak better Spanish, and whilst everyone else were handed knives and forks to eat with, we had to go looking for our own. I was starting to get the impression the owner didn't like the British.

For many years there has been a dispute between Argentina and the United Kingdom about the sovereignty of the Falkland Islands that sit off the coast of Tierra del Fuego. Although it lasted only two weeks in 1982, the two countries also went to war during a time of instability for the Argentinian government.

Over thirty years have passed since then though - could it really be down to that? It didn't matter really though; but it wasn't the best first impression for a country.

Moving on, we met up with Julieta for a tour of the Recoleta neighbourhood. This area has fancier architecture, and is an area for the wealthy. As we walked from the hotel to this neighbourhood we passed the Teatro Colón opera house - a nice looking building which also screens performances outdoors for people to watch for free. They also have tours which are thirty pesos for locals, and over one hundred pesos for foreigners.

It may seem odd that there's that difference in price; but I think it's fair. I've come across quite a few places where prices are higher for tourists - they do it so that the locals can still afford to visit these places whilst bringing in sufficient money from outside the country for the maintenance of the sights.

Whilst we were being guided around Recoleta we spoke to Julieta a little about the politics of the country - in particular what the people in Buenos Aires thought of the Falkland Islands, or as the Argentinians call them: the Malvinas. We were told that most young people don't care about the islands - it's only the government that cares.

That seemed fair enough, and I guess it made sense.

At the end of this walk was the Plaza Francia - a park with a very large rubber tree known as the Gran Gomero. Some of the branches are so big that it has metal support poles. The support poles reminded me of the Major Oak in Nottingham - a tree associated with the legend of a Robin Hood. However this tree was far larger with massive twisting roots, and new roots forming from branches. It was planted in 1791 by Martín José Altolaguirre, the owner of the land at that time, and so is actually much younger than the Major Oak.

Just beyond this tree is the entrance to the La Recoleta Cemetery, the final resting place of Maria Eva Duarte de Perón, the second wife of Argentine President Juan Perón, and known better to the world as Evita.

Due to the age of the cemetery you could expect all of the mausoleums to be old; but some families sell off their plots and new mausoleums are then built in their place. Otherwise, the families own the plots forever, with a small fee going to the government for maintenance.

Next door is the church of Nuestra Señora del Pilar - a very Spanish design that reminded me of ones in Peru. This one was built in 1732 by the Monastery of the Recollect Fathers, members of the Franciscan Order - the 18th Century order for which the neighbourhood is named.

That evening we took a taxi to La Cabrera - a place we'd reserved a table at long before flying out. It's one of the most popular restaurants in the city, making it difficult to get seats at; but it's one of the best places to try Argentinian steak.

We had been forewarned that portions at this restaurant are very large so it is normal to share dishes. With this in mind we ordered a 600g steak, fries, and a mixed salad. The steak was unlike any I'd seen before - it was bigger than what a Sunday roast would normally be! The quality of the meal was excellent, and along with a large bottle of water for the table it only cost 490 pesos, so the equivalent of about £15 per person. Considering the popularity of the place, not bad at all.

On our way back to the hotel the taxi ride cost twice as much; but with good reason. The roads were alive with the angry protests of locals. They had set-up road blocks with mounds of rubbish on fire, and to avoid them we had to take a longer route back.

According to BBC News the protests were due to power cuts across the city - a side effect of the heatwave which in turn meant people couldn't use air conditioning. It was nearing midnight; but the temperature was still 38°C - it was little wonder it was causing trouble.

Before our flight to Ushuaia, we had some time to wander around the city. The opera house runs tours every fifteen minutes, with English ones being once per hour - we thought this'd be a nice way to spend the morning so queued up outside.

Overnight the power situation hadn't improved, and we hadn't realised the opera house was a victim of this. We queued for over an hour hoping the power would be restored; but eventually we ran out of time. We had to head to the airport.

For this flight they had a stricter policy on baggage

limits which meant paying US$39 between us when checking in. It was expected though - we were both carrying a lot of heavy cold weather clothes.

Our arrival in Ushuaia was also one of the fastest baggage claims I've ever experienced - both of us had our bags just seconds after entering. From the outside I thought this airport looked like a ski resort with a dramatic backdrop of the snow-capped mountains of the Andean mountain range. It was quite a contrast to Buenos Aires.

The taxi driver from there to the hotel was insistent we weren't staying at the hotel we said we were. He went out of his way to call the tour company to check on this, and eventually agreed we were indeed correct. It's not the first country we've had taxi troubles in. Why can't taxi drivers just believe me?

This wasn't a bad hotel, it had a Christmas tree in the lobby; but you could tell that Tierra del Fuego, the southernmost city in South America, doesn't quite have the same money as Buenos Aires. It's also considerably cooler there; but we did only have around a thousand miles left to get to Antarctica.

Whilst we were there, James got an email that would change everything for him: he would be emigrating to Canada upon his return. It could complicate future trips; but it'd be an excuse for me to visit another country at some point in the future.

The culture in Ushuaia is very similar to other Spanish-influenced cities in South America - many shops will close around midday for a siesta. Most of the souvenir shops in this area had similar prices; but some of the larger shops had a better variety.

This morning was also a chance to try another recommended Argentinian dish - 'bife de chorizo'. It's basically a steak grilled over a charcoal flame with chimichurri relish.

Just before we'd arrived in Argentina we'd heard about a Russian research vessel getting stuck in Antarctic ice. By the time we boarded the Plancius, an icebreaker we'd be travelling on, we heard that the Chinese icebreaker that had been sent to rescue them had also gotten stuck. They were now having to wait out the worst of the weather until a helicopter could be sent. Whenever things like this happen, it's only natural to wonder if you'll experience the same bad luck.

On the pier that led to the ship, we passed a large sign.

"...we should remember that the Malvinas, South Georgias, South Sandwich Islands, and the surrounding maritime areas, are, since 1833, under the illegal occupation of the United Kingdom of Great Britain and Northern Ireland"

Well, that's awkward. I laughed as I read it - what else could I do? Maybe it'd be best if I avoided them seeing a passport stamp for the Falkland Islands when I eventually returned.

Onboard the ship we'd got a twin cabin with a fair-sized window rather than the porthole we'd been expecting. An upgrade!

I wouldn't normally unpack during a trip: I'm usually moving around too much; but we'd be on this ship for the next eighteen days. I felt I may as well unpack, and had finished this by the time the anchor had been raised. Our expedition had begun.

In a previous life the Plancius had been an Oceanographic research vessel built for the Royal Dutch navy. It was now a passenger vessel used by tourists, and by nothing but coincidence we'd be making landfall on Antarctica almost 103 years to the day since the Scott expedition reached the South Pole.

After the briefing and practice evacuation drill, I made my way onto the top deck with my camera to see what sea birds would be flying around the Beagle Channel. It was eerily quiet, so I instead attended the next briefing where they handed out champagne to celebrate the start of the expedition. At least they weren't doing this at breakfast - it'd been several months since East Africa.

The crew for this was made up of an atmospheric researcher who had once wintered in Antarctica, two ornithologists, a historian, and several other specialities including a doctor.

It hadn't really occurred to me before; but this was New Years Eve - we'd be at sea for the start of the next year, and it'd be almost February before we'd get back home. The crew had thought of this, and had prepared a quiz, and more champagne served in specially engraved glasses to mark the occasion.

As you'd probably expect, the ship burst into song

at midnight with just the first verse of Auld Lang Syne. Around this time we also passed our first milestone - we were out of the calm Beagle Channel and onto the open sea.

At some point overnight it had become cloudy and wet; but we didn't have anything to do so it didn't really matter. We attended lectures on the history of the Falkland Islands, and just how problematic they'd been even before the 1982 conflict.

Long before the confirmed discovery of the islands, the sovereignty of the Americas was in dispute between Spain and Portugal due to Christopher Columbus having met with King John II of Portugal before he got support from Queen Isabella of Spain. In 1493 Pope Alexander attempted to resolve this by splitting the New World in two between Spain and Portugal - this included any lands yet to be discovered whether people already lived on them or not.

It is believed a number of expeditions sighted the Falkland Islands after this time; but it wasn't until the late 1500s that it is believed it was landed upon by the English. John Strong then named the islands; but it was disputed twenty-three years later by the Spanish - they believed them to be theirs under the treaty of Tordesillas.

So that was our morning sorted, and our afternoon was taken up by a lecture of the birds we could potentially see on the Falklands. There was also a mandatory briefing on the use of Zodiacs - the rigid inflatable boats the Plancius carries.

A whole day had passed without seeing land; but overnight we'd reached the west coast of the Falkland Islands. The weather was still too bad though. To avoid it we were going to visit West Point Island instead of the planned Carcass Island. That's the way things go on expeditions - you need to be quick to adapt to a back-up plan.

Ashore, we were led by the expedition crew across fields, and up hills until we reached cliffs on the other side of the island. We had to stay five metres away from all wildlife; but it was close enough to see a colony of black-browed albatross with rockhopper penguins mixed between them. I don't think the animals here had heard the rules though - some penguins awkwardly waddled over to greet us to their home, and see what we were up to.

Wildlife is so fascinating to watch, especially when you start to anthropomorphise their behaviours. Some rocker hoppers looked as if they were having fun playing in puddles of water. Watching them made it almost possible to ignore the wind and rain.

When we got back to the ship we had to clean and disinfect our boots - we couldn't risk bringing anything on-board from the island that could potentially cause cross-contamination between islands on future excursions.

It wasn't too bad for a first excursion. We'd gotten back just in time for dinner which included a carrot and ginger soup. I mention the soup as whilst a waitress was passing with a bowl of this hot soup, one of the other passengers raised his hand into the air, and knocked it from her hands. The first I knew of this happening was when I felt something hit me in multiple places at once, and then the strong feeling of heat. Sure enough, I was covered from head to toe.

It was a rush to get changed again so I could resume my dinner, and the crew were good enough to sort out the cleaning of my clothes even though it had been caused by a passenger.

The weather still wasn't great, so we changed our afternoon destination to Port Egmont - the site of the first British colony in 1765. It was a rough ride; but we made it ashore safely so we could hike up to a memorial from the ruins of the old fort. My impression so far of the Falklands was that it rains frequently. Seems a lot like the United Kingdom to me.

Returning to the ship was somehow even rougher - the winds had picked up and we were now needing a second crew member on each zodiac to help keep the nose up. If the seas had been this rough earlier, we'd never have left the ship - they seemed to think it was now verging on being dangerous.

When morning came, we were once again going on an excursion. This time we headed over to Port Stanley which looks a lot like an English town, maybe somewhere in Yorkshire. The buildings were made from brown bricks, and had walled gardens and picket fences. It was no wonder that in their recent referendum in which 92% voted, all but three people had decided to remain British, and to not join Argentina.

Since my last trip I'd taken up running through

'Couch to 5K'; but hadn't been on a run since this expedition began. When I saw someone running around the town I felt a little jealous that I'd not thought of doing the same. It was still new to me, and I hadn't yet realised the benefits of running whilst travelling to new places.

It'd been suggested that we take a taxi to Gypsy Cove to see Magellanic penguins, though at first it seemed impossible to do so. We later realised there are only two taxis on this island, and they were spending most of the morning ferrying the passengers back and forth. It's a shame the tour company couldn't have arranged for a minibus; but perhaps Port Stanley didn't have any of these.

It's a short ride to Gypsy Cove, passing the rusty shipwreck of the Lady Elizabeth in Whale Bone Cove along the way. It's only a short journey; but still cost US $20 per passenger - they must have been making quite some profit that morning.

At the cove it's not possible to visit the beach itself due to fences. The reason is that during the last conflict there were landmines placed on the beach by the Argentinians. It had been cleared; but they couldn't be sure if more would wash ashore.

In addition to the king penguins and Magellanic penguins, there is a gun emplacement from the second world war at Ordnance Point. I hadn't expected to see this rusty piece of history there - it was part of their defences alongside the Falkland Islands Defence Force whilst many went to Britain to help in the war effort.

Back in Port Stanley, we looked around everything we could find. There's a post office, a museum that includes a lot of information about the 1982 conflict, and there's also a memorial to those that died.

Once back on-board the ship, this was the end of our time in the Falklands - our next stop would be on South Georgia and the South Sandwich Islands. We'd be one step closer to Antarctica. One step closer to that ambition of visiting all the continents, even though we were technically further away than in Ushuia.

20: South Georgia

Overnight we crossed the Antarctic convergence into the clockwise-flowing waters of the Antarctic circumpolar current. As we did so we changed time zone once more, and put our watches forward an hour.

The convergence is where the cooler Antarctic waters meet the warmer sub-Antarctic waters. The result is that inside the circumpolar current any travel from west to east is far quicker; but for those travelling west they'll find their journey slowed. A famous example of this is when the HMS Bounty abandoned its attempt to round Cape Horn in the months before the infamous mutiny. They had tried for days before declaring the sea had beaten them, and instead set sail for Cape Hope.

After breakfast there was a briefing in the dining room to talk about environmental protection and biosecurity, and how important it is to make sure outer layers of clothing and backpacks are cleaned before taking them ashore. These steps are to avoid the introduction of any new flora or fauna to these protected places. These guidelines are set by IAATO, the International Association of Antarctic Tour Operators, so must be followed by every visitor.

Due to less care in the past, South Georgia's habitats have already been contaminated with rats, reindeer, and dandelions. They are damaging to the natural ecosystem, and unbalances it.

Most of this day was to prepare for going ashore, but in the afternoon I stayed out on deck, and watched the waves crashing. I hoped to catch a glimpse of a whale. This time luck was not with me; but there was still time.

That evening I sat and ate dinner with French, German, Russian, and Singaporean passengers. It might sound like the set-up for a racially insensitive joke; but it's not. It was good getting to know them, and learning more about their respective countries, and cultures. They each talked about the adventures they'd already been on as well. They were like-minded individuals who all enjoyed seeing the world. From talking to them it might just influence my future travels, at any rate - we got to know them well enough that even years later I'd still be in contact with them.

Our conversations made us late to a lecture; but this didn't last long anyway - there'd been a sighting of a pod. I ran to the window to see how close the whales were, and saw numerous ones breaching the water. I ran to the cabin as fast as I safely could, grabbed my camera, and ran out onto the deck wearing just shorts and a t-shirt. There was a lesson there: take my camera everywhere.

It was cold out on the deck - the temperature had been dropping as we got closer and closer to Antarctica. I couldn't risk missing the chance to photograph whales though - I had no idea if we'd see any more.

Twilight made it increasingly difficult to take photographs from a moving ship. It became more sensible to get some warmer clothes, and then return to the deck to just stand and watch.

Another day dawned as we reached South Georgia, escorted by playful Antarctic fur seals alongside the ship. The ship, shrouded in a thick fog, was edging ever closer to the bay of Elsehul.

Snow began to fall through the fog, blanketing the decks of the ship with a fine white coating. I figured it'd make for some atmospheric photographs, though by the time we made it to the Zodiacs the sun was starting to break through the clouds, and was burning away the fog. The weather can change very quickly here.

Our navigator for this cruise was the Russian sailor, Igor. We saw an abundance of Macaroni penguins, and seals; but it seemed there was something else in the water. Something... bigger.

As we headed over to another part of the bay a southern right whale, partially covered in callosities, breached the water less than two metres from our Zodiac. Not one person on our boat was prepared for it, so whilst other boats started to head to our location, those of us in front of it were frantically trying to get cameras ready. It was a fantastic sight; but it disappeared beneath the surface as quickly as it had appeared.

Our boat was alive with chatter over the excitement of having seen the whale so close, so it came as a surprise when it resurfaced, and immediately blew smelly fluid from its blowhole - an action that was like it sneezing.

Covered in the pungent liquid it had sprayed, we soon soon put our cameras away.

This whale was called a 'right whale' because when they're killed, their carcass will mostly remain on the surface. It might sound an awful thing to do; but the term originates from the days of whaling.

South Georgia was already providing us with excitement, though we heard over the radio that one Zodiac was losing air after they'd hit a seal, and another had run out of fuel. Ooops.

I felt their were questions to ask there, such as how on earth did they manage to hit a seal with enough force to create puncture, and was the seal okay?

When we were all safely back onboard the Plancius, we continued on along the coast through a channel with Bird Island. Either side of us we watched snow-capped mountain peaks pass by. Or at least we did until the fog, and snow returned. Fifty knot winds were now blowing snowdrifts across the surface of the South Atlantic Ocean.

It'd been intended we'd go ashore in Right Whale Bay; but these conditions were making it unsafe. Perhaps we could in Prince Olav Harbour instead, though that was three hours navigation away.

These changes were becoming common - it's the way expeditions work. Whilst we waited, we sat and listened to a lecture on the famous Antarctic explorer, Ernest Shackleton. How different it must have been back then - we'd got it easy.

Unexpectedly it was announced we'd reached Rosita Harbour, and the conditions were good enough to go ashore. The expedition team hadn't visited this one before though, so had to do a quick reconnaissance first. The green light was given, and we raced to the Zodiacs. For this entire journey from ship to shore we were pelted by hail stones falling not far off horizontally.

On the beach there were Antarctic fur seals everywhere. We knew that they packed a nasty bite; but could make them back off or stop by holding out our hand firmly and commanding "stop". Never run away from them.

As we'd made good progress during the day from having visited this different beach, it meant that when we returned after the excursion we were able to reach Fortuna Bay early, and remained anchored there overnight.

Most of us arose early to go on what is known as the Shackleton Hike. For this we would follow the six kilometres of varying terrain that Ernest Shackleton took when seeking rescue.

This hike ascends steeply at first, and soon levels out. At this point we paused, waiting for the others to catch-up; but found ourselves lingering longer when a Japanese lady collapsed. The medic rushed over to her to assist quickly. It wasn't clear what had happened; but as they often do amongst groups, rumours spread quickly. They said that she'd collapsed from exhaustion, and hadn't had breakfast.

We passed a large glacial lake, and ahead of us were areas of thick snow. On the other side of this was a precipice overlooking the sea, and the route we'd be taking down to Stromness. In the distance through the falling snow we could see the Plancius had arrived in the bay, and wasn't far from the abandoned whaling station.

To reach our extraction point we needed to zig-zag down a snow-filled gully, and across a plateau with nesting gentoo penguins. We started slow, and I tried to help those that were less steady on their feet. One by one we reached a point where it was safe to slide down some of the mountain on our backs.

It was fun; but I'd not thought about the added weight of my camera backpack. I rocketed down the snow, picking up speed as I went. The only way to stop me was for a couple of people to stand in my path, and get ready to grab me. The force of stopping so suddenly tore my camera backpack away, and it tumbled down the slope. The horror! I'd got two lenses and two camera bodies hurtling away from me at speed.

Inside the bag was a lot of padding, though I had no idea if it'd survive. Someone stepped into it's path, and was able to grab it before it got too far. I'd been very lucky.

When we reached a plateau, some petrels were attacking gentoo penguins to get at the eggs they were protecting. You could see numerous eggs that had been cracked open on the floor, and the contents consumed – it was a shame to see; but it's the way of things in the natural world.

Beyond the masses of gentoo nests was a river bed that led all the way to Stromness Harbour. The closer we got to the coast, the heavier the snowfall until eventually it was like trying to see through a white sheet. It was necessary to be careful as not only were there fur and elephant seals everywhere; but also an exclusion zone around the abandoned whaling station. There was a sign which read:

"It is an offence to approach within the safety boundary markers of the whaling station. Danger of unsafe structures and asbestos."

It'd been in operation from 1912 to 1961, so when Ernest Shackleton had arrived here it had been their salvation. Having been closed for over fifty years meant that there was danger from collapsing structures that had succumbed to the elements and the passage of time.

Once everyone had made it back to the ship we begun our navigation to Grytviken for an afternoon excursion. After passing Cumberland Bay the weather quickly started to clear up, and the sun started to shine.

Here in Grytviken the scientists were racing against time. They'd spent £4.5 million on eradicating the invasive brown rats. They needed to raise another £3 million to clear the rest by March 2015. If they couldn't do it before then it was predicted the effects of global warming would cause the glaciers to recede enough to allow the rats to spread back out to the areas already cleared. It's impossible to deny that global warming is severely affecting the Antarctic regions.

Years after I returned from this expedition I checked up on the progress they'd made and found that they'd reached their target. The increase in South Georgia Pipit chicks the following year was a strong indicator that they'd succeeded in their task; but to be sure there was still the task of surveying the island. Conservation works, though the temperatures in South Georgia in the years since were still getting considerably warmer at a faster rate than the rest of the world.

Our first stop in Grytviken was a small cemetery with a white picket fence - it was the final resting place of arguably one of the greatest explorers of the south polar region, the 'boss' - Ernest Shackleton. It was precisely 94 years and 2 days since his death so we toasted to his memory whilst standing around his grave.

Not far from this is another abandoned whaling station. This one has been prepared for tourist visits so that it's possible to look around. I think this place isn't there to glorify the killing of whales; but to act as a reminder to humanity that this industry was misguided.

The small settlement there even has a post office, though I couldn't be sure how it worked considering the remoteness. Do Royal Mail have a ship pass by once a day for deliveries? I wondered what the difference between first and second class postage would be.

The following morning brought with it another challenge; but not one that was insurmountable. We'd arrived in Fortuna Bay to go ashore once more in conditions that were very bad. After a short reconnaissance trip the expedition team decided that the best way to handle the waves would be to go in backwards at the last minute, and to then disembark as quickly as possible.

After being led single file through masses of seals, and across streams I found myself very pleased that they'd taken that risk. A colony of King Penguins stretched for as far as the eye could see. It was impossible to guess just how many were there. It seemed very unlikely we'd ever see more penguins in one place.

Still amazed by the experience, a few of us were led away from the penguins in search of light-mantled albatrosses. We passed an old cave that had once been used by sealers and was partially bricked up to provide protection from the wind. I imagined it at first to be a smugglers cave like those you'd find in Cornwall.

Our guide came to a stop, though no birds were in sight. In fact, the beach was looking pretty empty. However, somewhere on the cliffside above was an albatross nest and the only way to see it would be to climb.

Before anyone could go up, we were told to only go up if we'd got a decent lens - we wouldn't see it properly without one. Of course I decided to make the climb, so slung my large lens over my back and begun to climb, pulling on tussock grass to maintain balance.

I don't think the climb had been expected as we found ourselves being late back to the ship for the navigation to Jason Harbour, though this was delayed further when the Royal Navy patrol ship HMS Protector blocked our path.

I couldn't be sure what transpired; but they eventually let us continue so we could make landfall and hike to one of the summits. Our guide found it wasn't so easy to get back down, and led us passed a crevasse, and back down a different route. With nothing around, the guide decided the best thing would be for a Zodiac to come and collect us.

Our last day on South Georgia was an 05:45 start. It was early, but it was worth it. Previously I hadn't imagined I'd ever see more penguins in one place than at Fortuna Bay, but I was wrong. We were going ashore at Gold Harbour which has also been nicknamed 'Penguin City'. When you see a place like this with your own eyes, it's easy to understand why.

It's crazy really; but despite the calm seas and the clear blue skies this excursion was almost cancelled. There was almost too much wildlife to safely make landfall.

Reports say that this harbour is home to around 25,000 breeding pairs of king penguins. They really do seem to be everywhere. They are however under the constant threat of attack from the lurking light-mantled sooty albatrosses.

There are as many penguins in this small bay as there are people in the borough of Melton in Leicestershire, England. These two places have considerably different geographical sizes though. I think it does give an appreciation of just how many penguins that is. Now imagine the amount of noise that many people would make; but translate it into chattering penguin calls. Combine that with the ever-present smell of guano, and this is what it was like to be there.

To get to the colony we first had to pass hundreds of sleeping elephant seals, being as careful and as quiet as we could be. Not all were asleep though: some were belching loudly and fighting with each other.

Amongst the penguins on the periphery of the

colony we caught an occasional glimpse of the eggs that some of them were balancing on their feet. Penguins do this so that they can keep their eggs warm from their body heat whilst still protecting them from the cold floor. It felt like this was the most incredible excursion, though we'd not yet made it to Antarctica itself.

The afternoon seemed fairly tame in comparison - we were in Cooper Bay to see chinstrap penguins, and to cruise around the rock formations. I have to admit though - they are pretty impressive and they made me think of the Gates of Argonath from The Lord of the Rings. Obviously they didn't have the carved figures, nor did this river lead to Gondor; but you get the idea - they felt imposing.

Our day came to a close with passing Cape Disappointment - named such by Captain James Cook when he realised what he found was not the continent he was expecting. Just like he had, we were now leaving South Georgia behind us.

We now had a day at sea so had lectures on things such as the environment, and how the future in this area looks bleak. A rise in sea temperatures has been melting the ice shelves from below, particularly around the peninsula so that they eventually break away. However in the western part of Antarctica temperatures have dropped due to the hole in the ozone layer caused by the use of CFCs. Whether humans have impacted this or not, it's still something that needs to stop.

As the day drew to a close the seas got stormier. Chairs in the dining room were sliding across the room, and the windows were awash with sea water. At some point it'd started snowing, and this was getting heavier and heavier. It was not a time to be on deck.

When midnight approached the clocks changed once more as we crossed time zones back into Argentinian time. The tumultuous sea had turned it into a night with very little sleep as we passed the South Orkney Islands, and continued on towards the South Scotia Ridge.

We thought perhaps we'd be going ashore on the South Orkney Islands in the morning; but with the weather as it was, it wasn't to be. We'd also heard reports that the ice around the peninsula was getting thicker and if we were to make landfall we needed to make good time.

Sure we were in an ice breaker; though moving at full steam would be too quick if we hit any of this thicker ice. We had to go slower, and take a longer route in order to avoid the worst.

On days at sea it seemed all we'd do is eat, sleep, and listen to lectures. At certain times of the day there'd be biscuits put out near the tea making facilities. We had the joy of watching icebergs floating by as the temperature dropped. I guess it was fortunate this wasn't the RMS Titanic - instead of killer icebergs, we had orcas on the port side that had killed a southern bottlenose whale.

Point Wild, part of Elephant Island named for Frank Wild from Shackleton's shipwrecked expedition, was our pre-breakfast destination. We couldn't go ashore; but they slowed enough to allow some photography from the ship. A thin layer of fog surrounded us and the island which combined with the stillness and quietness of the area made it feel eerie.

It would have been nice to set foot on the first of these South Shetland Islands; but instead we continued around the tip of Cape Valentine. In doing so we passed the largest iceberg we'd ever see - so big it seemed like an island floating passed.

We couldn't go ashore at Cape Lookout either, nor on Gibbs Island. It was a pattern that seemed to be repeating more and more. It was disappointing. It felt like the weather was against us once again; but every passing minute was now taking us closer to the Antarctic peninsula. In all honesty the crew couldn't yet tell how likely it was we'd be making landfall there either - their data on the Antarctic ice shelf was three days old. Morale was not good following this news.

Whilst we navigated the Bransfield Strait, the glacier expert and climatologist told us about her time wintering on a German research base in Antarctica, and how psychologically taxing it was. She'd seen tempers get shorter and shorter, and other times that caused immense depression.

In this context it made it even more amazing that Shackleton achieved what he did. What must have gone through their minds during their long expedition?

Maybe there was still some hope that we'd get to follow in his footsteps and land on the final continent.

21: Antarctica

The expedition had so far taken us from Buenos Aires in Argentina, to where we boarded the ship in Ushuaia, an Argentinian city in the province of Tierra del Fuego - a name literally meaning the 'Land of Fire'.

We'd navigated to the Falkland Islands, and then onward to South Georgia and a number of island clusters that circumstance prevented us from landing on. Our luck had been so mixed, yet the time had come for when it really mattered. We'd arrived in Antarctic Sound - an area between the mainland, and some islands named after Otto Nordenskjöld's ship which sank near Paulet Island in 1903.

Icebergs of varying sizes were everywhere; but the weather didn't seem too bad. Would they let us ashore?

With each passing minute we nervously waited, hoping more than anything luck would be on our side. Then it came: the signal to get ready for going ashore. We rushed to change, grabbed cameras, and boarded the Zodiacs. We were filled with the anticipation of the moment that now lay before us.

Adélie penguins were hopping around on some of the smaller icebergs - so close we could have reached out and touched them from the weaving Zodiac. Of course we didn't though - it's not allowed.

The day was January 13th 2014 - exactly one hundred years to the day since Ernest Shackleton announced his Imperial Trans-Antarctic Expedition to cross the Antarctic continent from the Weddell Sea to the Ross Sea via the South Pole.

This was it. As we stepped foot on the shore at Brown Bluff we had arrived on our last continent and completed a journey which for me had started six years before with the sands of Egypt.

I'd barely had an interest in travel at the start; but each country I'd visited had changed my view of the world. I hadn't even needed to be away from home or work for an extended period of time. What was left to do now? How could any other trip compare to this one?

This adventure was not yet over though. The vista before us was unlike anything I'd ever seen. There were ventifacts scattered across the beach which in places were also thick with snow. Behind these we could see snow covered mountains. Everywhere we looked there were Adélie and gentoo penguins.

Seeing Adélie penguins stealing stones from other nests to build their own reminded me of watching the Frozen Planet documentary series. There's something different about seeing it with your own eyes. It makes it more 'real'.

From there I started to climb a trail which I thought would give me a good view. I didn't get far before having to stop - there'd been a radio call saying we needed to head back as quickly as possible. The wind had picked up, and the ice was closing around the ship. The Plancius was having to move farther out to avoid getting stuck.

We all rushed back to the awaiting Zodiacs, and started back. We zigzagged around the majority of the ice; but for the smaller pieces we were zooming straight over making this a bumpier than normal ride. One of the other Zodiacs had gotten stuck doing this, and the passengers were shifting their weight to try and free themselves.

The Plancius was moving further and further away; but the Zodiacs were faster. We reached the ship first, and had to tie off against the moving ship to unload all the passengers so it could go back to the shore to collect another group. It was a race against time.

The Zodiacs headed back, each with one crew member steering, and another controlling the bow. Fortunately it could get back to the shore even quicker like this, and they safely collected the remainder of our group before the ship was forced to leave the bay. Watching the ice move, we'd all made it with minutes to spare.

It was time to move on, so we headed in the direction of the ominous-sounding Erebus and Terror Gulf. As we approached a heavy mist descended around the ship, hiding all but the surrounding icebergs. The air became still as the wind suddenly stopped.

Erebus is an ancient Greek deity personifying darkness, and was used to describe part of their underworld. It felt like perhaps this is where we'd arrived.

By midday this fog had mostly dissipated, and we

began to break through ice around Andersson Island. As the ship ploughed through we could hear loud cracking noises that were a little disturbing. It could have been the sound of the ship breaking. Looking at the bridge, the Captain was smiling - not only was this the normal sound of ice breaking; but also something he enjoyed doing.

This area around the Weddell Sea was exposed, and so much colder than anywhere we'd yet been. I tried to stay out in this so I could photograph icebergs; but everyone has their limit - eventually I reached mine.

It'd been planned we'd go ashore on the peninsular again, but the weather got worse and worse. Instead, they told us about the Nordenskjöld expedition, and how their ship had been crushed by ice. I guess that was a warning for what may happen if they ignored the conditions.

Twilight lasted long into the night with it never getting completely dark. During this time the ship had navigated to the South Shetland Islands, and into the McFarlane Strait where we dropped the anchor at Half Moon Island.

It was misty once more; but the sea was relatively calm. From the dining room we could see a building the Argentinians used as a research station: its red walls contrasting strongly against the snowy surroundings. There were also two communication towers just visible through the mist. To tell all visitors they were Argentinian properties they had painted their flag on the roof of each building. Subtle.

We went ashore and followed a trail passed these buildings onto the other side of the island where the snow was knee-deep. It was hard work; but worth it as we found a number of Weddell seals laying in the snow. One of our group walked over to one, far closer than we were supposed to go, and began to sit.

"Stop!" most of us shouted, stopping her in her tracks.

It seemed she'd been tired enough to think it was a rock she could sit on. I think she was very lucky that other people had been watching otherwise that could have ended very differently.

Despite this unexpected drama I got some photographs of the seal; it appeared to be smiling and hugging itself. It was practically posing for us.

On my way back to the other side of the island, I heard a loud rumbling and cracking noise that sounded like thunder. I turned in time to see the last part of a gargantuan block of ice crashing through the water across the bay - it'd just broken away from the glacier.

On the other side of the island a colony of chinstrap penguins were being attacked by giant petrels. One unlucky penguin family suffered tragedy as a pair of petrels were able to steal one of the chicks and flew off with it. They landed on a rock not too far away, and proceeded to bash the chick against the rock until it was red with blood. The chick was dead. When you're watching nature this sort of thing happens - it's the way of the animal kingdom and part of the circle of life.

Back onboard the Plancius we were briefed again for how our afternoon excursion would work. If we wanted to we could do what they referred to as a polar plunge on Deception Island. A polar plunge is the name they'd given to going for a swim in the Antarctic waters around this active volcano. In years past they'd been able to make the water a little warmer by making holes on the beach; but now the island is protected. If we wanted to swim it'd need to be in the open sea.

This being Antarctica it wouldn't be like going for a swim in the Mediterranean Sea-the temperature was predicted to be between -2.2°C and -1.6° C. The biggest consideration would be exposure: we'd need to be in the water for as little time as possible, and then get warm as quickly as we could. There was no doubt that it was something I wanted to try-there can't be that many people who can say they've deliberately swam in the Antarctic Ocean.

The ship passed through Neptune's Bellows into the caldera of Whalers' Bay. It was a tricky navigation for the crew - they had to pass close to avoid striking rock on the underside of the ship; but not too close to scrape the rock face.

This island was covered in pieces of whale bone, and parts of what presumably were once buildings - the wood now bleached white. The area around Neptune's Window is dangerous due to erosion underneath the ledge; but the expedition leader had marked off the limits of what would be safe to walk along.

Further inland there were remnants of the buildings that had once been a whaling station that had long since collapsed. Once I'd looked around them it was time for the most nerve-racking part of this expedition. The polar plunge.

I changed slowly into my swim shorts-aware how

crazy it seemed to be wearing just them whilst standing on an Antarctic island. Things were about to get a lot crazier.

In Antarctic waters you can expect your core body temperature to drop quite quickly, and cause hypothermia or even frostbite. After around fifteen minutes the temperature would cause a loss of consciousness, and after thirty minutes death is almost certain. These times are with some insulation; my skin would be exposed directly. Instead, it'd be more likely five to ten minutes would result in death. I wouldn't be in there that long; but I still needed to be careful.

I knew that when I was ready I had to just 'go for it' - I couldn't take my time otherwise it'd be too likely I'd back out. Standing on the beach I stood and thought about it for a minute before running out into the frigid water, and then diving under. I was underwater for less than a minute, several seconds at the most I had to assume; but I could feel how cold it was. The temperature made the water feel 'prickly' - though even then it didn't seem quite as bad as I'd imagined. Although we were inside an active volcano the water temperature was at best only a degree warmer than the open sea.

When I decided I'd had enough I stood up, and calmly walked back to the beach. This was when I realised how cold it was, and how cold my toes felt. They were starting to feel numb.

As I got back to the shore the ship's Doctor handed me a towel so I could quickly dry off and get into some clothes. I made quick work of drying off, but took some time to get dressed - I was being fussy about getting the ashen sand away from my toes first.

One of the group commented I looked like James Bond coming out of the water at the start of 'Casino Royale' - walking out slowly whilst everyone else was trying to get out as quickly as they could. Personally I didn't see that; but still an amusing comparison.

It's amazing how much warmer it felt after leaving the water - it now seemed too warm in all the layers I'd left on the beach, so had to leave them loose for the ride back to the ship. It reminded me of my time in Norway with the sauna.

Once everyone was aboard we were out on the deck for a special treat - a cup of hot chocolate with rum and cream. It was good enough to go back for seconds. Alcohol doesn't actually make you warm; but it's the feeling of the blood flowing that makes you feel warmer.

In the morning we navigated into the crystal clear waters of Wilhelmina Bay, escorted by humpback whales. As you'd probably expect, icebergs floated by, but this time we could see some of what was beneath the surface as well. Mountain glaciers were reflected perfectly in the water, except for the occasional ripple cast across them by the ship.

I'd have liked to have gone ashore one last time; but they decided the weather was too good and we'd have a cruise around the bay instead. That made no sense to me at all: why would we prefer a boat ride over walking on Antarctica again?

They took us close to a female humpback whale who was resting with her calf, though our proximity started to agitate them. Causing a change in behaviour is not ideal, so our driver backed off in the direction of an icy cliff. As we got closer to this a large piece of ice broke away and crashed into the water creating a small wave in its wake. We could see more was likely to break away at any minute. I guess we couldn't go that way either.

The driver rammed the Zodiac into a small piece of land that was no more than a few metres across. Sure it was an unconventional way of getting ashore, but it worked.

I walked to the peak of this landmass, and started to reach for my camera. One second I was standing, and the next I was supporting myself from my elbows with my legs dangling into emptiness below me. It appears I'd walked across a small crevice that had been hidden by a thin layer of snow - it'd then given way beneath me.

Lucky to have not fallen through to water, I struggled out of the hole whilst another Zodiac came ashore on the other side of this island. Jokingly they claimed this island as their own, and a snowball fight broke out. It was a nice bit of childish fun to end our time in Antarctica.

By lunchtime we'd returned to the Plancius, and had navigated to the Gerlache Strait - an area named for the Belgian expedition leader Adrien de Gerlache. He'd led the very first expedition to stay in Antarctica over winter. I can't imagine what the conditions would have been like - summer is cold enough.

Once we'd crossed the Schollaert Channel into Dallman Bay and beyond, we were back out into the rough seas of the Antarctic Ocean. Soon we'd be reaching

Drakes Passage - an area of sea that is notoriously rough. Throughout history there have been stories of how bad it is, and during the exploration of the New World it often resulted in shipwrecks. Our expectation was that it'd be unlike anything we'd come across before.

After all the violent rocking of the ship we'd experienced, it came as a surprise to find that Drakes Passage was relatively calm. Even the snow that had been falling constantly the day before had stopped.

The day was mostly lectures, with something sinister spreading in the background. A computer virus.

Memory cards owned by passengers had become infected and were now showing as empty; it had even spread as far as the unprotected computer in the library which in turn spread it to the computer on the bridge.

Passengers were worried about their photos having been lost, but in fact it was the virus hiding them. I spent the rest of the afternoon working on cleaning memory cards, and USB sticks as well as trying to remove the virus from affected machines without having an internet connection available for any reference or anti-virus pattern updates.

It was the last thing I'd expected to be doing on a ship in the Antarctic Ocean, and it was hard work. I was however fortunate to have a small portable computer on me known as a Raspberry Pi - the Linux-based operating system I was using could not be infected by this, so I used that to disinfect everything one at a time.

The crew wouldn't let me fix the one on the bridge, so instead I wrote instructions on how they could do it themselves. It'd taken me so many hours that by the time I was done we were approaching Cape Horn and the islands off the tip of Tierra del Fuego. We were back twelve hours early.

During breakfast on the next day, the pilot arrived to guide the Plancius through the Beagle Channel. It's not something the government allows the ship crew to do themselves.

From the port in Ushuaia we headed to their maritime museum - built inside an old prison. There was a wing converted into an art gallery, and another one dedicated to the history of the area, whilst yet another wing had been left as it had once been. This wing was now derelict with holes in the floor.

When we left we found ourselves continuously bumping into the crew and passengers of the Plancius. I guess it's something that's bound to happen when you're in a small town.

From the Sous Chef we heard that the other ship that had gone out, the Ortelius, had broken down after just five days. I couldn't help but feel sorry for them, especially as that is the more expensive ship equipped with helicopters for locating Emperor penguins.

That afternoon we returned to the airport and after a bit of confusion going through doors we weren't supposed to, we eventually made it to the right gate, and onto our flight back to Buenos Aires.

The eventual flight home from Buenos Aires was a memorable one. When going through passport control to leave they took my passport from me, and stared at the page containing both the Argentina and Falkland Islands immigration stamps. Why did they have to stamp that page?!

She continued to stare at the page for long enough for it to become uncomfortable, and then proceeded to write what seemed to be an essay on her computer. A few minutes later she looked at the passport once more, passed it back to me, and waved me through. I'm sure they must do that to unnerve people who have been to those contested islands.

This trip had been an experience with no equal. Sure enough it hadn't gone entirely to plan, but then I think the best trips are those that provide unexpected adventure. We'd done it though, we'd visited the last continent.

22: New York City, NY.

I couldn't leave it another year before travelling again, so decided that I'd end the year with a return to North America. I'd considered going to San Diego Comic Con again; but I couldn't find any friends that wanted to go. When I started to consider New York Comic Con instead, my sister expressed an interest. It'd be her first holiday without our parents, and her first time outside of Europe.

I could finally put everything I'd learnt from travelling to use by planning this trip, and helping my sister with what she'd need to know. New York City is made up of five outer boroughs known as Bronx, Brooklyn, Manhattan, Queens, and Staten Island. The majority of tourist attractions are in Manhattan, so this is where we'd be staying.

I started to plot sights we wanted to see on a map, and then figured how we could get around these the most efficiently. Part way through this planning, James decided he'd hop down from Canada for a few days to join us. In the months between trips he'd finally made the big move across the pond.

After I'd returned from Antarctica I'd continued running, and had in the months since then built up the distance enough to now be preparing to run my first marathon. Ideally I needed to be starting this trip off with a twenty-one mile run, but with an early morning tour of Liberty Island it didn't seem realistic.

We'd arrived in the evening, and had gone for our first meal at a small bar called The Jolly Monk. Whilst I'd been eating a turkey burger, my sister felt unable to eat as the flight had not been kind to her. I got just five hours of sleep after this, and found myself wide awake. Jet-lagged, I looked at the clock, and realised at just 03:35 it was early enough to be able to fit in the miles I needed. Thirty minutes later I was ready, and out on my way to Central Park. With how many people I passed on my way there, it really did earn its name as the city that never sleeps.

Signs outside the park indicated I couldn't run inside until daylight, so I started to run around the perimeter instead. Although there was no traffic about, I'd heard about jaywalking laws in the US so was stopping at every red light.

Time passed by quickly. I looked at the buildings I ran passed, and watched the homeless being fed from a food cart that arrived around sunrise. Raccoons were scavenging for food as well - I wish I'd had my proper camera with me. I also ran along boards that were being put down ready for the thousands of people that would soon be watching the New York City Marathon. Maybe one day I'd be one of the ones running too.

Three hours had passed, and I'd completed twenty-one miles - around three laps of the park. Whilst eating breakfast back at the hotel, James arrived ready for the three of us to head over to Battery Park for our tour of the Statue of Liberty. I'd heard tickets would be difficult to get, so I'd booked some with access to the statue's crown ahead of time.

To get to the park we each bought a seven day metro card - it'd be the cheapest way to get around. It was in fact about a third of the price a similar card would have cost in London. I was seeing more and more how much our mass transit systems in the UK were overpriced compared to other countries I'd visited. I had after all travelled by train across Italy for less than a ticket would have cost me for Leicester to London.

Once onboard the ferry it provided views of Manhattan as well as the best views we were going to get of the statue. On Liberty Island I think we were then a little too close for taking pictures. Instead of hanging around we headed straight up to crown.

On the way up we had to hand over our backpacks - we could only take water and cameras up. It's not just a security measure really, there simply isn't the space for bags on the corkscrew staircase up.

The pedestal hides a museum that details the design by French sculptor Frédéric Auguste Bartholdi, and the construction of the national monument after the statue was gifted.

James and Lindsay both suffer with heights. James rushed on ahead so he wouldn't have to think about it, and my sister took the final climb one step at a time with me behind for reassurance.

From the crown windows you can see out over the

surrounding Liberty Island, and down at the tabula ansata that the statue holds - the tablet of law inscribed with the date of American Independence. If I looked out at just the right angle I could also see part of the torch that the statue holds aloft. The torch would have allowed a higher view though access has been closed to the public for safety reasons since 1916.

Knowledgeable park rangers told us about the statues history; but I was interested in it for its role in the Ghostbusters II film. It's one I'd seen at the cinema when I was younger; even though I hadn't quite been able to see it all. An Irish Republican Army bomb went off outside the building at around the time we'd have been going back to the car if we'd seen our intended showing. I'd never have imagined back then that I'd one day be standing inside the statue.

The statue rocked gently in the wind, and my mention of this encouraged James and Lindsay to return to ground level. We didn't linger either - we headed straight to the ferry that would take us onward to Ellis Island.

Ellis Island is famous as being one of the major immigration points for the United States in the past. A lot of the landmass comes from land reclamation that took place in the early 1900's using mostly waste from the construction of the underground:this allowed for the facility to grow in size to accommodate the massive demand.

There may be those that complain about immigration now; but it is estimated that one in three

Americans can trace their ancestry back to immigrants that came through Ellis Island.

Since the damage left in the wake of hurricane Sandy, the artefacts they once had there had been removed, and were expected to make a return the following year. Not too dissimilar to my luck with the Acropolis museum in Athens.

Once we'd seen all there was to see we returned to the mainland, and began our walk from Battery Park up Broadway to the Trinity Church. Timing, as always, is hit or miss. This time it was a miss, as just like our visit to the Acropolis in Athens, this building was covered in scaffolding.

A walk down Wall Street from there led us to the September 11th Memorial where the twin towers of the World Trade Center once stood. It was a day that many of us around the world will remember forever. I think everyone knows where they were, and what they were doing when the news first broke.

Sunk into the recesses of where the towers once stood are pools of water with continuous waterfalls flowing down into them from a parapet with inscriptions of the names of the 2,977 people killed that day, and the 6 killed in a 1993 bombing. White roses are placed on the names when it would have been their birthday.

In New York City there are a number of foods I think you're pretty much expected to try, one of them being doughnuts. We stopped briefly to try some from a popular chain before continuing our long walk across the Brooklyn Bridge.

For non-motor traffic there is a path that is split

into two: one side for pedestrians, and the other for cyclists. Both lanes were incredibly busy, and the pedestrians were particularly fast moving. In fact, there were so many pedestrians that they kept crossing into the path of bicycles much to their annoyance.

We walked as far as the first pylon before turning back - we never quite made it into Brooklyn during this trip. On our way back a runner ran straight into my sister, and then just carried on as if nothing had happened. New Yorkers have the reputation for being rude and in a rush, but we hadn't found that at all - except for this one incident. Sometimes all it takes is one person to ruin an impression.

Our walking continued on through Little China and Little Italy until we eventually made it back to the hotels. It'd been a long day of walking, and before the day was over I'd covered over thirty miles on foot.

Next morning we had breakfast at a diner near Central Park. I'd seen some of Central Park from my run, but this time I could really take it all in - we'd be spending the morning wandering around.

We visited Strawberry Fields - a memorial to the late John Lennon, and close to the Dakota Apartments building on 72nd street where he'd once lived and was murdered. Further north we walked through The Rambles to Belvedere Castle, and the Turtle Pond.

Unlike previous trips I'd been on, we were taking regular breaks and we weren't trying to see absolutely everything. After one loop of the park we exited into Grand Army Plaza where we could see the famous Fifth

Avenue Apple store.

The entire avenue is filled with expensive shops; but the Apple store is one that catches everyone's eye due to the impressive glass cube that houses a stairway down into the store below.

Just off this avenue further along is the Grand Central Terminal - the main railway station in New York City. The exterior is as impressive as the interior - it feels grand, but is poorly lit.

Whilst James and myself attempted to photograph the main concourse, my sister rested on the steps besides us. Two police officers walked up to her and demanded she moved. They don't allow people to sit on the steps. They should probably have a sign for that if they don't want people doing it.

On our way out we bought a hot dog from a stand, another typically American thing to do. It wasn't great if I'm honest - the sausage wasn't much thicker than a pencil. Maybe if I'd like onions it would have been a little more substantial.

The Empire State Building had ticket hawkers on the streets; but without clear evidence they worked there we decided it better to join the queue in the art deco lobby. For this there are various ticketing options available; we decided as we'd got other places to see we'd go for the basic ticket up to the 86th floor - I was hopeful it'd be almost as good as the observation deck twenty floors above.

I expected it to be like Melbourne: to be indoors and behind glass. Instead we stepped outside into the open air; but protected from the wind by a perspex barrier. In every direction we could see across Manhattan and beyond. At this point I couldn't compare the skyline to any other I'd seen.

The most southern part of Manhattan we visited that day was the iconic Flatiron building. It was owned and constructed by the Fuller Company in 1902. It became one of the first skyscrapers in New York City to be built using a steel frame after local building laws were relaxed.

In the evening we didn't have to go too far to find good food - we came across a small family-owned pizzeria on 48th with some fantastic pizzas; but an overpowering smell of incense from their neighbours. Whilst there the sun had set, and the sky was finally getting dark - the perfect time for visiting Times Square to look at the brightly lit signs.

We weren't there long though as I was taking my sister to a Broadway show, having bought her a ticket for her birthday. It was a little cooler in the theatre than expected as we were located underneath one of the air-conditioning vents. I didn't have a great view either as the person in front of me seemed to be a giant. It was however great fun with plenty of classic songs we could enjoy.

Our hotel didn't do breakfasts so we had no choice; but to either buy something from a convenience store for each morning or to find somewhere to eat. For James' last day with us we settled on the Carnegie Deli for bagels and cinnamon toast. The food was good; but the waiter wouldn't let us sit and talk, he insisted on talking to us throughout the meal. It's good that they're friendly there; but sometimes it's just too much.

After breakfast we parted ways. James headed back to his hotel en route to the airport, whilst we headed to an exhibition - the first of our Comic Con themed activities.

By midday we'd arrived at the USS Intrepid Air and Space Museum: an aircraft carrier that was built for the second world war; but also served in Vietnam. Most of what we learn in English high schools is the European theatre of war, so this aircraft carrier wasn't something I knew about - it had served in the Pacific.

The flight deck is filled with many aircraft, including a Lockheed A-12 'Blackbird' built in the 1960's as part of Project Oxcart for the CIA. As impressive as the craft is, it's not the main attraction on the flight deck. Adjacent to a marquee where they're restoring a plane, there is the Space Shuttle Pavilion.

Here they have the space shuttle Enterprise, a name known to Star Trek fans everywhere. This was the first space shuttle to be built by NASA, designated OV-101; but was not suitable for spaceflight. Its purpose was as a test craft that would lead to the construction of the Columbia, and later the Challenger, Discovery, Atlantis, and Endeavour.

Space has interested me for a very long time, and I never imagined that I'd get to be in the same room as a space shuttle. I took my time trying to take in every detail about it. It's an impressive sight, considerably bigger than the die-cast one I'd had when I was younger.

Also on this dock is the USS Growler, a unique Grayback-class submarine from the Cold War. It was one of only two of this class, the other having been sunk, and was built to carry four Regulus I and II nuclear cruise missiles.

I'd never boarded a submarine before so didn't really know what it'd be like. We boarded through a modified missile hanger, and gradually worked our way to the aft. It didn't take long at all; but I was glad we'd seen it. We never got chance to look inside the Concorde that they also have there.

From there we took the metro to Tribeca, the location of the Hook & Ladder 8 fire station. It might not sound special, and to many maybe it isn't. It is however the fire station used in the Ghostbusters movies. I didn't even need to look that hard for it as when leaving the metro a police officer came over to me, and pointed me in the direction of it without even needing to ask. I was after all wearing a Ghostbusters t-shirt and carrying a camera, so it was pretty obvious.

Everywhere you look in the city you're bound to find something that was used in a film or a television series. Not that far away we also found the apartment block that was used for exterior shots in Friends.

Our legs by this point were incredibly tired from a busy day of walking despite the use of the metro. When we reached the High Line, a 1.45 mile long stretch of park on disused raised railroad, we decided to only walk along it for a couple of blocks. The sun was starting to set by the time we got there, so it was perhaps for the best.

Getting passes for entering New York Comic Con was far quicker than it had been in San Diego. It wasn't yet time for the event itself, so we had one last day of sightseeing. For this day we decided on a 'Sun and Stars' ticket for the Rockefeller Centre that would get us onto the 'Top of the Rock' during the day and then again for night-time.

Contrary to what I thought, the Rockefeller Centre isn't just the massive skyscraper; but the whole complex of buildings around it including the Radio City music hall. It was constructed and funded by John D. Rockefeller Jr. and was originally intended to be the home for the Metropolitan Opera. The land was owned by Columbia University and was only leased until the Rockefeller Group bought the land in the 1980s for $400 million.

Unlike the Empire State Building, in 30 Rockefeller Plaza it is a single lift that goes up seventy floors to the observation deck. As the lift started to ascend the ceiling turned transparent to reveal a lift shaft illuminated with little blue lights to make it look like you're travelling into space.

I stepped out the elevator to see an impressive panorama of Manhattan in three directions. To see more we took an escalator up to a higher level with a full 360 degree view.

With that done, we headed by metro to Pelham Parkway in the Bronx. I wasn't entirely sure if we'd taken the best route there; but it was easy to find their zoo from there. Admittedly I'm not too keen on seeing animals caged up like this; it was however the best chance Lindsay would get to see some of the animals I've seen on my travels so far.

Their tiger seemed too skinny, and their rhino has no space to move - a reminder of why I dislike zoos. My hope was that next time I saw a tiger it'd be in the wild or in a decent sanctuary. The only positive here was that the animals were safe from poachers.

We'd got some time left before we needed to be back at the Rockefeller Center, so we took the metro over to another borough - Queens. I guess it's not really a common tourist destination; but I knew it was home to Silvercup Studios which had featured in a Queen music video for the first Highlander film.

When first arriving at the metro station in Queens we saw three police officers putting two sets of handcuffs on someone. I wasn't sure why they'd use two sets of cuffs; but I'm sure there must have been a good reason for it.

When we got back there about ten minutes later the officers were still there, and recognised us. One of them asked me about it so I explained what we'd been there to photograph. The officer was then kind enough to open the barrier for us so we could pass through without needing to use our metro cards again.

The Rockefeller Center was far busier than it had been in the morning; but due to our ticket we could bypass the ticketing queue. It was getting ever closer to sunset; but we made it to the top in time and found a good spot to stand and wait. For the next hour I stood almost motionless, taking photographs every few minutes to capture the slow transition from day, to dusk, to night.

By the time the last of the light left the night sky we were also getting hungry as we'd barely eaten all day. It was a struggle to find anywhere open, even though it was only just passed 20:00. I thought this city never sleeps…

Over the days that followed our time was spent mostly in the convention centre, with lunch being snacks we'd bought from a local grocery store to save time.

San Diego's entry had been organised; but here there was a stampede of people rushing to the front, some running up escalators the wrong way just to get ahead. What was at this convention that would drive people to such madness?

This convention was a very different experience all around - the focus felt like it was more on the show floor than the panels. One stall was run by Jordan Hembrough, a vintage toy dealer made famous by his 'Toy Hunter' TV series. My sister, a fan of the series, couldn't resist the temptation to buy something from them, and have her picture taken with him.

Here they will also empty the halls between panels which gives everyone a fighting chance of seeing what they want to. Rather than needing to queue all day, you queue at the start, and they will give you wristbands to use when returning later. Even this made it so different to San Diego.

On our second day we got a wristband each for the 'Elementary' panel which premiered an upcoming episode, and then featured a question and answer session with the stars. Lindsay had never seen the show before; but this was enough to get her watching it.

Over the years I've come across quite a few famous faces, particularly from the world of science fiction. When we headed over to the autographing area to waste a little time by seeing who was about I found that the majority of the 'Star Trek: The Next Generation' cast were in attendance. I'd met most of these before; but there was also someone from the original Star Trek series. It was William Shatner - the actor who had played Captain James Tiberius Kirk. He was charging US$80 for signing; but I couldn't pass up this chance.

Having paid more for a signature than I had ever done before, I then queued for each of the other cast members. These were only charging US$40 each; but it soon adds up. Brent Spiner joked about remembering me from San Diego Comic Con, and my sister had a good chat with Marina Sirtis: the Next Generation cast really are good people.

That night we went to one of the few off-site events for the convention at the Manhattan Center. This was a live interview with the Star Trek cast, hosted by William Shatner.

People say that time flies when you're having fun, and for the two hours that passed whilst we were there it seemed like time had run out in the blink of an eye.

One morning I ran along the Hudson River, and beyond where we'd visited the High Line to cover around eight kilometres. Unlike in the UK where I can run for hours and not see another runner; I encountered so many here. The morning after that I did one last fourteen mile run around Manhattan to see a few last sights before our last day not just at the convention, but in the city.

The highlight of this day was the panel for the

thirtieth anniversary of Karate Kid. Ralph Macchio and company talked about what it was like behind the scenes filming the first film, and how things have gone for them since then. There were a few comments about the remake; but the actors remained professional and never gave their opinion on it.

Our time in the Big Apple was now over, and my sister had a taste for what travel could be like. Maybe the travel bug would bite her too.

23: Mexico

Six months after my trip to New York City, I was ready to be on the move once more. Over the last few years I'd started to get a reputation amongst my colleagues for what they considered to be adventurous holidays in crazy places. So where would I visit next?

South America and the area historically referred to as Mesoamerica are two regions whose history have interested me for some time. I'd seen some of the ancient ruins; but there was so much more to see. Mexico seemed like a good chance to see more.

My flight connected through Toronto where I met up with James before arriving in Mexico City just before midnight. Even at that time there were restaurants open. There were people celebrating as apparently May 10th is Mothers Day - it's celebrated in such a big way that it's common for people to not turn up for work.

When our tour began several hours later the roads were empty. Every Sunday morning the roads are taken over by cyclists and runners. It's an incredible thing for a city to do-it cuts back on pollution just that little bit whilst promoting a healthier lifestyle. Part of me wanted to be outside, and joining in on the running though I was also eager for some sightseeing.

At the start of our tour the guide took us to the Hidalgo metro station to get us to the Zócalo. The official name is Plaza de la Constitución but the locals know it better as Zócalo, which is Spanish for 'plinth'. During the precolonial times it was the ceremonial centre of the Aztec city of Tenochtitlan and today remains a major gathering place in the historic centre.

The metro station can apparently get quite warm and is not air conditioned so they have barrels of water which the locals can drink from for free. I got the impression that it's pretty rare for the locals to see ghostly white tourists on the metro as we were watched constantly.

We were led into the National Palace - the residence of the Mexican President built under the orders of the Spanish Conquistador: Hernán Cortés. In precolonial times this was also the site of the royal palace of King Montezuma - the ninth tlatoani of Tenochtitlan, who reigned from 1502 to 1520 during the Spanish conquest of the New World.

To construct this palace the Spanish had used the stones from Montezuma's original palace - a practice we'd seen in other Spanish conquered settlements such as Cuzco.

Once inside, our guide took a seat, and started to talk about various types of cacti and the production of tequila. Above the courtyard there are murals by the Mexican painter Diego Rivera.

One of the murals depicts how Tenochtitlan was once a floating city built by the Aztecs around an island in Lake Texcoco. The Spanish occupation resulted in this lake being drained.

Although I'm not a big fan of art, I did find these paintings to be interesting because of what they were depicting. I couldn't wait to see what they had in the Anthropological Museum; but we had to delay our visit due to reports that it was overcrowded.

Instead our guide took us to another local museum - the Museo del Templo Mayor. The outside section of this consists of some Aztec ruins of pyramids discovered during some construction. They demonstrate how every time the Aztec needed to increase the size of a temple pyramid they built over the top of the existing one. Inside the museum they have a lot of archaeological finds from all over Mexico City. Eventually our guide left us to go around the museum ourselves.

Next-door is the Mexico City Metropolitan Cathedral of the Assumption of the Most Blessed Virgin Mary into Heaven. Quite a mouthful. It's not just the name of the cathedral that's big; apparently it's the largest cathedral in the Americas. It has unfortunately been a victim of one of the common problems in Mexico City: subsidence. No doubt a problem caused by the previous geography of the region.

From the outside it's not easy to spot the damage as some work has been done to reduce the amount it leans by. We were told that at one point the pillars inside were noticeably leaning, and the government had to spend a lot to try and save it. At the time we visited their attempts had not succeeded; they were only prolonging the inevitable.

In the afternoon we switched from experiencing their metro, to having a short drive around the city. It was short-lived but they did at least drop us off at the Anthropological Museum.

The admission for this museum was 64 pesos at the time, so the equivalent to less than £3 - a bargain for getting to see everything they have on display. On one side of the museum it covers the stone age with exhibits such as a partial woolly mammoth skeleton, and then proceeds from there all the way through to pre-colonial times, and eventually more modern years.

Outside in the courtyard they've also set-up an Ōllamaliztli court, a Nahuatl name which in English is known as 'the ball game'. This was a game that the Aztec people used to play and is believed to represent the passage of the sun. My only real knowledge of this game comes from watching an animated film set in the fictional El Dorado.

Even at our 'breakneck' pace around the museum it took us almost two hours to cover the majority. We finished just in time for an evening meal, so went to a local restaurant where the staff couldn't speak English.

There was a time that'd have been a problem; but after having visited a few Spanish speaking countries with James already, I'd picked up enough from him for ordering. With it being away from the 'touristy' areas, it also meant the food was incredibly cheap.

Our guide met us the following morning to take us

to Teotihuacán; but not before a brief visit to the Plaza de las Tres Culturas. Our guide told us it's because the buildings belong to Aztec, Spanish, and Russian cultures. If the internet is to believed, which isn't always possible, our guide was wrong and the third was not strictly Russian but one belonging to the Mestizo nation-a Spanish term describing people of mixed descent. It's strange how often local knowledge differs to what the 'accepted' version is.

Around Teotihuacán we could hear the constant drum of fireworks from a nearby village that was celebrating. Ants were marching alongside us on the path to the pyramids. Not in rhythm to the fireworks though; which was a shame.

When we reached the Avenue of the Dead our guide said he'd meet us at the crossroads in two hours. That seemed fair enough-though so far our guide had worked hard at doing as little guiding as possible. It was fortunate I'd read about Teotihuacán before, and had seen the occasional documentary; so I was our tour guide for the time being.

It is not known who built the city of Teotihuacán-it was once thought to be the Toltec civilisation however with it beginning construction in 100 BC it was far too early to be from them. As the Nahuatl word 'toltec' also means 'master craftsman' it does not necessarily refer to that civilisation. The current name we use came from the Aztecs.

The smaller of the two pyramids, the Pyramid of the Moon, was the first one we climbed-it's the one situated at the head of the Avenue of the Dead. I could see tarpaulin covering archaeological excavations underway at the foot of the pyramid; but it was still okay for us to climb these steep stairs to the top.

I ran up the steps and turned around at the top to look back over the avenue. Either side there are pyramids after pyramids for hundreds of metres. Beyond them were mountains. What had this looked like in its heyday? If only we had a true window to the past.

I headed over to the Pyramid of the Sun, and this seemed considerably higher. I thought it'd be more of an effort to climb so took it slowly. At the top of this one black butterflies were performing a behaviour known as 'hill-topping'. It was strange we hadn't seen any elsewhere since butterfly hunting is depicted in the Aztec 'Paradise of Tlaloc'.

There wasn't really anything left to see - we'd looked around some of the other buildings between scaling the two pyramids.

We sat at the top of one of the sunken terraces for a while thinking we were at the meeting point. We could see a reasonable way in each direction; but the guide was nowhere to be seen.

Thinking that we may have misunderstood the instructions, we walked further down the avenue to the next crossroad, and found our guide resting under a tree. He advised us to go off and climb to the Temple of Quetzalcoatl as he pointed at another structure behind us.

The climb and subsequent descent of the Adosada platform in the heat was worth it to get to this temple. It was more like what I was hoping to see in Mexico-an impressive style of architectural detail with decorated snake heads protruding out of the stonework. Preconceptions about a place don't often match reality; but in this case this was exactly what I'd imagined.

This temple may not have been Aztec in origin; but it summoned a memory from infant school when this same imagery was used in a theatrical production about Aztec culture. I think that may have been the first time I'd learnt about the Aztec, and their encounter with the Spanish Conquistadors; but it had stayed in my mind for all those years.

Eventually we had to leave this world heritage site behind us to look for food. We exited through a market, and found a small restaurant where our guide advised us to try their cactus-based foods. It being this early into the trip I didn't want to risk a dish that may have been washed in tap water so went with the safe option: enchiladas served with a green sauce that was allegedly hot.

On our way back to the hotel we stopped by the Basílica de nuestra de Guadalupe. Again this was another building where subsidence was causing the building to split. In this case it seemed like it was now two buildings.

In Mexico City at this time of year it is common to get thunderstorms because of their geography, and how humidity would rise throughout the day. The thunderstorm arrived whilst we were eating in the evening. With a flight to Tuxtla the following morning neither of us wanted to be packing wet clothes in our suitcases. The solution was to run as fast as we could through the heavy downpour to get back to the hotel.

Sometimes being a runner is useful.

When we arrived in Tuxtla the following morning we found our driver didn't speak English. We were told this could be the case; but that it wouldn't be a problem. He'd got instructions to give us though, and we couldn't understand him.

Unsure what he'd said, we set off for Sumidero Canyon - a river located in the Chiapas region. For this journey our eyes were fixated on the driver as he hurtled around the bends of a winding road with a mobile phone to his ear. Perhaps it's not illegal like it is back home.

The midday sun had disappeared behind rain clouds when we boarded a canoe that would take us along the Rio Grijalva. For the next two hours we were on the boat with no English speaking guide, and nobody able to translate for us. At various points the guide stopped and gave a description of the area - this much we could tell, just not what he was actually saying. Being told we wouldn't need an English guide for this day was a lie.

At the Chicoasén hydroelectric dam we could go no further. It was now 14:00, and we'd not eaten since a light breakfast. A small dugout boat was selling a dark-brown coloured drink called 'Indio', and packets of tortillas covered in dirt. I thought it best to not trust food that questionable.

It rained for most of the journey back; though quick drying clothes, and the warmth of the bus meant we'd dried off by the time we'd driven to Chiapa de Corzo.

We weren't completely sure how much time we had

as it was difficult to figure out what the driver was saying with our limited Spanish - it sounded like he said fifty minutes. Just in case we decided not to go too far so only wandered as far as the Santo Domingo church.

The church appeared to be closed, so we took the opportunity to buy a snack from one of the shops around the square. The drinks here were about a third of the price back home, but chocolate was about the same.

The minibus eventually took us up into the mountains along a road that weaved around the edge of the mountain. It took us higher and higher until we were above the clouds, and we could no longer see the valley below.

Along this road there were various signs which people familiar with the highway code would know indicate that you're not supposed to overtake. It seems our driver, and many other drivers, didn't seem to realise what this sign meant. They also didn't seem bothered about overtaking in heavy rain on a winding road with a very long drop on one side. I guess it's one way to make sure passengers stay awake until they reach their destination.

The city of San Cristobal de las Casas has an obvious Spanish colonial feel to it. The roads are a combination of cobbles and stonework, and the buildings have wrought iron balconies and red roofing tiles. There is no conformity between buildings and most are painted in either neutral or bright colours.

When travelling you shouldn't be afraid to ask for directions, and that is how we managed to find a restaurant hidden down an alleyway near the Zocalo. It'd been a long day getting to this town, and I think neither of us had been so happy to get a meal. From that point on we decided we'd always have a chocolate bar in our backpacks just in case we had to miss another meal. Perhaps we hadn't learned our lesson in China after all.

Mornings in San Cristobal de las Casas are of course quieter than they are in Mexico City. The traffic was almost non-existent so it meant we could get to the village of Zinacantán in thirty minutes. In the Nahuatl, the name of this village is 'Land of the Bats'. Why it's called that I have no idea, though I suspect it has nothing to do with Batman - just as the Batman Avenue I'd seen in Melbourne has nothing to do with the superhero either.

This village is one which has its own laws. One of the most notable laws here is that you cannot take photographs inside churches, and can be imprisoned if you're seen to. It would be a bad idea to try and take a sneaky photograph - the consequences would be harsh.

We started off by looking around a church, so obviously not taking photographs, and was then led into the front room of a nearby house. Inside was dark, and the floor made from stone; there was very little decoration - everything was practical.

In this house they made fabrics in one of the back rooms, a process that they demonstrated whilst we were there. Adjacent to this larger room was another small dark room which was lit mostly by a log fire burning away.

Three ladies were making tacos using a large metal dish over the fire. One had bowls in front of her with different fillings to use. Each filling tasted dry and powdery; but it was nice of them to make us lunch.

Behind this house they also had a greenhouse for growing flowers and beans; though they'd make almost no money from this produce. All the profits would be obtained further up the chain - we'd seen the same in Africa as well. Seeing how hard they work, and how little they'd make on this produce when we knew how much it'd sell in shops for - it felt wrong. The poor struggled on to make the rich even wealthier. Travel can be a real eye-opener into how people are treated, if you're willing to see.

Chamula, another nearby village mostly inhabited by the Tzotzil Maya people, was our second destination. This culture has stood up for itself for a long time-first it didn't accept fealty to the Aztec culture, and then it refused to be taken over by the Spanish Conquistadors. This area reportedly takes the law into its own hands, and will beat and burn its criminals. Pleasant.

It's illegal to take photographs inside churches here as well. Inside this one the floor was covered in grass cuttings with the occasional gap where candles had been placed. Between the grass and the banners hanging from the ceiling, it was a fire waiting to happen.

In this church apparently some of the people praying were 'professionals' - people paid to pray for people's health. They also insist they don't like to be called shamans.

When we arrived back in San Cristobal de las Casas the minibus pulled up in the Zocalo, and told everyone to get off. They drove off without even pointing people in the right direction - it was lucky we'd explored the evening before, and knew the mile long route back to the hotel.

Most of the afternoon remained, and we'd not really got anything left to do. Being a runner now, I decided the best thing to do was go for a run. At 2,200 metres above sea level I knew that it would be harder work than normal even over just two miles. I was right.

During the night I could hear the frequent noise of people passing by. When 04:30 arrived I'd barely slept, but it was time to move on. Fortunately this was a hotel that could provide a packed breakfast for the journey - a possibility I've found useful to know on later trips elsewhere.

The drive up into the mountains was dark, winding, and bumpy. At every half mile we'd hit a severe speed bump in the road which would cause the driver to slow to below 10 mph; yet still it felt like a sharp jolt keeping us awake.

After the sun had risen we started to notice people walking along the roadsides, some carrying machetes. In most places back home that wouldn't be an everyday sight.

Eventually we made it to Agua Azul for a ninety minute stop. There's a lot we could do: we could look around and take photographs, swim in the clear waters of the falls, eat, or shop. Time was limited so we decided to get the photographs we wanted first, and to then see what we could fit in afterwards.

It was a shame we couldn't have spent more time at

the falls. We knew we'd be getting into Palenque early afternoon despite this being considered a full-day trip. Getting to swim at these falls would have been a good way to cool off in the sweltering midday sun. It would also have given us time to have some lunch. It seemed that missing meals was becoming a common occurrence on this trip.

With one further, albeit brief, pause at Cascadas de Misol Há, we eventually made it to Palenque. The temperature there had soared to 37°C with 89% humidity. Even inside the hotel it wasn't much cooler. Every step we took out in the sun was akin to being cooked like lobsters. At any rate, I was beginning to look like one. Although only fifteen minutes away, the walk to their supermarket to get water was almost unbearable.

That evening we took advantage of the hotel Wi-Fi to book a trip to Uxmal for a day we had free later.

One of the highlights of this trip for me was knowing I'd get to visit the ruins of Palenque - one of the largest cities of the Mayan kingdom. An English speaking guide was waiting for us at the ruins, and told us that our day trip would actually be one hour; but for an extra five hundred pesos each we could have an optional one hour excursion through the jungle.

I think we'd both learnt that in future we should ask for an approximate length in hours for any tour we booked. Saying it's a 'day trip' and it lasting an hour feels very dishonest.

Once we'd paid the additional fee we were led through the trees to our first Mayan temple. The largest of the ruined temples is the Inscription Temple where they found the remains of K'inich Janaab' Pakal; or as we'd more likely know him, King Pacal the Great.

Our pace was swift, and left us little time for taking photographs. It seemed our guide was impatient; but even lingering with our cameras I was sure we must have been moving quicker than most groups he's had.

Climbing the Temple of the Cross gave us an impressive view of the Mayan city; but our hour was at an end. He led us back to the Temple of Inscriptions, and disappeared briefly. When he returned he led us through a roped off area to begin the jungle hike.

The jungle vegetation has taken over many of the buildings, and it's likely only 10% have been found. It wasn't these our guide was looking for though, it was howler monkeys. We could hear their calls echoing through the trees somewhere out of sight. What we could see though was a large termite mound protruding from the side of a log with hundreds of them scurrying about their business.

Eventually the guide gave up, and led us to what he called 'The Forgotten Temple'. It was a relatively intact temple in the middle of the jungle; though some of the lower parts were damaged by tree roots growing through it. Starting to feel like Indiana Jones, we climbed the stairs to look around.

There might not have been adventure there, but we did find a cave populated with roosting bats. Sadly, even though I'd brought my flash with me, I'd not brought any batteries for it. A tripod may have been better to avoid disturbing them anyway - a long exposure would have been more effective.

Maybe I didn't get to photograph them, but sometimes it's the experience that matters more - and we did get to see a howler monkey up in the tree canopy too.

When we got back to the entrance to this site we found the entire tour had been thirty minutes short. Frustrating, though we probably wouldn't have seen any more by hanging around any longer.

The taxi driver wasn't quite ready for us, so we had to wait for him to finish his beer. It wasn't even midday yet, so when he dropped us off back at the hotel we decided we'd wander around the nearby town in the blazing midday sun.

We passed live chickens in cages for sale, and so many different types of shop we hadn't seen in other cities. It gave us an idea of what Mexico was like outside of the busy tourism centres.

Our supposed air-conditioned drive to Mérida was on a bus that may have once had air conditioning; but it'd probably been some years since it'd last worked.

During the course of the day, the bus stopped a few times to drop people off, and take on new passengers - we were never stopped for more than twenty minutes though. This was why it was essential we got supplies from the supermarket in Palenque before setting off so we'd have something to eat and drink on the way.

The only other stops were at checkpoints where the military boarded the bus to check passports. Time did pass relatively quickly the closer we got to our destination; but the insect bites I'd got in the jungles around Palenque weren't helping.

When we left the bus we were directed out onto the streets; but there was no sign of our ride to the hotel. Sixty pesos lighter, a taxi took us to the hotel which felt like its drab brown decoration had come straight out of the 1970s. It seemed likely the furnishings hadn't been replaced in that time either.

Not long after arriving we got a call put through to the room. It was the tour operator. They claimed they'd sent someone to pick us up, and had been waiting at the bus station for two hours. We can say without a doubt that when we exited the bus station, he was not there. If there was more than one exit to the station it wasn't something we'd had a choice about either. He met us at the hotel with details for when we'd be picked up in a couple of days time, and gave us a map of the town.

Exploring this city we found it being the capital of the Yucatán state gave it a very different feel to Palenque. This city was obviously wealthier, and had a more Spanish colonial feel to it. The pavements seemed to shine, and each of the buildings we passed were painted in a different colour.

Unfortunately we had no idea when we'd be picked up by a tour company in the morning. We'd been expecting them to email details through to us, or to provide them to the hotel; but they'd done neither in the days since we'd booked it.

The best option seemed to be to wait in the lobby early, just in case. Whilst waiting I was able to get an internet connection on my phone for the first time in days. Overnight I'd had an email from the tour company to say we'd need to phone a different tour company to confirm we'd got a place on the tour, and what pick-up times would be. This was despite having received an email from them that confirmed everything other than the pick-up time.

A little confused and exasperated we called the tour company asking them what was happening. At first they claimed we weren't there waiting for them, and then they decided they'd meet us in twenty minutes. *Excellent.*

The tour company sent two people to meet us, and they told us we'd not be doing the tour as we'd missed it.

"Great," I told them calmly - a very British way to show unhappy we were.

To resolve the problem they decided they'd pick us up in the afternoon, just after lunch, to go on a two hour tour of Uxmal. The meal would now include a soft drink at no extra cost, and to apologise for their mix-up they decided they'd take us back to the ruins after the meal for a sound and light show after dark.

Fortunately our plans for the afternoon could easily be moved to the morning, so we accepted their gesture. So instead we found ourselves looking around the Government Palace which is quite similar to the one in Mexico City.

We were collected on time, and joined four Argentinians for the tour of these iguana-infested ruins. We walked around the main site of the ruins, and passed the Pyramid of the Magician and a pokolpok court to reach a temple we could climb. I was the only one in our small group to climb the stairs - it was worth it for the views.

Pokolpok is what the Yucatec Maya of this region would have called the ball game that the Aztecs had called Ōllamaliztli in their Nahuatl language.

When I got back down I realised I'd lost a strap from my backpack; but even with retracing my steps I couldn't find it. For the remainder of the tour I found myself constantly thinking about when I'd last seen it, and where it could be. Once the tour was over I ran around the site once in the hope that I'd find it. I did not - losing anything on a trip is frustrating, and this was the first time I'd lost anything other than a map.

After the included meal we decided we'd pay to go around the Chocolate Story museum as we had enough time before the light show. This museum starts with the story of how cocoa beans are gathered and processed, and then moves on to the dangers that the Maya used to face when gathering.

Surprisingly they have cages demonstrating the dangers - one containing monkeys, and then a pair of cages containing one male jaguar, and one female jaguar.

The tour ended with a demonstration of the production process, and a chance to make your own chocolate drink by combining the different ingredients. Mayans would use annatto, cinnamon, allspice, hot pepper, and sugar; but the taste was still a little bitter.

When the time came for the light show, we were led to our seats on the high wall of the nunnery. From there we could see the rounded walls of the Pyramid of the Magician were now illuminated.

Although the sound and light show is advertised as

being available in both English and Spanish, it was in Spanish that we saw it. This was a story told through lights with a pre-recorded voice-over. Different coloured lights were shone on different parts of the ruins to indicate where the story was taking place and to a degree reflect the story being told.

My Spanish is almost non-existent so I couldn't really understand the majority of what was happening. What I could understand of the dialogue indicated that there had been a drought, and then I believe it talked about a priest offering a sacrifice to the gods, and this being answered with rain clouds that saved their crops.

During the night drive back to the hotel we found delays from police breathalysing every driver, and bush fires causing smoke to billow across the road.

Our tour guide for the drive to Playa del Carmen just happened to be our guide from Uxmal; but was now working through a different company. A strange coincidence, though I guess local experts offer their services to multiple companies to find enough work.

During this drive we took the opportunity to stop by a cenote, Ik kil. A cenote is a type of sinkhole - a place where underground erosion has caused the ground above it to eventually collapse. In the case of a cenote the collapse has revealed groundwater. This particular cenote is sixty metres in diameter and drops twenty-six metres before you reach the water which is then around forty metres deep. Many of these cenotes are around the rim of the Chicxulub impact crater - one currently associated with a mass extinction event.

Around the edge of the cenote there are a number of long vines hanging, and carved steps that lead down to the level of the water. It felt like a place that could have been straight out of Indiana Jones; if you ignored the modern buildings around it.

Further down the road we stopped at Chichen Itza - the most visited archaeological site in Mexico. The first ruins we saw was a temple called 'The Temple of the Thousand Warriors'. Our guide told us there was a column for each of these warriors, though it looked more likely there were only a couple of hundred. It's not exactly the first time a guide has exaggerated to us.

The pyramid in this plaza features architectural styles from both Maya and Toltec civilisations. It was tempting to get many more photographs of close-up details; but with no shelter from the sun I was finding it hard to concentrate in the heat of the midday sun.

The famous pyramid, Temple of Kukulkan, was the only place I allowed myself to linger. There are ninety-one steps on each of the four sides adding up to a total of 364 steps, with one final step at the top to make it equal to the number of days in the year.

Their study of the world around them didn't stop there either - around the spring and autumn equinoxes the shadows cast by the steps represents their feathered-serpent god Kukulcan. It's an incredible example of ancient architecture, and their understanding of the world. It proves them to be anything but the primitives that Europeans saw them as. These indigenous American cultures deserved better.

Two sides of the temple are in excellent condition,

whereas the other two were undergoing some restoration work. Unlike the Parthenon in Athens, at least here I could get photographs that wouldn't show the restoration work.

Three hours after leaving Chichen Itza, we arrived at the hotel in Playa del Carmen.

Breakfast wouldn't be served at this hotel until after we'd gone, so the night before we'd bought a few bits from a local store. Once we'd eaten we were collected by a scuba diving company, signed some forms, and gathered what hire equipment we'd need.

Our first dive was a cenote called Chac Mool which has two entrances into the Kukulkan cavern system. After the usual buoyancy checks we began our descent into the cavern following the guide ropes.

The entranceway was dark, but shafts of light shone down through the opening. Once inside the system it was completely dark with the only illumination being from our torches.

At around thirteen metres I found it difficult to equalise the pressure in my right ear, and after surfacing at the end of the dive I found my hearing muffled.

Our surface interval was short - just long enough to drink some water and prepare the next tank. The second dive was from an underground entrance hidden from the sun, so felt cooler already.

Again my right ear just wouldn't equalise, and at one point was getting painful. Stalactites underwater made ascending difficult - something which may have alleviated the discomfort. Eventually we reached an air pocket in the middle of this route where we could take off our masks and regulators to talk. The most noticeable feature of this underwater air pocket was the tree roots above our heads,some of which extended down into the water.

One quick chat later we were back underwater and navigating our way around the system to the exit point where we could remove our masks one last time.

"He's covered in blood again. Why is it he's always covered in blood?" James exclaimed.

"Huh?" I wondered what he was talking about. This Harry Potter quote was directed at the blood that now covered my face. At first I thought perhaps it'd been when James had accidentally kicked me in the face; but it seemed to be a nose bleed instead. My ears wouldn't clear either which made me wonder if I'd damaged them.

After a day of diving, the best thing to do is relax and refuel. So that's what we did: utilising the hotel pool, and only wandering around Playa del Carmen when it was time for food. Relaxing is not something I'd really done much of on trips so far; but we had another day of diving to come.

Another early start meant another day without breakfast. My ear still hadn't improved, so I thought I'd have to miss the dives. Fortunately, our dive master for the day had experienced the same in the caves before, and had found it to be inflammation from the frequent pressure changes during the multi-level dive. Maybe it'd be okay to risk then.

For this session we'd be using the same entry point

for both dives at Dos Ojos - a name meaning 'two eyes'. Much of the eighty-two kilometres of caves remain unexplored. Through the use of tracking dyes it's been determined that it exits into the ocean, though no human has yet been able to follow it all the way through.

As I got into the water I noticed a steady stream of bubbles from my BCD - it was leaking air. When I spoke to the guide he looked at the BCD and the tank, and couldn't figure out what was wrong with it. He suggested I should dive anyway.

To me, diving when your equipment has a known fault is just crazy. Yes, I could probably have gotten away with it; but it's not worth the risk in case the fault gets worse. Instead I exited the water, and another dive master was able to fix it.

The first guideline we took allowed me to stay higher than the dives at Chac Mool and Little Brother. Again my face was covered in blood, though I noticed that I more or less had working hearing in both ears which was a nice surprise. Even if it was short-lived.

The tank changeover was our quickest yet, and we continued diving along the second route through tight gaps between rocks and stalactites. I enjoyed this dive far more than the previous dives. I was more in control of my movement, and was able to work on technique whilst trying to keep my air usage to a minimum.

Maybe my ears had issues, and there wasn't really any marine life to see; but the experience was incredible. It was like being in an abyss of nothingness that rendered my new underwater camera mostly useless.

Once back in Playa del Carmen we wandered

around, trying to decide what we'd do on our last day. By chance we stumbled across a street vendor selling snorkelling tours in Puerto Morelos. It sounded like the perfect way to end the adventure.

With the end of the trip in sight, no longer would I need to eat the dreaded refried beans that are a staple of Mexican diets. Hopefully it'd also be the last time for a while that I'd be seeing watermelon for breakfast.

For this morning we were told nothing would be a rush: we could all take it easy, and things would just happen. Don't believe everything you're told.

Most of this group hadn't snorkelled before - they had their feet below them, and kicking up sediment. Many weren't too aware of their surroundings either as they'd bump into each other frequently. The guide was unimpressed and hurried people around, not wanting people to linger in any one spot even if they were looking at the fish around them.

Most of the fish were too fast for me to photograph so I concentrated on one that wasn't moving too much. Of course I didn't know at the time it was a barracuda, nor that they tend to be a little ferocious. I guess I got lucky as even when getting a bit too close to it, it just swam away without attacking.

In between trips there was a buffet lunch, and nobody knew when we'd need to be ready for the next trip out on the boat so it became a rush to get ready. On this last one though I did get to see a swordfish.

When the snorkelling sessions came to an end they gave us just ten minutes to dry off, queue for the changing rooms to get changed, and to hand in any borrowed equipment. For a supposedly relaxed tour I don't think there was a single moment when we weren't getting herded from one thing to the next with haste.

It was a nice day, but I think it's one of those places we should have read the reviews for first. It was all over now, and all that remained was our flight to Canada.

24: Toronto, ON.

Flying from Cancun to Toronto was the journey home for James; but for me it was a continuation of the sightseeing adventure.

Our trip to the airport had been in silence. We'd wanted the airport transfer to arrive at 07:00; but the tour company insisted on 06:45. When it arrived at 06:30 and had to wait for us the 'guide' was angry. It was probably the least professional behaviour I'd seen on any trip.

During this flight I noticed that my ears had returned to normal. Whilst in Mexico I'd suffered hearing loss in one ear due to the multi-level diving; but the pressurised cabin fixed this problem perfectly.

A few hours later the aircraft begun its approach into Toronto as normal, and had descended most of the way down to the runway. At the last minute the aircraft pulled up, and went into a holding pattern over the Toronto airspace. There had been debris on the runway that needed clearing.

Immigration didn't go much better for me either. They questioned why I was arriving in the country for the second time in two weeks, and led me to a different room to ask additional questions. Long waits like this make me paranoid about being rejected entry into a country.

One hour after this we'd left the airport, and was at my friends apartment.

Being in Canada meant I could finally have a change from scrambled eggs and refried beans for breakfast. I don't particularly like either; but had put up with them in Mexico because it's all there was. James made us blueberry pancakes topped with maple syrup. Lots of them. So many in fact that there were more than we could eat. I pondered whether or not Canadians would bleed maple syrup when cut.

On our way to the port for the Toronto Islands we stopped by a number of metro stations, one of these being the Union Station. Although this station only opened in 1927 it is in the National Historic Site of Canada registry. It may seem very recent, but in fairness it's probably one of the oldest buildings in the city.

In some ways the Great Hall reminded me of the main concourse in New York City's Grand Central Station - just a bit smaller.

The ferry ride to Ward Island was a cold one as we were blasted with the cold air blowing across the water. If we'd not arrived from the blistering heat of Mexico, perhaps it wouldn't have seemed so bad. It's also possible the islands actually were colder than downtown as the wind would also have been cooled by Lake Ontario.

Center Island has a number of buildings, and some places to get food. It also has a bit of a theme park as well, though most of the buildings around this area are aimed at young families. We stopped briefly for a burger, but carried on our walk to the far side of the islands, to Hanlan's Point.

On our way to the ferry we came across a lighthouse at Gibraltar Point which was open as part of the Toronto Open Doors day. This is a day a bit like the Heritage Open Days back home where many old properties are opened for free. Some are even ones which aren't usually open to the public too. It was a bit of a wait to go up the lighthouse as they'd only allow four in at a time for safety reasons. From the top you could see all over the islands, and of course the Toronto skyline. It's apparently one of the oldest structures in Toronto, and has a ghost story surrounding it dating back the the early 19th century.

When we got back to the mainland we had no idea what to see next. The old town hall was part of the Open Doors day, so perhaps that would be worthwhile.

Further along the road we could see a number of people standing around, and some police cars. Then I saw a crashed helicopter. My first thought was wondering what had happened, and why people were so close to it. Could it have been a tragic accident, or a terrorist attack? As we got closer I realised that it was being set-up as part of a film shoot.

Once I was close enough to photograph it I could see the rotors on the helicopter were mangled and it had been set-up to look like it had crashed into a bus. I noticed one of the police cars said 'Midway City Police Department' on the side - it was familiar but I couldn't quite place where I knew it from.

When I realised this was a Warner Brothers set, I knew what it was - this was Suicide Squad. It'd have been nice to hang around in the hope of seeing them shoot a scene, but we'd already lost enough time. Unfortunately it was already too late - we'd missed the chance to look inside the town hall.

Instead we headed over to Yonge Street, a road which stretches for almost thirty-five miles. Again we found a reason for pause when we encountered another crowd of people.

A street performer had started off with juggling, and then moved on to juggling fire. To maintain the interest of the crowd he added in a little variety in the form of a demonstration of how to use a whip. Then set it on fire. I found it entertaining that this was the point he got some audience participation.

For the finale of his show he set fire to a tennis racket that had its strings removed. It didn't seem that amazing, but then he dislocated his left shoulder, then his right shoulder, and then squeezed his entire body through the flaming tennis racket. Now that was a finale. How he never set his long hair on fire during this was also something of a mystery.

The following day was the one sight I really wanted to see in Ontario - Niagara Falls. To get there we hired a car using a local service that James had an annual subscription for.

Niagara-on-the-Lake is surprisingly more commercialised than I thought it would be, though I'm not sure what I really expected - I hadn't really imagined a town besides it. I'd always believed it to be in the middle of nowhere.

Finding parking in the area isn't too bad; but it's easier to find once you've passed the falls. What this means is that you then have to walk back following the flow of water and you only get to appreciate how immense the falls are once you finally pass the edge.

On the Canadian side of the falls you can easily see the three waterfalls that are collectively known as Niagara Falls: Bridal Veil Falls, Horseshoe Falls, and the American Falls. From both the American and Canadian sides of the falls there are boat rides out to the Horseshoe Falls on the boats known as the 'Maidens of the Mist'. From the Canadian side you can also take a tunnel almost down to the water level in order to see behind the falls.

I'd have been interested in either of those, but I hadn't realised it was a possibility until it was too late to find something I could protect my camera equipment with. Once again I needed to remind myself to research a place properly before visiting. There's not much else to do in the area really; though it's possible to try another Canadian staple: food and drink from Tim Hortons.

It was now the working week so it meant that James was back at work, though I'd got the first of these days as vacation time. I'd gotten used to using the subway system in Toronto so I decided I'd visit Fort York.

I was surprised that my sense of direction worked out okay on this rare occasion. Perhaps the years of travelling had helped me to overcome being locationally challenged quite as often. Maybe.

Originally the fort had been built strategically by the British due to its natural harbour far enough from the United States. In later years it was also garrisoned by Canadian militia, but the original buildings were destroyed in the Battle of York in 1812. Years later the ownership transferred to the City of Toronto. The buildings there now are the ones which would have been present during the first and second world wars.

The entrance to Fort York is a modern building where the windows are covered in sheets of steel that give it a defensive look but they lift up to act like an awning. At the time I visited there was also an exhibition on recent warfare. All the buildings around this feel out of place with the skyscraper backdrop; but it's a rare reminder of where this city started.

The next few days had very little tourism as I was working remotely - an advantage of the job I do. It was another new experience though. As I was waking up early I was starting far earlier (ignoring the time difference) than I normally would, and could eat breakfast whilst I worked. This meant I was finishing mid-afternoon to allow for a bit more exploration.

On the first of these days I went to the Rogers Stadium to watch a baseball game - the Toronto Blue Jays and the Chicago White Sox. When we got to the stadium there was a bit of an issue with my camera to start with. As I'd got my 150–500mm lens attached they said that without a press pass I wasn't going to be allowed to use it. My only option was to let them lock it up, and to collect it after the game.

When we got to the place where they lock up valuables the manager there decided that as we were sitting up in section 535 that it'd be okay for me to keep my camera with me as long as I kept it out of the way. As it turned out we were almost the only people sitting in that section as the majority were further down - closer to the action.

Before the game began, the national anthems of America and Canada were sung by performers that walked out onto the field. I didn't really know much about baseball, and to be honest I still don't. I watched as two teams I'd not seen before took it in turns to try and score points - something that they didn't do for a number of innings.

After a few of these had passed I'd decided that as I'd not yet eaten I should do what seems stereotypical for baseball games and went to get a hot dog. It was better than the one I'd tried in New York, so that was something. To make it even better the teams finally started scoring and for most of the game they were tied.

My hope was that there'd be a victory after nine innings so I could get some sleep; but it wasn't looking good for the Blue Jays - the White Sox at the end of their last innings were ahead and it seemed it was all over.

Eventually it got to the last ball for the last batter. There were runners on each of the bases ready to go if he could hit it - they just needed to score one to get level, or two to win. Amazingly he hit a home run propelling the team to victory. I was told it was an ending you don't often see in baseball, and I was fortunate to see a home team win like that.

In the days that followed I visited the CN Tower, and also one of their indoor markets. The tower is one of those places which is nice to see, so you can appreciate the size of the city; but it's hard to take photographs due to the reflections of lights on the glass. I spent enough time up there to see it go from dusk to nighttime, and to see the city light up.

The indoor market sold all sorts: fresh meat, dairy, cake, and also less perishable things such as souvenirs. It's not really the sort of place I'd seek out deliberately; but it was something to do.

Another adventure had come to an end; albeit one with a delay. Not long after boarding the aircraft I had to 'deplane' due to them finding one of the lavatories didn't work. It caused hours of delay, and by the time the aircraft was ready there was a further delay due to the pilot going off shift. As with all things, this eventually passed and I made it home - ready for my next adventure.

25: Five States

Time changes everything. Entropy causes a gradual decline into chaos, whilst experience can bring order for the short term.

When I went to Egypt I had no idea what I was doing, and everything was new. It felt the most chaotic of any of the trips I'd done and it felt like it'd gone so terribly wrong. However, there and on other trips I'd got someone else with me as back-up. Whenever things went wrong it'd been a joint decision on what to do next.

When I went to San Diego I was alone for the journey for the first time, and then repeated this when I went to Mexico. The next step was to travel alone, and then be by myself for the majority of a trip. Had I learnt enough? Or was this all going to go wrong?

I returned to the United States once more for a work trip visiting customers in three different states. Unfortunately I'd be starting in Texas so couldn't get there through a direct flight - there'd be many.

My flight leaving New York's Newark Liberty International Airport was running thirty minutes late when I arrived, and I realised this would give me a very tight thirty-five minute connection in Houston. Tight, but possible.

I waited patiently, but the flight was delayed even further, and then again once more. The pilot was able to recover fifty minutes whilst in the air, but it was not enough time. The flight to Tyler had already left the terminal. For the first time in my life, I'd missed a flight.

Remaining calm is important in situations like this: every problem can be solved. For the next hour I queued at the airlines customer services desk hoping they'd be able to sort something. During this time the number of staff working there had halved which meant they were getting through potential passengers even slower.

I explained to them that their delayed flight had caused me to miss the next one, and they arranged for me to be on the next flight a few hours later and without asking gave me a $7 food voucher as compensation.

Okay Houston, we've had a problem here. Crisis averted, and I'd be on my way to Tyler in no time. Now I could satisfy my hunger.

I was tempted to eat at the first place I could find, but I didn't have that long until my rescheduled flight so needed to find somewhere that'd serve quickly. If I missed this flight there wouldn't be another until the following day which would cause me to miss my meeting.

The food I chose came to more than the $7 voucher so I gave them some money as well which I'd need change from. Confused by this the employee commented that they can't give change for vouchers.

That's fair enough, but I explained that I was using the full value of the voucher and wouldn't be using the full value of the cash I was giving him. He insisted it didn't work like this, and I gave up on trying to explain this before the discussion got too heated. Despite this, he still gave me the change but refused to give a receipt.

The final flight of the day was on what the locals called a puddle jumper. It's the name they give to a light aircraft used for short 'jumps' between cities like a stone being skimmed across water.

"So where are you going?" one passenger asked another during the flight.

"Tyler," she said in a deadpan voice. They were both on the same aircraft heading to a small airport that serves the same airports as Houston, and had no further flights that day. It seemed the answer should have been obvious unless they expected to parachute out along the way.

This airport is small enough to use the same hall for arrivals, baggage collection and departures. There wasn't even a place for ordering taxis from.

I walked outside and stopped. I contemplated walking for two hours along a dark, unlit road carrying my suitcase in a place I didn't know. Getting lost was a strong possibility.

Common sense prevailed, and I went back inside the terminal to ask at the car rental desk if they knew of any public telephones I could use. Fortunately they let me use theirs, and I called the taxi number.

"Good evening. Could I order a taxi, please?" I asked the operator.

She replied in a heavy Texan accent, "With an accent like that you can order whatever you want"

I was taken aback by the reply, surprised that Americans here still found the English accent novel. I'd assumed by now, with TV in particular, they'd have become accustomed to it. Admittedly it'd resulted in comments at San Diego Comic Con, but nobody thought twice about it in New York.

I often find that when I change timezone I don't sleep much to start with, even off the back of a long day. This time I awoke at 03:00 to a cacophony of noise from the fridge humming along to the whirring of the air conditioning unit. I tried to sleep as well as I could, but after a few more hours I decided I was better off getting up for a run.

Tyler is the sort of place that doesn't have sidewalks - everyone travels by car. This meant I was running along quiet six-lane roads, and the occasional grassy embankment.

It was difficult to run even that early in the morning. I was drenched with sweat from the humidity, and could barely see from it dripping into my eyes. It was my first real experience of running in very hot weather, and although difficult, I was glad to have done it.

After my work meeting was over it was already time to move on - I needed a taxi back to the airport so I could begin a weekend of tourism.

For the entire taxi ride the driver was leaning back over his broken chair, his weight causing it bend beyond its limit. Instead of keeping his eyes on the road, he was looking back and talking to me - telling me his life story. He'd been in prison for five years, but had realised he'd done wrong and was filled with remorse. It's good that he'd turned his life around; but I was wishing he'd turn around and watch the road as well.

This airport didn't have an x-ray machine for luggage so I had to remove the lock and put it inside my suitcase so they could search it prior to the flight. I wasn't too keen on the idea, but I didn't really have a choice. At least the flight to Houston was short.

I awoke in Houston, and paid US$70 for a taxi ride to the Lyndon B. Johnson Space Center. It was expensive, but it was a place I'd read about from a very young age.

I'd planned ahead and knew to head to the tram tours first - they'd be the ones that would fill up the quickest so joining a queue early would be a good idea. The first one was for the Historic Mission Control - used in the days of the Apollo missions.

Eighty or so steps took me up to the Mission Operations Control Room 2, or MOCR-2 as it's known. This room had been where they'd monitored nine Gemini and Apollo space missions from.

On the 20th of July 1969 this was the room where they first heard words from human beings on another astronomical body. This was where they'd been monitoring the Apollo 11 lunar landing from.

"Houston, Tranquility Base here. The Eagle has landed."

Six hours after they'd received this communication, the American astronaut Neil Armstrong became the first human to set foot on our moon. An action that inspired a generation, and continues to inspire today. I'd never imagined being able to stand in that room, nor had I imagined what I'd get to see in the Rocket Park.

Outside there are a few rockets such as the Mercury-Redstone, and the Little Joe II. Inside though is one of only three remaining Saturn V rockets in the world. The rocket itself will not have been into space as the old Saturn Vs were disposable, but it is real. This behemoth in front of me was a rocket I'd been so interested in as a child, and there one was.

As soon as I made it back to the main building I joined the queue for the next tram. I felt it important to get these done first as I didn't want to miss a thing. For this one it visited the Space Vehicle Mockup Facility. Sure they've got mockups of ISS modules there, but they also test new equipment such as the Small Pressurised Rover.

The final tram was for 'White Flight' flight control. Unlike the previous mission control I'd seen, this one had been refurbished with new equipment. It was about to become a temporary flight control for the ISS; but would one day be flight control for the Orion missions.

Back in the main building I finally started to look around the exhibits. There wasn't really anything special there; however in the Astronaut Gallery they did have the restored prop of the Galileo 7 Space Shuttle used in the filming of the original Star Trek TV series. I'd not expected to see it, and it was incredible to find it there.

When this prop was sold at auction in 2012 it had been in complete disrepair. The purchaser spent a lot of time and money, enlisting the help of the original builder in order to restore it to its former self before donating it to the space centre.

It's quite an educational place too. One interesting fact is that the water that they reclaim from urine on the ISS is actually cleaner than the water we drink here on Earth, even that which is in bottles. It's the sort of technology that makes you think whether one day it could be used on Earth in places where water is scarce. Solving problems for living in space have a habit of also benefiting life on the planet as well.

I'd made pretty good time at the space centre though it'd been a rush to see it all in the five hours that the taxi driver had given me. It gave me time in Houston to find somewhere to buy food from before looking for the Amtrak station.

I asked at the hotel for directions first; but they didn't know what an Amtrak was, or that they even had a train station. Though as it was around a mile away I found their claims doubtful. I used their Wi-Fi, and was able to see where it was on a map, and with my suitcase dragging behind me I made my way in its general direction. Somehow I found my way there okay.

Before the train arrived I had to hand over my luggage as this would travel on a different part of the train. Though stupidly I left my food in my suitcase which meant me having to try to get access to it before the train arrived. This was done in a back room of the train station where employees were sitting around and joking with each other.

The train was a two-storey one, with some carriages having beds. I'd opted for a spacious seat that would recline instead. I was hopeful I'd get to relax a little before getting into San Antonio at 23:30.

Even at midnight the Alamo had tourists standing around taking photographs. The hotel wasn't far from there, and easy to find. Alas, this was not the end of my night.

They told me that despite my prepaid reservation that they were overbooked and had arranged for me to be in a motel - one so far out of town that it was almost at the airport. I was too tired to argue; but I made sure that they paid for my taxi to get me there. I was not happy, but there wasn't really anything I could do about it. It would have made more sense though, and I'd have been happier, if they'd booked me into a similar hotel somewhere in the vicinity of The Alamo or the Riverwalk - the two reasons I'd booked this one. The place they'd booked me into was not even in a similar price range. I didn't find this even remotely acceptable.

I arrived at the motel at 00:40. The air conditioning didn't work, and the neighbours were noisy. The place looked like the sort of motel you'd expect to find criminals hiding in if it was a film. Hopefully none of the neighbours were murderous.

I didn't need an alarm to wake up - I was awake at 05:30 after what at best would have been three hours of sleep. It was however perfect timing for getting a pre-breakfast long run done. I had planned to run fourteen miles; but I was in the middle of nowhere now - at best I could manage a four mile loop that I'd need to repeat a few times.

During my first lap of this route I was chased by two different dogs that had been left out by their owners overnight. This exhausted me quickly, and I overheated. Even this early in the day it was hot and humid.

Breakfast at the hotel was possibly worse than the room - all they had was coffee, which I don't drink, and a lukewarm pot of porridge oats. Fortunately I'd learnt to take cereal bars everywhere. I can thank China at least for that.

I felt drained, and angry at what had transpired. So much so that I drafted a letter of complaint. Was it harsh? Maybe; but the experience had annoyed me, and reduced my time in the city. Even after all that they were very reluctant to let me leave my luggage with them to save on time later.

In the time since I'd left the Alamo at midnight, a queue had grown for getting in. I hadn't realised though that this was actually a queue for just the main building that had been used as their last stand.

I took a slow walk to the San Fernando Cathedral to take more photographs; I arrived there just as Sunday mass ended which meant again it was difficult to get a shot without people in view. So, I wandered over to the City Hall and the Spanish Governor's Palace, and then back to the steps down to the river.

With my free time on this trip at an end, I needed to make my way to the airport for the overnight flight to Wichita via Dallas. During the second of these flights I witnessed an incredible thunderstorm that flashed with increasing ferocity. It was amazing; at times there were flashes from multiple places at the same time. On one occasion there were multiple bolts one after another in what appeared to be the same place - who said lightning doesn't strike twice?

At 01:00 the airport in Wichita was deserted. With no airport shuttles available my only choice was a taxi to El Dorado. It wasn't a pleasant journey though. The taxi driver was chewing tobacco creating an awful smell, and was trying very hard not to fall asleep at the wheel. It wasn't until an hour had passed that he thought to tell me his credit card machine wasn't working so would need to be paid in cash. It took most of my remaining cash. It felt like the last twenty-four hours had been one problem after another. Even though in reality the issues were few. Had that missed flight early on been an indication of what this trip would be like?

Again it was another hotel room with a faulty air conditioning unit, though this time it caused the floor to vibrate. It didn't matter though - I was too tired now to be kept awake by it.

For the rest of the week I'd be with a colleague who was based in Kansas. After our first meeting of the week we travelled along the interstate to our overnight stop. I'd expected to see masses of corn fields, and barns - just like you see on television. It didn't really seem like that though. In fact, Kansas City isn't entirely in Kansas either - some of it is in Missouri. It meant I'd already travelled through three states on this trip, and would have another two to go before the end.

In the city we stopped by the Liberty Memorial, a place that towers over the city in remembrance to those that died in the First World War. Our second stop was to get food.

Apparently Kansas is famous for barbecues, so my colleague took me to a barbecue restaurant. The dish I went with was a combination one that had crown prime beef ribs that were thick with meat, chicken, burnt ends, hickory pit beans, and cheesy corn bake.

It tasted amazing, but there was also an incredible amount of it. I guess American portions is one of those things you have to get used to, or let food go to waste.

Running in Kansas was more bearable than in Texas. Just. It was still warm though, but not warm enough to make me stop. It felt good to get it in before another day of travel. My next meeting was in a small town called Wayne - we'd be driving through Iowa and Nebraska to get there. If there was a place that was the farthest from civilisation, then it sounded like this was it.

On the way we stopped in Omaha - another city that straddles two states. This one felt more European than the sort of American town I'd visited so far. Hours later we finally made it to our final destination in Nebraska.

By American standards Wayne is a very small town where at last count the population was around 5,660 - a lot of which were employed by or attending the college there.

The town is so small that it's about two miles from east to west, and a little over a mile from north to south. It's not densely settled either, and large parts of this town were fields. At a guess, I'd have estimated that the college accounts for almost a quarter of the surface area of this town. It'd make it challenging coming up with an 8.5 mile route for the following morning.

The only food place seemed to be a sports bar called The Max. Seeing the name from the outside I thought it'd be like the place of the same name in 'Saved by the Bell'; but actually it's grittier and darker. Isn't everything these days though?

All food there was fried and very cheap. A hamburger, for example, would cost under US$2. It was greasy, yet somehow was still better than some of the places I'd eaten at during my travels over the years.

My morning run covered the extremities of the town in each direction, but I'd still not covered the required distance. I found myself using the running track at the college to finish off.

Once the run and my work meeting were over, I was back in Omaha for an overnight stay before flying home. This was my chance to do one last bit of exploring whilst looking for an evening meal.

I walked across a grassy bank from Iowa into Nebraska, and the Heartland of America Park. Along this stretch of the Missouri River had been one of Lewis and Clark's landings during their discovery expedition.

Sometimes journeys are long and tiring, and may not go entirely to plan; but that is the price of travel. It's often the experiences that make us remember the places we visit, and give us stories to tell.

26: California

I was now seeing more and more of the world at an increased pace. Instead of just one trip a year I was now making two or sometimes three trips. Following my work trip across five states, I returned to the USA one last time that year for a Big Sur road trip.

The plan originally had been to go Arizona with my sister; but unfortunately she took ill not long after I'd done the London Marathon. With her time in hospital it meant she wasn't going to be able to fly again for at least a year.

James however had the idea of driving the Californian coast. I created a spreadsheet to help us plan, and then between us we put ideas together very quickly. I even went so far to estimate where we'd be each day, and how long we'd want at each stop.

It was a new way for us to be planning, spun out from the sort of comparison spreadsheets we'd created previously. There were bits we weren't sure if they'd work out, but it was a learning experience.

For me the biggest challenge would be driving with an automatic gearbox instead of a manual, and being on the 'wrong' side of the road.

Unusually my flight landed in Newark an hour earlier than scheduled. It was a relief after my last experience there. From there I flew to Denver, and met up with James for the last leg of the journey to San Jose.

I was tired when we eventually arrived, but could only sleep until 02:00. After that I was kept awake by constant noise, and people shouting in the corridor.

Even though we'd provided all our details online, the car rental place still required us to provide it all again. They'd got James' credit card on record; but they needed mine too in case there were any fines accrued.

The mention of fines raised a good point. What did I know of the traffic laws in the US? Nothing. I should have done more to learn these before travelling. I did at least know that in some states you can turn on a red light. James had reminded me enough times on that one anyway.

With the paperwork completed we were led to the car we'd have for the next week. It'd be great to drive down the empty US highways, with music playing - just like in the films. Oh, wait, no. Neither of us had thought to bring music with us.

With only the local radio stations to listen to, we began our drive with a stop in the small town of Capitola. This place had been recommended to us as a good place to buy lunch from.

The next stop planned had been Point Lobos; but we saw signs for Marina Dunes Preserve and thought it'd be worth investigating. The sand there was fine, and the beach completely deserted.

There wasn't that much to see though, so we continued on to our planned stop. We started with the Cypress Grove trail; but paused during this one to eat the lunch we'd purchased earlier. On paper this trip looked busy, but so far it felt relaxing.

At the end of this first trail we could look down on sea otters, sea lions, and harbour seals relaxing in the sun. A couple of park rangers had set-up spotting scopes and were talking about the wildlife of this area. Apparently it used to be possible to get down to where the seals were, but it had been observed that the seals had been moving further ashore so they'd closed the path to protect them. I like how thoughtful they were here.

By mid-afternoon we'd moved on, but had still only made it to the start of the winding road of Big Sur. Our first proper stop was the historic Bixby Creek Bridge. Prior to the building of this bridge the locals would often be cut off during bad weather due to the trails that flooded.

We couldn't really get much further as we were now an hour away from sunset. Instead of going any further we headed back into Monterey County to the city of Seaside.

My early morning run, although not quite as early as intended, took me around Seaside and along the undulating coastal path. The closer I got to the coast, the more I was convinced I could hear a crowd of people.

I carried on in the direction of the noise, and stumbled across the start of the Bay of Monterey Half

Marathon. I'd arrived just in time to see the elites starting off! If I'd known about this race prior to visiting I think I'd have entered it. It'd have been nice to combine actual racing with a sightseeing holiday - maybe something for the future.

A great start to the day got even better with our first stop of the day being at Pfeiffer Big Sur State Park. At the trailhead there are many impressive redwood trees - some of the tallest trees in the world. At first I was reminded of a resort in Sherwood Forest due to the paths through trees, but those trees are tiny compared to these. These were like skyscrapers surrounding the road.

Once away from the road, the trees started to remind me of the forest moon of Endor from Star Wars. As it happened those scenes were filmed a little further north in the Redwood National Park.

When we reached a fork in the trail, the route we took led us down to a waterfall. Whilst climbing over a rock to get a better view I knocked the cap off my biggest lens, and watched in horror as it dropped. It's not the first lens cap I've lost in a waterfall - last time I was unable to retrieve it. This time I watched it bounce onto some rocks below, and then slowly roll into the flowing water. It was swept up by this water until it was stopped by a branch.

The lens would have been left unprotected for the rest of the week so I decided the best thing to do was to climb over the rocks, and to carefully lower myself down to the waters edge.

I was standing on some rocks, but couldn't reach the lens. I decided my best option was to jump across to the other side and to try from there. I landed safely, and edged forwards to reach out to retrieve the lost lens cap. Mission accomplished.

It was difficult climbing back out; but I did it, and stayed dry. This fun led us to start talking to Aaron and Caitlin who had been watching. They're professional event photographers that were working their way up Big Sur.

They recommended Ragged Point where apparently they have a large number of Hummingbirds you can get close to. This sounded to me like a great idea for something to do. I wasn't that happy with my hummingbird photos from Ecuador so this was another chance to get it right.

Our next stop was a little further along Big Sur at Julia Pfeiffer Burns State Park. This second state park has a coastal trail that provided a reasonable view of McWay Falls. Though with the ongoing drought it made it little more than a trickle.

Limekiln Trails wasn't a place we'd planned on stopping; but when we found it we thought it was worth checking out. At the trailhead there is a small bridge, taken out by a tree which had fallen and broken through. Our only option was to cross the gentle stream below.

On the other side the, the trail leads to some old lime kilns on one fork, and a waterfall on the other. Once again the waterfall had been reduced to little more than a trickle by the drought.

There are four lime kilns, all of which are damaged to some degree revealing the inner workings. This is what I felt made them interesting: a piece of abandoned industry in the middle of nowhere.

The area is partially roped off with a sign saying it's dangerous to go up to the kilns. It makes sense - these rusty towers might not be stable, and there's a lot of stone rubble around them. The rope doesn't fully block the path to them though, so it's possible to have a closer look if you're willing to take that risk.

These kilns were built in the 1890s to convert limestone into lime. Once processed it was then transported from the kilns in carts along the local road to the Everett area. None of the structures that were used for loading the carts still exist, but you can still see the various ports for stoking the fires that were used up until the 1930s.

By the time we got back to the car, time was racing towards sunset. With a failed attempt to see hummingbirds at Ragged Point we headed on to San Luis Obispo.

That evening, after finding a barbecue, was our first time filling up with fuel in a foreign country. We tried to pay by card but that required a US ZIP code to be entered. Obviously we didn't have one of those so we tried the one for the hotel thinking it just needed to be a valid code; but this didn't work.

Instead, what we needed to do was to go into the gas station to prepay an amount, and then go back for a receipt after. If we paid more than we took, then they'd also refund the excess. Such a strange way of doing things.

Before setting off on this trip we'd organised some surfing at Carpinteria Beach, Santa Barbara. It was however 110 miles away from where we woke up, and we needed to be there by about 08:30.

It was nice to be driving along this coastal road, but the sun peaking over the horizon provided a downside - it was difficult to see anything without sunglasses.

At the beach we changed into wetsuits, and the instructor led us across the beach to our first lesson: standing up on the board. You'd think standing up would be easy - we get lots of practice at standing in life, but on the water it's a different kettle of fish.

When I got into the water for my first attempt I started to paddle when the instructor told me to, and then pushed up to standing position when he called again. Amazingly, and almost unbelievably, on my first attempt I stood up quickly and rode the wave in all the way to the beach. The next few attempts weren't so fortunate and I found it was actually quite difficult to do when using my own judgement.

Towards the end of the lesson the coolness of the water caused cramp in my left calf, and it made the remainder of the session even more difficult. It was bad enough that James had to take over the driving to get us to Santa Monica. It was lucky I wasn't on my own, and have friends I can travel with now and then.

As we approached Los Angeles the roads began to widen to as many as six or seven lanes in each direction. I'd never seen anything like it.

After a brief stop so James could see his work colleagues in the area, we continued on to the impressive Vincent Thomas suspension bridge next to the battleship, USS Iowa.

I've been on historic ships before, and this one

wasn't really all that different. It was a rush though as even though we'd got an hour before closing time they were already preparing to close.

For the next couple of nights we'd be staying in a hotel on Santa Monica Boulevard. I found the drive there to be one of the most stressful ever. Seven lanes of heavy traffic in the dark, and many switching lanes from either side without care, into gaps not much bigger than their car. Mental!

As the sun rose on a new day in Los Angeles I decided to head out for an early morning run along Santa Monica Boulevard to the ocean and back. With the exception of a taxi pulling off a driveway almost into me, it was a pleasant experience. It was also proof for me that pleasure piers do exist outside of the United Kingdom.

Our plans for the day included a deluxe tour of the Warner Brothers film studio; but we hadn't realised just how bad LA traffic would be. Glacial and chaotic is probably the most accurate description of rush hour in Los Angeles. I sat and watched as our ETA increased until the point the satnav was predicting we'd arrive at the studio one minute before we needed to be there. The traffic seemed to move so slowly that I was sure I could have run to our destination faster.

The satnav really didn't help us either - it kept trying to make us take U-turns into traffic that would only save us at best a minute. It wasn't worth the risk. We did however make it with minutes to spare.

At least that's what we thought. When we got there we found the details on the ticket were wrong, and it actually started thirty minutes later.

This tour had been worth the panic. It started with a video about the history of the studio, and then continued by cart into the backlot. Apparently any building there, even if it's in use as an office, could be redressed to be used as exteriors for television shows. It's one of the ways they try to save on space, and save on money so that their money can be spent more intelligently. I think Harry Warner would have been proud of their frugalness.

The guide even pointed out one section of trees that had been used for a chase sequence in Jurassic Park. The most notable thing about that is the film was Universal and not Warner. The explanation is that film studios will often lease resources out to each other.

Our lunch was in the same place as where crew and cast eat which meant we weren't allowed to use cameras. It makes sense, if you were them, would you want people taking photographs of you eating your food during a busy schedule?

Around the corner from the dining room was the museum with two exhibits: the 50th anniversary of Batman, and another for Harry Potter. The Batman theme continued on in their garage which contains many of the Batmobiles and other vehicles used in the films - including one that had not at the time been seen on screen.

We also got to look around an exterior set being used for a show called The Middle; but as they were filming we had to ensure we stayed off camera. Filming did however prevent us from looking around the popular soundstage used by The Big Bang Theory, so instead we had to look around another used by Two Broke Girls.

For the sound stages that are used in filming short episodes with a live audience they will have all the sets lined up in a row with bleachers facing them. The ones used most frequently by the production are in the middle, directly in front of the audience, whereas the lesser used ones known as swing sets are made up as necessary and are off to the sides.

Some of the other sound stages are used for scripted dramas so are configured differently. The one we saw was for Pretty Little Liars, and had a number of different locations we could walk between such as a school and a coffee shop.

The remainder of the tour took us through the prop department, and to the final self-guided part of the tour. This section looks at pre-production on films, such as modelling and artwork. They do however have a replica of Central Perk from the Friends sitcom that you can walk around.

We'd learnt a fair bit about Hollywood and specifically Warner Brothers during the course of this tour. One of the things they didn't tell us about though was the studio zone which is more commonly known as the Thirty Mile Zone - a name later borrowed by one of the industry tabloids run by Time Warner.

This thirty mile radius around the studios is what labour unions in the 1990s decided would be considered 'local' so that filming within this would be at a lower fixed rate. Outside of this radius it would be considered to be 'on location' and workers on productions would need to be paid more.

It was getting dark and chilly, but our day was not yet over. It was time to visit the Griffiths Observatory. The winding road up the hillside was busy with parked cars and runners with head torches. I wondered if it was a night race, but couldn't be sure.

The observatory itself did however bore me. Most of the information available inside were things I'd learnt at school, or in my own time. We probably spent an hour there before heading for food.

Tired legs meant my second morning in Los Angeles did not include a run. We'd got a busy day anyway, and needed to find somewhere to park near the Hollywood Walk of Fame. If I've ever thought parking back home is expensive, then it's a good job it's not like Hollywood Boulevard. The place we found charged US $2.50 for every twelve minutes of parking so we thought it best to be as quick as we could manage. They really know how to milk tourists of their money.

Along Hollywood Boulevard the main attraction is Grauman's Chinese Theatre-built during the golden age of Hollywood. This theatre is famous all over the world for the films that have premiered there including Star Wars in 1977. The cinema is also famous for the concrete blocks that the famous leave their hand and footprints on.

From one Hollywood attraction to another, we went looking for Canyon Lake Drive which I'd read was a good spot for photographing the famous Hollywood sign. It being a residential area did however pose some problems as a lot of the houses now have tall trees to obscure the view. It makes sense why they'd want to discourage the arrival of tourists.

Other sights we saw that day included the California Science Center - the home of the space shuttle Endeavour. The first thing I noticed is how you can see the wear and the discolouring from nineteen years of service, and the twenty-five missions it completed. It made it very different to the Enterprise in New York City.

This one had been constructed after the destruction of the Challenger in 1986 - a disaster that resulted in a thirty-six month hiatus of the space shuttle program. The Challenger disaster was a reminder that space exploration is a dangerous business, and things can go wrong when you're strapped to gallons of highly explosive rocket fuel. It is a price that has been paid many times since the 1960s when those first astronauts began training.

To finish off our sightseeing of Los Angeles we visited the Bradbury Building. It's home to the LAPD Internal Affairs division so some of it is restricted to visitors. This isn't what interested me though - it'd been the building used in the final scenes of the first Blade Runner film when Harrison Ford's Rick Deckard had chased down the rogue replicant.

Our next destination would then be our final stop of the road trip, but first we had to drive out into the Mojave desert to get there. The drive was long, and eventually the bustle of the city gave way to desert and a wind farm unlike any I'd seen before. For miles into the distance, an impressive array of wind turbines stood generating power for the city. Eventually these too were behind us.

We passed a sign for Joshua Tree, a name I'd heard mention of once before from a friend living in California. Perhaps it was worth us checking it out, but the fuel gauge was getting close to empty.

Mile after mile ticked by and no fuel stations were in sight-at least not ones we could see from the road. In reality there were ones down turnings we'd passed-we just hadn't seen them. Nervously I kept an eye on the needle, concerned that we'd be stranded. As luck would have it, we found fuel in Yukka Valley, just before we arrived in the park.

We didn't know it was Veterans Day until then, and we found this meant free entry into state parks. This was the sort of place where once entering you can drive from viewpoint to viewpoint with very little hiking required. We could see people also used this park for rock climbing, and for camping. We were short on time, but still wanted to see as much as possible.

One of the most obvious and prevalent parts of the landscape is the Yucca brevifolia, the Joshua Tree for which the park and town are named. The trees look very different to what you'd see in England-their branches are thick and point mostly upwards with their needle leaves. They wouldn't be short on sunlight, but they would be short on water-especially during this drought.

At another stop we walked amongst the trees and the rocks to where we saw a large rocky outcrop. I decided to climb the rocks there; but found the surface to be incredibly abrasive.

As I climbed there was a moment when I lost my

footing and thought I was going to fall backwards. With my camera slung over my back I couldn't risk landing on it so had to go forwards. I had two options: I could use my hands to help regain my footing, though the abrasive surface could make it unpleasant. The other option would be to try regaining my balance using my legs; but if I was unable to do so successfully then I'd fall sideways onto a rock, and might not be able to move my leg fast enough to avoid a break. I'd only got seconds to stop myself from going over, and eventually time made the decision for me.

I reached out with my hands and regained my balance; but in doing so I'd cut open my hand. It was minor which meant I could wash it and dress it back at the car.

The trail leading to Barker Dam was the only proper trail we took, and we knew that the setting sun would stop us from seeing any more. We remained at a steady pace along the trail of sand and grit; but the sight we saw at the end of it was not what we'd expected.

California's severe drought had reduced what should have been a large body of water behind the dam to be nothing more than a shallow pond. We could see evidence of where the waterline had once been. California needed rain, and soon.

Before we'd left the park, the sun had set and darkness descended quickly. It was like we were driving through a never-ending abyss. All we could see was what little could be illuminated by the narrow corridor of light from our headlights, and the occasional blinding light from an oncoming car.

It wasn't the easiest of journeys; but we made it to

Palm Springs.

My plans for running hadn't gone well. I'd hoped to run in Palm Springs to get some exploring done, but tiredness meant I never made it out.

Our motel booking included breakfast at a nearby diner, the sort you'd see on television with the small booths against a window and stools around the bar. I guess this was one of those American experiences we'd not previously encountered.

The day ahead of us would be a long one though - before the day was over we'd have driven 450 miles in around seven hours to reach San Jose. When you're driving that many miles, a quick diversion to the Coachella Valley Preserve doesn't make much of a difference.

This preserve is a park on the San Andreas fault-line, with a number of different hikes you can do. We decided on the McCallum Trail as it's supposed to be only 2.4 miles - something we could cover pretty quickly.

The trail begins on a boardwalk over the marshy land of the 'Thousand Palms Oasis', but this soon falls away to a dusty trail of sand. For most of this hike we were at the mercy of the ever-present sun.

On the furthest point there was some respite where some volunteers were working in one of the hot springs. In just the right light we could see gas escaping through the water in streams of bubbles.

The way back to the car wasn't as direct. I'd been trailing behind due to taking photographs, so when we reached a fork in the road it seemed James couldn't hear me call that I thought we were going the wrong way. Before we knew it we'd found private residences and a dead-end. I really should have repeated myself before we'd gotten that far. Though with my lack of directional sense, and I didn't really know if my suspicions were right or not.

For the first leg of the drive back to San Jose, James took the driving seat. Miles ticked by as the landscape changed from desert palms, to barren landscapes, and then to a cityscape when we skimmed the outskirts of Los Angeles towards the Pasadena area.

At around the halfway point we stopped in Bakersfield to stretch our legs, have food, and switch over. The drive was long and monotonous - it had been a straight road at a constant speed for hundreds of miles.

The last hour of the drive became more difficult. The road was now winding around the cliff face in the direction of the setting sun. As the sky got darker, the roads got wider and busier.

Once we'd dropped off the car, our road trip was over. One last lesson we learnt from this is that not all airports have a fuel station close to their car rental drop-off points.

Constant noise around the hotel resulted in a very restless night. Before the sun had even risen it sounded like large metal containers were being moved outside. This was not a hotel for a restful nights sleep.

After the first of the flights that day, we parted ways as I'd be heading from Denver to Newark for my eventual flight home - hopefully I'd have more luck there this time. It was going to be tight though.

I stared at my watch frequently, hoping that time would just stop. When the aircraft's wheels touched the tarmac in Newark, the gate for my next flight had already been open for some time, and my chances were getting slimmer by the second.

Flight attendants requested people remained seated so that those with tight connections could disembark first. As if anyone ever listens. It was a struggle; but I got off and ran across the airport not daring to even look at my watch now.

I arrived at the gate just five minutes before they closed the cabin door. Despite the odds, I'd made it.

27: Russia to Siberia

Every now and then I have an idea of somewhere I'd like to visit. I've seen photographs of the abandoned city of Pripyat in Ukraine - a place frozen in time. I'm sure I don't need to explain that it found infamy when reactor four of the Chernobyl nuclear power plant there exploded during a routine safety check.

It'd been thirty years since this disaster, and I was looking seriously at options to visit. If I'm going to visit, then why not make it into a longer trip and see Russia? However, at that time the border was closed which would have prevented visiting both. Reluctantly I decided Russia would be the better option, and along with frequent-travelling friend James, we found a trans-Siberian adventure to Mongolia.

From watching 'Long Way Round' I knew that getting a tourist visa can be a bit of effort, so we decided that for booking this it'd be advisable to use a company. In theory this should make life so much easier. In theory.

As James was about to get his permanent residency in Canada it made him getting a visa that little bit more difficult. As luck would have it, he'd be in England over

Christmas and had a couple of days that overlapped with the Russian embassy opening times. It was a small window, but there was hope.

Whilst we'd been solving this, we found the Mongolian visa requirements had changed for British citizens - we now needed one. With James back in Canada it meant he had no way of getting to the UK for this before the start of the trip. It was looking like we'd need to change plans.

All was not lost though - he found a company in Canada that was able to obtain the visa for an increased fee.

After receiving my passport back from the Russian Embassy, I was back in London to visit the Mongolian embassy in an old town house on Kensington Court. I buzzed the door, and waited. No reply.

I tried the door again, and still nothing so I knocked instead. This time someone opened the door and then walked off into what appeared to be a waiting room with a counter against one wall.

I handed my form, passport, and other paperwork over at the counter. She quickly checked through it, and told me I could collect it on Monday. It was now Thursday so would have a few days to wait, but it meant another seven hour round trip to collect it. They couldn't post it like the Russians had.

She then handed me a slip saying that the £40 for the visa would need to be paid at the nearest HSBC. She repeated that it had to be HSBC, and not any other bank.

I wandered out onto the Kensington High Street with the slip in my hand. I wasn't really sure where I was going; but I'd got thirty minutes to find HSBC before the embassy was due to close. In these situations it's good to not be afraid to ask for directions.

Finding the bank was still not the end of it. After queueing I handed over the slip to be told that this bank would not accept debit cards for paying at the counter and that it had to be cash. I rushed to find the nearest cash point, got the money for the visa, returned to the desk to queue and was finally handed a receipt to take back to the embassy.

I'd never before had visas for a trip take so much time and effort. It seemed ridiculous that a bank wouldn't allow payments with a debit card.

I eventually got my passport back following another visit to London, and was ready with the necessary visas for another adventure to begin.

Whilst James was flying across the Atlantic, I was 'fortunate' enough to not need a taxi until 03:45 on the day of our adventure. It was difficult to stay awake, but the driver insisted on talking. I did notice he'd put some tape over the 'check engine' light to hide that there was an issue. Maybe the talking was actually a distraction tactic.

The flights were easy, and a concerned guide was waiting for us at the airport in Saint Petersburg - she wondered what had happened to us. The guide had panicked when we'd not arrived on a British Airways flight from London, and had called her office to find out what was happening. They'd not been able to help her despite them being told repeatedly, and confirming repeatedly, that we'd be arriving on a different airline from Munich.

Thirty minutes from the airport we arrived at a hotel next to Saint Isaac's Cathedral, with a room overlooking it.

For me a Sunday does not mean a day of rest. It means a day to get up early and go for a run-usually a long run. Just because I was in Saint Petersburg I didn't see a reason to make an exception to this recent trend. Due to the runs I'd done during the week it meant I could keep this one shorter-just eight miles, which would equate to around an hour. It's like a quick reconnaissance of what there is to see. From this point onwards I started to find early morning runs on trips useful for this very reason; sometimes it'd even mean being able to get photographs of places before tourists started showing up.

After my run, our guide took us to the Palace Square for the State Hermitage Museum. The first of the buildings is the Winter Palace, but the museum expands into other buildings along the Palace Embankment-the Menshikov Palace, Museum of Porcelain, a storage facility at Staraya Derevnya, and the eastern wing of the General Staff Building.

This palace was once home for the Russian Tsars; but in 1917 the Russian Provisional Government took it over during their revolution. Unhappy with this coalition government, another revolution led by Vladimir Lenin and the Bolsheviks took control. It was the start of the Soviet Union, and signalled the beginning of the end of the Great War.

Our guide moved swiftly through the museum, and

we had to slow her down so we could take photographs along the way. Her intention was to get to the art gallery quickly as this is what her interest was in. The latter part of this tour is one I found boring, but at least there were a few pieces from the great masters Leonardo da Vinci, Raffaello Santi, and Rembrandt. They were artists I would at least pay attention to.

The media has often projected an image of Russia that is cold, utilitarian, and sometimes dark; but I could see the Hermitage was far from this-it was a reminder of what Imperialist Russia was like before the iron curtain of Communism swept across the country.

We had a rough idea what to do with the afternoon-we knew we weren't far from the Peter and Paul Fortress and thought that might be worth seeing. We went the long way around to it so we could stop by the cabin of Peter the Great along the way.

The cabin is said to have been constructed by Peter the Great in May 1703 - the date when Saint Petersburg was founded. Despite being over three hundred years in age, the cabin is preserved very well due largely to a brick construction having been built to protect it. You can't go inside the cabin itself but there are windows open so you can see into each room.

Whilst Peter lived in the cabin, work had begun on the fortress. Although it had originally been built as a citadel, the fortress later got converted into a prison by the Tsars.

Inside the fortress we found there was a museum of Cosmonautics and Rocket Technology, but the exhibits were minimal. Most of the other exhibits are included in the 'full' ticket we purchased. When we finished looking around the rest of the fortress, we left across the wooden Ioannovsky Bridge. It'd been there in some form since the construction of the fortress. It did look old.

Our wandering took us around more of the city, and eventually to the front of the Mariinsky Palace next to the hotel. The setting sun gave everything a golden glow and I was finding that Russia so far was feeling very European. Our first full day had been a good one.

In the morning we explored a little by ourselves, following the Neva river to the Admiralty building. Outside there is a large fountain which I think would have been good for photographing as a long exposure, but I didn't have my tripod for this trip. Sadly hindsight is often better than foresight.

As we'd got time to spare we decided to look around the cathedral. The interior is sculpted from marble with numerous paintings from Russian masters. Looking up from the middle of the room you can see into the cast iron structure of the dome.

When you're ready to see the colonnade you exit the cathedral at the rear, walk back around to the front of the cathedral and then enter through a different door onto a winding staircase leading up to a narrow passage.

This passage leads out into the open air onto the roof of the cathedral. From there you can walk single file up a metal ramp across the roof onto the colonnade to get a 360° view of the city. When I was there around midday it was very crowded as they don't seem to control numbers.

On our way along Nevsky Prospekt to find somewhere to eat, we spotted the unusual design of the Singer Company building. It was designed by Pavel Syuzor as the first metal framed building in Saint Petersburg. The initial idea was that it should resemble their building in New York City, though due to the height restrictions here they had to adjust it. Today it's a book shop named 'Dom Knigi', so had a quick look around.

For the afternoon, the guide met back up with us and took us to the Tsar's village. After the revolution, the Soviet Union renamed it as the Children's Village during their effort to eradicate any remnant of the Tsars; but the locals know it as Pushkin.

The summer palace in Pushkin was occupied by the Germans during the second world war. When they left, it was a burnt out shell of its former self. Since then they've used the extensive documentation of Soviet archivists to rebuild it.

Our guide decided that the best place to start the tour was in the gardens whilst the sun was shining. The first part of these are French in design - a style where they are arranged in geometric shapes with a feature in each section such as a pavilion or a statue. These are all about imposing order upon nature.

French language and culture was common amongst the aristocracy in Tsarist Russia to the point that by the time of the French invasion, some of the aristocrats knew very little Russian. This was one of the lasting influences from Catherine the Great and her royal court, and is something that is touched upon in 'War and Peace' when we learn some are taking Russian lessons.

Inside the palace we found ourselves trapped amongst an obnoxious tour group. Maybe that sounds unfair; but as we went up the stairs into the museum they'd be constantly pushing passed, bumping into other tourists, and whenever possible jumping the queue. They had a 'me first' mentality. Whenever we tried to take a photograph they'd walk straight in front of our camera to take their own photographs with a tablet device. There was no consideration for others from them. I think this sort of attitude can spoil travel and tourism for others - everyone is there to enjoy the sights; but fortunately it's one of those things I've not seen happen often.

The guide had asked us to be ready and waiting promptly at 09:30 the following morning as we'd be short on time; but the driver was late. With only eight hundred metres to where we needed to board the hydrofoil it was a surprise we didn't just walk there.

Unlike other boats I've been on, we had to stay seated for the forty-five minute ride to Peterhof. Upon arrival we needed to queue to get tickets for the palace. It didn't take long for a British tourist to accuse our guide of pushing in front. Sure, she had, though they'd done it to her first - and they were in the queue for guides, not the queue for individuals like they were supposed to be.

Whilst we walked along the canal to the palace we could still hear him cursing loudly. That was until exactly 11:00 when music started blasting out from the palace with dozens of accompanying jets of water from the various fountains.

It was impressive, but our guide didn't let us stop. She insisted we had to get to the palace to join the next queue. Again, this was another palace that was no more than about fifty years old after Germans had destroyed the original.

Many of the rooms are very similar to those in the Catherine Palace, with the exception of the Chinese rooms. These rooms have black lacquered panels that are highly decorative. To control the humidity in the room they limit your time - you can't stop moving.

Our eventual return to Saint Petersburg was by car, so it meant we could be dropped off at the Artillery museum. What we hadn't realised though was that they were closed on Mondays and Tuesdays. I guess our guide didn't know that either, though to be fair she couldn't be expected to know everything. We should have done our own research.

With one failed attempt at sightseeing, we moved on to the Kazan cathedral. There was however a service, so again we moved on; this time to the Church of the Saviour on Spilled Blood - the one that has the colourful spires.

Almost every inch of the walls are covered in colourful mosaic with lots of blues and golds. The architecture and the design was unlike any church I'd been in before. This one gets its name from it being the location where Emperor Alexander II was fatally wounded by an anarchist's bomb.

When the Soviet government came into power the church interior was damaged, and was not reopened as a museum until 1997 after years of restoration work. I think it's awful that governments can damage or destroy parts of their history on a whim; but it's the same story we'd seen in communist China.

We continued along Nevsky Prospekt and soon found the Fabergé museum. The decorative eggs there were created by the House of Fabergé - a jewellery company based in Saint Petersburg who had been tasked with creating an Imperial Easter Egg for Tsar Alexander III to give to his wife. The company was eventually nationalised by the Bolsheviks, and the loyalist Fabergé family fled the country.

For our evening meal, we found something peculiar that was repeated time and again whilst in the country. In other countries, I've found that usually everyone at a table would be served their food at the same time; but here food is served as it becomes ready. This meant I was frequently finishing my food just as James was receiving his.

Our guide eventually collected us from the hotel lobby, after James was told off by the hotel staff for falling asleep in a chair, and took us to the train station. At 23:00 we boarded the sleeper train for our journey to Moscow.

The train carriage reminded me of ones in old James Bond movies, and in Harry Potter. Instead of open plan like most trains back home, this one was made-up entirely of compartments with seats facing each other and a table in between. I could have imagined we were on our way to Hogwarts School for Witchcraft and Wizardry.

We were short on space with our suitcases, but managed to make enough room to fold the seats down to reveal beds. With a bit of luck, we'd get some sleep before arriving in Moscow as sleeping on trains is something we'd need to get used to in the near future.

I was still tired when breakfast was served in the morning. Throughout the night the train had bumped along the train tracks, and jolted me awake whenever I was fortunate enough to have fallen asleep.

Vlad, our Moscow guide, met us in the rain at the train station and took us to Revolution Square where the most prominent feature is the statue of Karl Marx. Already this felt very different to Saint Petersburg.

In Red Square, Vlad told us about the 'GUM' - a centre of trade since 1812, and nationalised by the Soviet Union. We passed the Church of the Intercession of the Most Holy Theotokos on the Moat, or as most locals know it: the Church of Vasily the Blessed.

Ivan the Terrible, the Russian Tsar who conquered many neighbouring territories, began construction of this church in 1555 to commemorate victory over Kazan. The site of this church was on the grave of Saint Vasily, a historic figure who would shoplift to give to the poor-a sort of real-life Russian Robin Hood.

Vlad then led us to the nearby metro station. It was cleaner, and felt grander than any I've seen in London. Though a lot of the stations we visited were filled with Communist imagery.

Our tour took us around the city seeing sights such as the Moscow State University, though time was short as Vlad had us on a schedule for visiting the Moscow Kremlin at a specific time.

Kremlin is the Russian term to describe a citadel, so when people refer to 'The Kremlin' it could technically mean one of many, but the one in Moscow is the most famous and important of them - the one that everyone usually means.

This Kremlin is located at the side of the Moskva River and has been inhabited since the 2nd century BC. Sometime after this it became a fortress but was then destroyed by the Mongols in 1237. In 1339 the fortress was strengthened with oak walls; but only thirty years later these walls were replaced yet again with the white limestone that was used in many buildings around Moscow.

The Kremlin was abandoned during the reign of Peter the Great, and was damaged during the occupation of Napoleon's forces during the Peninsular war. During the Soviet-era the capital moved back to Moscow, and the Kremlin once again became the seat of power as symbols of the Tsars were destroyed.

With every few steps we took, Vlad would stop to talk in great length about the history of the Kremlin. Even if he'd already told us, he'd tell us again. Some of the things he told us, such as the history of the Tsar bell were not entirely correct either according to the historical record.

Our feet were tiring from days of walking, and our ears were growing weary. It was starting to feel like Vlad was a vampire - sucking the life and any interest out of us with every word he spoke.

In the armoury we came across the opportunity to look at the Russian Diamond Fund - a collection started by Peter the Great. It was an extra 500 rubles to look around, but it would be some respite. Eventually though we had to rejoin Vlad for the remainder of the tour. He led us to every exhibition, describing every item on show. It was an impressive amount of knowledge, yet also a relief when members of staff asked him to hurry up so they could close. It's nice to have a knowledgeable guide with lots of enthusiasm; but there are limits.

This brought the tour of the Kremlin to a close, so we now needed to collect our camera backpacks from the security desk. This was not so easy.

A concert was about to take place in the Moscow Kremlin, so they'd closed off one entrance, and were directing people around to another. When we got there, Vlad and James walked straight through; but a guard raised his hand to stop me from following.

I was confused: whatever it was he'd said in Russian, his intention seemed clear - I wasn't getting passed. I tried to explain I needed to get my bag; but still he wouldn't let me through.

"James!" I shouted to get their attention - I'd got the token required to collect our bags, so they at least needed to get it from me.

This caused some other nearby armed guards to approach and stand behind me. I was now surrounded by them. It felt like things were not going to go well.

James came over to see what was happening; but they now made him leave as well. It was getting more, and more frustrating by the second. It's difficult to know what will happen when you don't understand the language; I had a feeling we wouldn't be seeing our bags again.

"VLAD!" I shouted at the top of my voice - finally able to get his attention. I explained to him the issue, he nodded, and took the token from me. When Vlad returned, he had our backpacks. Such a relief!

Once the drama was over, Vlad asked us if we wanted to walk over to Red Square or go to find some food - we opted for food as we weren't sure what we'd be able to get at the airport. Instead our guide decided he'd take us for a walk, and then asked us again what we wanted to do - again we repeated that we'd like to go for food. We appreciated his eagerness to tour; but we needed to eat before heading to Irkutsk.

He ignored us again, and took us back to where we'd started the tour where he called for the driver. Instead of going for food, he took us to the airport. Although it was many hours until we needed to be there it was lucky we'd left early. An accident had resulted in delays that meant we only just made it in time for the check-in to open.

Since we'd got business class tickets we started to head over to the virtually empty queue; but Vlad insisted we joined the long economy queue instead.

Business class is a nice experience, and was worth what little extra it cost for the slightly bigger seats. When breakfast was served it was done so with real cutlery and ceramic pots; not the normal plastic ones I'm used to on flights. The breakfast was of higher quality, but it wasn't anything I was keen on so I ate the bread roll and left the rest.

We arrived in the Siberian capital of Irkutsk having barely slept or eaten over the last twenty-four hours. I was beyond tired, and now starting to feel strangely awake again. It's strange how that happens; but not the first time I've encountered it.

Our next guide met up with us in the airport, and she gave us thirty-five minutes until we'd be starting a tour of the city. It's a settlement that is young in terms of Russian cities, though it has also played an important part in the history of Russia.

After the failed Decembrist revolution of 1825, those involved were exiled and eventually allowed to settle in Irkutsk. When they arrived they brought new culture into town.

The October Revolution, which saw a civil war between the 'white' and 'red' armies brought further changes to the city. The anti-Bolshevik Soviets gave hydroelectricity to the city though this itself caused issues for others. It's strange how two revolutions almost a century apart are described by a month.

In more recent times the Irkut Corporation was the main employer in this town with their product being aircraft parts. Originally this was for the Soviet Air Force; but in more recent years this switched to commercial aircraft parts for companies such as Airbus.

Our tour led us to a monument to those lost in war. School children of about fifteen years in age were practising marching and standing guard. Our guide was surprised they didn't have rifles; but then said that their marching isn't about showing power to the west, but remembering and honouring their ancestors.

I think it's an interesting viewpoint, as from our side it often looks like a show of power. Maybe there are political motives behind it; but to the people that live there, they believe that to not be the case. I guess in some ways it's their equivalent of having scouting and guiding.

Our tour continued at a place connected to the Decembrist revolt-Trubetskoy Manor, the home of one of the Decembrist exiles. It has long been a museum, and recreates the interiors of the times. The items within are all ones which belonged to the different exiled families.

Out of all those that were exiled, only nine of them had their wives join them as in doing so it meant they would lose their wealth, title, and status in society. I'm not sure if it says more about the people, or about the society in which they lived in if they cared more about those things than their families. They were different times though.

Once the tour was over we went for food, and opted to try Russian cuisine - beef stroganoff. It seemed we were now on a 'not eating much' part of the tour - we'd missed lunch and this was our only meal of the day. It meant that most days we were opting to try a different dessert too - just for the extra sustenance.

We'd got a day at Lake Baikal; but stopped at the Taltsy Museum of Wooden Architecture and Ethnography on the way there. They had over forty different buildings from both Russian and Buryat history demonstrating different parts of Siberian life.

Sixty-seven hectares of land in the pouring rain, which only seemed to get heavier as the morning went on.

I have to admit it was worth the visit - the architecture there was impressive, as well as the workmanship in piecing the wooden parts together.

Whilst waiting for access to one of the buildings we sat in the warmth of their cafe where I bought the three of us a warm drink for around twenty-five roubles. We sat and talked with the guide about life in Irkutsk until she decided it would be a good idea to return to the wooden house.

We were told about how each living room in a house would have a corner that would have a religious 'icon' which they would pray to before each meal; but only the matriarch of the family would be allowed to touch it so it could be cleaned. For this reason, this would be where they'd stash their salt supply - a valuable commodity in often remote communities.

Our next stop was the small town of Listvyanka. It was supposed to be a photography stop but the winds were driving rain across the lake so strongly that we couldn't really turn to face the waves it was creating for long. Instead of lingering on the pebble beach that looked like it could be busy in their peak season, we headed over to their market square where they sell the locally caught fish called 'Omul'.

Our guide asked us what we'd like to eat so we both said we wanted one of the kebabs. Whilst these were being prepared we went upstairs to a seating area that looked out over the corrugated metal roofs of the stalls.

When the food arrived it became apparent that the guide had misunderstood, and had only ordered one. I let James have that; but I felt it was too late to order another due to the time it would take for them to cook it. If we'd had to wait then we'd have missed out on visiting the Baikal museum.

The next stop was the church of Saint Nicholas which has a lot of original religious icons. The number is because some were saved from the churches in Irkutsk, and brought to this one during the Soviet times. This one in Listvyanka had managed to remain a functional church throughout.

The rain had finally eased off a little whilst in this church. Our guide actually spent quite a bit of time in there talking to a lady - in hindsight this would have meant there would have been time for me to order food after all. As Douglas Adams would have said, "You live, and learn. At any rate, you live."

The Lake Baikal museum is mostly uninteresting except for the Pisces XI - an oceanology submersible sitting outside, and the small aquarium they have indoors. They have a few fish, but the main attraction were two female Baikal seals. They were nice to see, but it's always a shame to see animals in captivity - especially in such small enclosures.

When we got back to Irkutsk, we needed to get some shopping done as it was possible the Trans-Siberian Express we'd be taking next might not have a restaurant carriage. The only guaranteed thing was a hot water urn - so powdered soup was one option.

Back at the hotel we got ready for the morning, and found something concerning - it said our train would be at 03:15 in the morning; but our paperwork had said 07:53! James quickly called the tour company in England who had booked the tickets for us. If there was a mistake, and these times were correct then it could mean we'd need the guide to pick us up a lot earlier than they thought.

We were promised a phone call back once they'd figured out what was going on. Whilst we waited we went down to the hotel restaurant for some food. I was more than ready for a proper meal, and even went as far as to finally try their Russian honey cake for dessert.

With still no sign of the promised phone call we asked at reception about the tickets in case we had misunderstood them. They explained that in Russia they will issue tickets based upon Moscow time. At least this finally made some sense.

It was now 21:00, but I was finally able to go out for a five kilometre run. I started to walk down a side street next to the hotel whilst waiting for my running watch to get a signal. I was then approached by someone, talking to me in Russian, and showing me some sort of ID.

"Sorry, could you repeat that in English," I asked him. He replied with something brief in Russian and walked off. A little confused by this, I carried on walking as my watch was taking it's time to locate a signal.

Even when I got back to the hotel afterwards, the tour company had not returned our call. It's true that we now knew the answer; but they didn't know that. As far as they knew, they were ignoring panicked tourists on the other side of the world.

28: Mongolia

In Berlin the trains had been for the most part clean and punctual. In Naples the experience had been quite the opposite. For this journey I had in the back of my mind an image of a steam train, and old fashioned carriages.

The reality was that it had no doubt seen better days. The railway between Moscow and Vladivostok was completed in 1916, though the Trans-Mongolian branch wasn't completed until 1955. I couldn't help thinking that the train and it's carriages probably dated back to the original opening of this branch.

The carriage had a narrow corridor that was just wide enough for a suitcase to be dragged down. I noticed the exposed pipes of the hot water urn at the end of the carriage - that'd be our way to have warm drinks and soup during the journey.

As I walked along the corridor I looked at the doors to each compartment until I spotted the one with our ticket number on. I opened the door and found that it was going to be a little cramped for the next twenty-four hours.

The tour company had told us they'd booked a four

berth compartment to give us more space, but it turned out to be only two berth-apparently this happens sometimes depending on the train.

Underneath the window was a small table we could use; it was about the size of a laptop. On one side of the table were bunk-beds, and on the other was a chair. There was however a single power socket in the cabin so we'd be able to take it in turns to charge devices.

By the time we'd figured out a way of storing the suitcases so that we'd have some standing room, the train had left Irkutsk and was now passing Lake Baikal. I stood out in the corridor with some of the passengers, watching as the world passed us by.

The attendant for this carriage had opened a number of windows which meant it was possible to take photographs of the lake without reflections. They didn't mind people hanging out the windows, but it was something you did at your own peril. The fact that it was into the path of potential oncoming trains was the main risk.

I accepted this risk a few times when the train was on a bend-at these points it was easy to see it was safe, and it gave a good view of the curvature of the train with Lake Baikal on the left. This was the more scenic part of the journey.

As time marched on we could see the snow-capped mountains getting closer until we left Lake Baikal behind and started to travel across fields. The landscape could now have been any country, and there wasn't really anything to photograph at the speed we were moving at.

I returned to the compartment and started on some

of the food we'd brought with us for a late lunch. It was a simple meal but it was better than nothing. I think it adds a little to the adventure of the trip to have cobbled together meals. The best bit though was a chocolate bar I'd bought just in case I needed it.

In the hours that followed I split my time between reading and sorting through the photographs I'd taken in Russia. There were a few stops along the way, though I wasn't really sure where we were.

I'd imagined the journey would be filled with sights to see, and would be full of adventure. It was in reality just time spent waiting, and getting to know some of the other passengers.

When the evening arrived I used the hot water urn to make some soup in the travel mug I'd packed.

Around 20:00 IRKT we reached the border crossing between Russia and Mongolia. Most border crossings I've done before this have been ones either between countries in Europe, or have been at a port of some sort. This was a completely different experience.

When we came to a stop we were boarded first by Russian customs officials who searched the compartments and the luggage as they passed through the train carriage. This included opening our suitcases so they could see inside.

Once they'd passed through, a second group boarded with a sniffer dog whilst a third group was going from compartment to compartment to check passports and collect the Russian immigration cards we'd completed when we arrived in Saint Petersburg.

With this complete they left the train so that after

this hour had passed we could continue on our journey. Two hours later they gave us cards to fill in for the Mongolian customs. Once they'd passed these out we'd got thirty minutes until we stopped for the Mongolian border control.

As we'd changed time zones during the crossing it was now 23:30 ULAT. Not the best of times to be reaching a border: people would be getting tired, and possibly short-tempered. The officials asked us to keep the window blinds closed until after the crossing was complete.

Again the train was boarded, this time by Mongolian officials who started off by handing out immigration forms. We weren't really given enough time to fill these in before they collected them and disappeared with our passports.

Whilst the border crossing was taking place there were sharp shunts that shook the entire carriage followed by what felt like moving backwards and forwards periodically. I suspected a different train engine was taking over.

The Mongolian customs passed through the train once more, whilst another team were walking up and down the corridor shouting out names to give passports back. If they'd grouped the passports by cabin, and kept them grouped, it'd have been far quicker.

At around 01:15 we began to move again after over four hours from reaching the Russian border. It was a long and tiring process, though now we were in Mongolia and on our way to Ulaanbaatar.

A conductor walked along the corridor waking everyone up at 06:45, even though some passengers would be continuing all the way to China. I'm sure they appreciated that after the long night.

The Mongolian steppe could be seen from the window as we got closer to our destination. We arrived later than scheduled, but our guide was there waiting for us. The drive to the Hustain Nuruu Steppe Reserve would take around ninety minutes.

Mongolia's population is around 3.1 million with just over half of this living in the city of Ulaanbaatar. The majority of the rest are nomadic, as is traditional for their people. As there are not enough buildings yet to support the population there is a shanty town of sorts made from gers in a ring around the city. A ger is the Mongolian name for a yurt: a round tent that is covered in various materials.

The small population has also caused issues with them trying to build their own industry as well - they struggle to find a workforce. Prior to the Soviet Union they were still mostly nomadic, and the buildings they have now were mostly built during the Soviet-era.

Under the Soviet Union, raw materials from the country were all sent to Russia. The Mongolians would then buy the end products back building a reliance on them. Since the 1990s they've struggled to produce any sort of export which has caused their economy to struggle. It seemed like they were thrust into the ways of the western world; but left without any way to help themselves.

At the reserve we were shown to our ger: the only

one with its own bathroom structure. There was some power there, provided by solar energy, but it wasn't quite working as it should so we had to wait for an electrician to finish.

Eventually we had the opportunity to wander around outside of camp until lunch. We headed up into the hills which at altitude was a little more work than normal. We didn't spot any wildlife, just endless hills with nothing for as far as the eye could see.

When we went back out after lunch it was with a local guide who didn't speak much English - she was going to help us find some wild horses. The Takhi horse, also known as the Przewalksi, had died out in the wild in the 1960s; but due to them being taken in large numbers to zoos at the turn of the twentieth century it meant it was possible to start a program in the 1990s to reintroduce them into this national park.

We were miles into the wilderness; but it seemed like we weren't going to find any of these horses. Our only chance to ever see them was passing by. Just before we were ready to turn back we spotted a small herd.

Having left the vehicle behind us, we started walking up to the top of the hill, getting as close to the horses as we could risk. We got within two hundred metres of them before they ran away. All except one, who stood watching us, before chasing after the rest of the herd. It was like watching the Gallimimus run together in Jurassic Park.

That evening we ate at the camp - a starter made from seaweed, and a main course of stewed beef, mashed potato, carrot, and Grechka.

When morning came we were on our way back to Ulaanbaatar to visit the winter palace of Bogd Khan:the last ruler of Mongolia before the formation of the Mongolian People's Republic.

Pollution was hanging over the city like a shroud. Smoke from the coal power stations to the north of the city would blow south across the city and then get trapped in by the mountains.

These power stations were constructed during the time of the Soviet Union, and it is likely they hadn't considered such things at that time. It's now becoming such a big problem that the pollution is five times worse than Beijing, and eighty times the recommended level defined by the World Health Organisation. Perhaps we should have researched more and packed face masks like we had for China. Not that we'd actually used them there.

In order to use my camera at the palace I had to pay an additional US$26. It's a lot; but I wanted to have photographs to look back on. The inside of the palace comprises of a number of buildings;most of them being Buddhist temples. We went around most of them, and was told about the purpose of the buildings, the history, and about the artefacts that were on display inside.

Not all of these buildings in the palace are of the same Chinese style. After Mongolia declared independence from China they eventually joined the Soviet Union and around this time buildings were created in a western style like you'd see in Moscow and other Russian cities.

This wasn't the only influence they'd had. In Russia

the Communist party had destroyed or damaged anything that linked to the Tsars, and in China they had destroyed any links to the Empire. Here in Mongolia we were learning they'd been the victim of mass cultural destruction as well.

On the southern side of the city we visited the Zaisan Memorial - a reminder of Mongolia's tank contribution to the Soviet military. It seemed like this memorial was in honour of their partnership; but it was created by Russia to remind the people of the 'debt' they allegedly owe.

It just happens to be a good viewpoint too - we could see just how much construction was going on. Winters in Mongolia are harsh, and during these months all construction work ceases until the snow melts. What this means is that during the few warm months they have each year they will rush to complete as much work as possible.

After we'd checked into a hotel, we were taken through heavy traffic to see a Mongolian cultural show performed by Tumen Ekh. This show is a strong reminder that the country had been under the rule of China for a long time before its independence in the early 1900s. Despite the similarities, there were differences too that set them apart from their close neighbours.

One of the traditional dresses worn by a performer was very similar to one we'd seen in the palace earlier; but it also bore an amazing resemblance to a costume worn by Queen Amidala in one of the Star Wars films. I think it's good to see where filmmakers and other artists get their inspiration from.

That evening we tried another local dish: a Mongolian barbecue. With this we had to take a bowl and fill it with the meat, vegetables, and noodles that we wanted. Their chefs would then pour the sauce we wanted with it onto a flat pan heated by a fire pit. They would use sharp swords, which they'd toss into the air and catch, to then slice up the vegetables as they cooked. It was certainly a dining experience, and tasted so much nicer than the Mongolian barbecue I'd tried in the UK.

After the sun rose on our last day in Mongolia I was out running five kilometres. I'd intended further, but the frequent stops for traffic were preventing me from finding a rhythm. Perhaps for the best in that pollution.

Sometime after this the guide collected us to take us to the nearby Tibetan-style Buddhist Gandantegchinlen monastery. A lot of this monastery was destroyed by the Communist Party but some of it survived as a museum.

Inside this monastery there had been a copper statue of Avalokiteśvara-the tallest indoor statue in the world since 1913. The Soviet army melted this down in 1937 to cast bullets with; but a new one was produced in 1996-six years after the Mongolian democratic revolution.

Our next stop on this tour was in the city centre at Chinggis Square. It is named after the first great Khan of the Mongol Empire: Genghis Khan. This large open square was one of the busiest places we'd seen in the city as a number of schools were using it for graduation photos. They were also setting the square up for Mother and Children Day which is one of their national holidays.

When we reached the square we were told to get out of the car whilst the traffic was stationary. Being quick off the mark, I'd got the door open and was half out of the door just as they changed their mind and started to pull away again. I dropped to my feet, fortunately uninjured, and stood to one side watching them carry on until I saw them stop again.

The guide apologised and seemed to be horrified by what had happened. There wasn't much to see in this square other than a statue; but there were also a few shops about too should we want to do some souvenir shopping.

The lunch stop today was 'The Castle': a castle-shaped restaurant hidden away inside an amusement park, and surrounded by a moat. The castle was empty except for one table indoors that was set for us and the guide. The staff there were really good though as even though we were awkward in suggesting a table outside, they didn't hesitate to move us.

We learnt a lot more about Mongolia during this meal, such as the British and American TV shows that they'd often watch. The time after this however was a waste as we'd got an afternoon free with nothing to see or do until the train back to Siberia was scheduled. There weren't even any suggestions from the guide before she left.

The train back was a little nicer than the last one, and there was a tiny bit more room due to it being 4-berth for the two of us. This one didn't have any power sockets though so we realised power for devices for the next day on the train would be limited.

We arrived at the border station of Sükhbaatar later than we'd anticipated, and was awoken by a Russian conductor shouting, "Border crossing toilet outside". This really didn't make much sense to us at the time. We were tired. When she insisted we left the train, we did as we were asked.

From the platform I could see the other carriages had gone, and there was no train. We wouldn't be going anywhere anytime soon. We walked up and down the platform a couple of times before we found someone who explained what the conductor had meant. We'd got until 09:00 to use the facilities here at a cost of 10 roubles each before the border officials would be boarding the train. Once boarded they'd be on the train for two hours.

The process of crossing the border was then very similar to before, with the exception of the Russian side taking photographs on entry. By the time we were ready to move it was 15:00. Most of the day had gone.

Once the train started moving they tried to sell everyone souvenirs, and when nobody would buy anything one of the conductors locked the door to the washroom. Passengers still refused to buy anything and started to complain, so the other conductor put an end to it and unlocked them. It wasn't the only annoyance on this trip though: someone was smoking on this non-smoking carriage.

It was another sleepless night on the train: I was awake at 04:00 to see the sunrise over Lake Baikal. Our breakfast had been so early that by the time we arrived back in Irkutsk we were looking for a second one after what had felt like an arduous journey. This train journey didn't quite feel like the big adventure we'd hoped; but was worth it to see Mongolia.

Most places in Irkutsk didn't seem to open until 10:00 or later which isn't ideal for breakfast. We eventually found one small coffee shop where their 'small' cups of Earl Grey tea were served in cups that seemed to be the size as my head. I can only imagine their large cups being the size of buckets.

For the rest of the day we followed the 'green line' to visit the thirty sights it passes. The route marked out on the pavements is supposed to only be five kilometres, so in theory shouldn't take too long to do. Theories are good, but in practice the line was difficult to follow where it was well worn - we'd actually walked over fourteen kilometres in four hours to see everything.

I'd long since learnt that domestic flights all over the world will open two hours before their scheduled time. So when the tour operator insisted on us arriving three hours before, it meant an hour waiting at the airport before we could check in.

Airport security seemed to think my shower gel and toothbrush could be an explosive device, but after emptying half of my suitcase onto the airport floor they were convinced it was safe. Knowing my shower gel isn't going to explode is always good to know.

The check-in lady for business class made the assumption we'd got the wrong queue, and pointed at the sign. It seemed that us turning up in shorts was enough for a little prejudice.

This airport has so few flights every day that the planes will actually taxi down the runway and turnaround before take-off instead of approaching from the correct side. This is something you'd never see at Heathrow.

We arrived in Moscow in the early afternoon, but got delayed on the way to the hotel by long traffic queues trying to get passed the Kremlin. Apparently there was a VIP arrival which had closed the road.

It was worth the wait though: the Metropol hotel, located next to Red Square, was one of the most impressive hotels I've ever stayed in. It's had famous guests such as Steven Seagal, Sylvester Stallone, and Michael Jackson.

After all these years, we still didn't feel that navigation was a strong point for either of us - so we decided to use an offline map to find our way through the torrential rain to the Memorial Museum of Cosmonautics. We weren't that far from a metro station so we ran to get out of the rain quickly.

Just as I reached the metro station my foot slid across the wet surface of the steps, and my ankle twisted with a loud click. I dropped to the floor. *Is it broken?!*

James helped me up, and I limped across the platform to sit down waiting for the next train. Perhaps it'd be okay; but it felt bad, and I couldn't put any weight on it. I thought about it some more, and I wasn't prepared to let it prevent us from reaching the museum, so I limped onto the train when it arrived. The metro ticket cost fifty roubles per trip; so not only were trains here quicker and more frequent than back home, they were also a lot cheaper.

By the time we arrived at the museum I was hobbling a little better; but it was hard work and painful. Even with these difficulties we got halfway around the museum in what seemed like no time at all, and then paused to have some lunch in the cafe there. Just being able to get the weight off my feet was a relief. I didn't dare to take off my shoe to look at it in case I couldn't get it back on afterwards.

The cafe was styled to look like an American Diner with stools at a bar, and booths. They served burgers and fries; but it couldn't really be counted as fast-food when it took thirty minutes to prepare.

The exhibits to see in the museum were a mixture of genuine pieces, and mock-ups. For me, it was definitely worth seeing; despite the price. It was considerably better than the exhibits in the Peter and Paul Fortress in Saint Petersburg. In the first room it reminded me a little of the entrance to the Johnson Space Center: it has a large focal point to the room and is then surrounded by smaller exhibits, which in this case includes a Vostok descent capsule.

When we left there we returned to Red Square. This time there was a market of some sort, and the government had set-up a security checkpoint to search bags on entry.

I limped to Saint Basil's cathedral, though after having seen so many Russian Orthodox churches this didn't feel all that special. I think maybe sometimes the order you see things in is important. It's something I'd have to consider when planning other trips.

The exterior is impressive - it's an iconic part of Moscow's Red Square. Inside there is a maze of rooms on multiple floors, with many different areas for prayer. I found it difficult to keep track of where we'd been in order to ensure we'd seen everything we could.

After a disappointing meal where James' was served cold, we returned to the hotel so I could finally remove my shoes. My ankle was a purple, bruised mess that had swollen to an absurd size. It was the sort of size that if I told anyone about it later without showing them a picture they were unlikely to have believed me. Having hobbled on it for all this time I no longer thought it was broken, so took some anti-inflammatories in hope that with some care it'd improve before the morning. One thing was for sure: my plans for running in Moscow were unlikely to happen now.

Breakfast at the Metropol was impressive. The waitress greeted us, and when we replied in English she switched to a perfect British accent. The room was large with intricately detailed decorations, and a lady playing a harp on stage. Each note was being amplified by the cavernous glass ceiling.

Vlad was to be our guide again today, and his plan had been to take us to the Novodevichy Convent. It was however very good of him to agree to take us to Lenin's Mausoleum first.

We first passed through security to enter Red Square, and then again to join the queue for the mausoleum. They request that once you enter the building you remain silent until you leave. Of course they might request this, but it didn't stop a group behind us from talking all the way through.

It was strange to see a dead body in front of us. Sure I've seen skeletal remains before, and even the ancient remains of mummified Egyptians, but this was different. Lenin had been preserved so incredibly well as part of their embalming process that his skin texture now made him resemble a wax figure. It looked like he could have died yesterday, not ninety years ago.

Outside the mausoleum there are plaques for notable communists whose cremated remains have been placed inside the Kremlin Wall Necropolis. One such person is the Russian cosmonaut Yuri Gagarin - the first human in space.

From the mausoleum we were driven to the Novodevichy Convent, and spent an hour walking around the grounds. Most of the buildings there were ordered by Sofia Alexeyevna, but begun construction under the reign of Prince Vasili III, the Grand Prince of Moscow. The buildings are in the Muscovite Baroque style which is common to many buildings in the area.

You'd think after spending an hour there it wouldn't be a problem to carry on walking to look around the adjacent necropolis; but instead we were driven around the corner to see the tombs of Boris Yeltsin, and Anton Chekov.

We then reached the grave of Mikhail Gorbachev's wife.

"Gorbachev should not be buried in Russia - he is a traitor," Vlad exclaimed. We were both shocked by this, but said nothing. It was suddenly clear that Vlad was a strong supporter of Communism.

Gorbachev had been the last leader of the Soviet

Union, and was responsible for perestroika which restructured their political system by allowing for other candidates. In just four years the changes caused the Communist party to lose control and brought about the dissolution of the Soviet Union, and the formation of the Russian Federation.

Just as the Soviet Union had ended, so was our time in Russia. At the hotel Vlad confirmed that the tour company had given him the wrong flight details as we'd predicted, so estimated we'd be collected at 02:30. We'd got one last afternoon to explore by ourselves. Perfect timing for a thunderstorm.

We decided we'd head to the Tsaritsyno museum and park: a thirty minute metro ride out of the city. These grounds were originally owned by Tsaritsa Irina, sister of Tsar Boris Godunov, but later taken over by Catherine the Great. With more time, and fairer weather I think we could have spent quite a bit of time there. Of course it'd have helped if my ankle had been in better condition too. There could have been hours of photographic opportunities.

29: Arizona

In 1997 my Grandma died of liver metastases. She'd seen a lot of places in her life, but one of her most memorable had been her last: Arizona. I promised my sister we'd see Arizona ourselves, and our itinerary would be filled with the places she'd seen. Hopefully it'd be an adventure we'd both remember.

In the time since getting back from Russia, my ankle had mostly healed. I'd still be careful though.

The fun started pretty much from the moment we arrived at Heathrow's check-in desk. We were told we'd been lucky we'd checked in the day before as the flight was overbooked. It's not uncommon for flights to be overbooked, but for a long-haul flight it was surprising. This was then followed by having to give Lindsay an injection of Dalteparin due to her having been seriously ill a year before.

Ten hours of flying later we arrived in Phoenix. James had flown down from Canada to join us, and the first thing we had to do was collect the rental car. Of course they attempted to 'up-sell', though this time we decided a larger car wouldn't be a bad idea - an SUV would be more comfortable for the three of us. It was pretty much a tank.

When we left the hotel in the morning we bought enough water to last the week whilst trying to avoid the heavy downpour the best we could. Buying water in bulk is always the most cost effective way, and it seems like a good idea to always have water to hand in a desert environment.

Tombstone looked like a frontier town with a combination of wooden and stone buildings. It's the sort of place you'd expect to see in a spaghetti western where the locals gather in the saloon whilst their horses are drinking from a trough outside.

Maybe if we'd been strangers riding into town on horseback it'd have been easier to find parking - what they have seemed to be well hidden. The rain had at least stopped before we arrived.

We booked tickets for a reenactment of the showdown at the OK Corral, and wandered around the old-fashioned shops whilst we waited for it to start.

The reenactment of the gunfight at the OK Corral started off with introducing us to some of the backstory. Billy Claiborne, Ike and Billy Clanton, and Tom and Frank McLaury were cowboys. They were the villains of the story who had been antagonising and threatening the Earp family - all of which were lawmen in Tombstone.

Doc Holiday and the Earp brothers confronted these outlaws outside of the CS Fly Photography store, not the OK Corral. When shots were fired, three of the outlaws were killed, and two of the Earp brothers were wounded. One of the surviving outlaws, Ike Clanton, filed murder charges against the lawmen, though these were eventually dropped.

There wasn't much else to see in town that interested us, other than the old newspaper building for the Tombstone Epitaph. I think our time in this town gave us the chance to have some understanding of what the Old West was like, the sorts of dangers they faced, and how they lived.

With troublemakers like these it seemed like you could be shot for any reason, at any time. We think of those times as 'lawless'; but there were lawmen as the Earp family proves. It almost seems like those days were no more dangerous than today. In 2016 alone there were 17 days of mass shootings in the United States with more than one victim killed and others wounded. Just months before we arrived there was an incident in Florida where 49 people were killed, and a further 53 were injured. Just like at the OK Corral there was a shoot-out with lawmen, and the gunman was killed.

Based on the Global Peace Index, the United States ranks below places such as Kenya, and China. In fact, in terms of safety the United States isn't too different to Egypt. Many developing countries which the media coverage encourages us to believe are unsafe, are actually safer than one of the most developed countries in the world.

Our plan for the afternoon was to move on from history and culture, and to see some of nature in Madera Canyon. My Granddad had recommended it to us due to the amount of bird life he'd seen during his own visit. The satnav couldn't locate the canyon so we had to do it the old fashioned way - using a roadmap to navigate for ourselves.

Getting to Sonoita and onto highway 83 was easy enough, but we had to be careful not to take the wrong turn. If we took the wrong left we'd be on a road that wouldn't have any further turnings until crossing the border into Mexico. My Granddad had managed that when he visited the canyon.

It seemed our map reading skills weren't too bad. After passing the road for Mexico we found a left turn like we'd been looking for. However, the road quickly deteriorated into an unmaintained gravel path that slowed progress.

We had no idea how far along this path we needed to continue, we were just guessing based upon how the map looked. The winding trail opened up into a clearing with a map printed on a board.

Above the map it read 'OHV'. I wasn't sure what it meant, but the map indicated we were still miles from the canyon. We crossed fords to continue the path there, but one of these was blocked by a fallen tree. I climbed out of the car and walked over. Stupidly I tried to move it by myself, but it wouldn't budge. Instead we decided that if me and my sister got out of the car, we could guide James through the gap between trees instead. Slowly but surely we did it.

Soon we reached the end of the road. Literally. A fence was blocking any further progress: it seemed the rest of the trail was intended for off road vehicles. That's when we realised OHV meant 'Off-Highway Vehicles'. Well it was a new lesson, and if anything it was a bit of an adventure.

Further down the main road we found another turning along a mountain pass. It climbed up and up, improving our view across a valley. This was the turn we should have taken.

The visitor centre for the canyon was closed, but they have honesty boxes in the car park for out of hours. To be honest, I wasn't that impressed and felt it too late in the day to see anything. Though whilst I was looking up in the trees, James spotted a tarantula crawling across the floor.

Having never seen a wild one before, you might guess at what I did next. I ran back to the car, grabbed a macro lens, and then laid down on the floor in front of the arachnid. Other tourists started coming over to see what I was doing, and took their own photos - just from much further away than I was.

As there was nothing else to see we decided we may as well drive to Tucson for our overnight stay. The hotel happened to be next-door to a barbecue restaurant - the very thing I'd promised Lindsay she'd get to try. The taste of barbecue was almost as good as I'd remembered.

Before the sun had risen Lindsay had been to the gym. I should have gone out running, but I did not. I felt I needed the sleep more ahead of our drive to Flagstaff.

Our first stops of the day were actually in the opposite direction - the Mission San Xavier del Bac, and the Titan Missile Museum. For the latter of the two we made sure we arrived before the time of the first guided tour.

The Titan Missile Museum is one of many missile silos around the Tucson area that were built in the space of a few months during the Cold War as a nuclear deterrent. This was the United States' reaction to their belief the USSR wanted world domination, just as the USSR thought the same of the USA.

Both sides were building arms they claim they didn't want to use and it led to the creation of a massive stockpile. All that anyone could be certain of was an attack would mean mutually assured destruction. It was mad!

The majority of the stockpile was decommissioned once the USSR cut their military spending around the time of the dissolution of the Soviet Union. I'd already learnt a little of this during our time in Moscow.

Underground there are four blast doors which are made from concrete and steel. They would protect the people inside the base in the event of a nuclear attack. Anything that was critical was also mounted on springs so they wouldn't be damaged by the shock of a blast.

The first room inside the base was the important one: it was where two of the four man staff would wait for a launch order. If they received one then the two officers would verify the order and with the launch codes would prepare the missile for launch.

Just like the Sith in Star Wars, they had a 'rule of two' on the base. Nobody could ever be alone unless they were in the downtime room. The paranoia of the Cold War meant everybody was always watched - anyone could be a double agent.

When two officers turned the keys - this was the point of no return which would mix the fuel that would propel the Titan missile. They just had to release the concrete blocks to let it soar out of the silo. A devastating nuclear war would then have followed.

This installation was filled with history and gave us a glimpse of the other side to what we'd seen in Russia just months before. The robustness of this place, and the size of the missile demonstrated just how serious things had gotten.

For the original rocket, they had to fill it with fuel on demand which meant forty minutes of launch preparation. This later changed to a butterfly valve which allowed them to store fuel in the rocket, and respond within fifty-eight seconds.

This silo reminded me of the one used in Star Trek: First Contact. Though in this film a rocket had been changed from a weapon of mass destruction to an instrument of discovery. If only all could be like that.

Hours passed on the road up to Flagstaff, and the famous Route 66 with few stops on the way. Darkness had fallen by the time we checked in to the motel there. We could only find one restaurant nearby; but our roast dinner there was served cold.

Long before the sun had crept above the horizon, I'd been out running along the streets of Flagstaff. It was colder than I'd expected: shorts and a t-shirt were not ideal for sub-zero temperatures. At 7,000 feet above sea level the extra effort it took meant I could warm up after a couple of miles.

Once again we were back on the road with our first stop being Meteor Crater - a meteorite impact site which is more formerly known as the Barringer crater. Although it's far from unique, this one mile wide crater dates back fifty thousand years meaning it's one of the youngest known impact sites.

In the centre of this barren crater you can see where previously there had been a mineshaft sunk into the crater for mining precious rocks. This was an unsuccessful mine however as Barringer never found the iron ore that Roosevelt had allowed his company to dig for.

This was one of the places my Grandma had visited, and the next was the Petrified Forest and Painted Desert which was just east of where we were. This would be our next stop.

In some ways these parks are similar to Joshua Tree: you drive around by car from one stop to the next in order to see the points of interest. At some of them you can go off hiking if you want to, but we didn't have the time to do them all. What we could see was a landscape filled with different shades of whites, pinks, reds, and even some greens.

Some of the stops in the petrified forest offered views of petroglyphs dating back 650 to 2,000 years ago. One of the stops is named 'Crystal Forest'. It's a place where you can walk amongst pieces of petrified wood, and to get a better understanding of why the place is named as it is.

We'd lost time during the day from having to find somewhere to eat - we should have taken a packed lunch with us, and we also spent longer in the parks than we'd intended. As a result we began our two hundred mile drive around two hours later than intended. I should have investigated food options beforehand.

To start with we continued along Route 66 into New Mexico, and would be heading up into Colorado. It was now dark, and we'd changed time zones as well. After passing Gallup, it was like we'd left civilisation behind us. Without street lights it was like driving through a never-ending abyss.

The area we were now heading through was not far from where almost forty years ago the Church Rock accident happened. We all know about Chernobyl; but a lesser known story is how a disposal pond at a uranium mill breached its dam and contaminated all of the ground water in the surrounding area. Even after all this time the radiation lingers, and few people know about it. We hadn't whilst we were there.

Twenty two miles of roadworks with a varying speed limit between 45 and 25 mph made this journey seem to last forever. James did a great job of maintaining concentration for what felt like an eternity.

With two hours left to go, we made a stop at a gas station to make sure we'd have enough fuel, and to find out where the nearest place to get food would be. We'd not eaten for around seven hours, but the nearest place was in Shiprock: another hour away.

If we couldn't find anything there, then it was likely we wouldn't get to eat until morning. The first place we found was a popular worldwide fast food chain I'm not that keen on - I'd not eaten in one for around seven years.

It was something to eat though, and better than nothing.

Eventually we crossed the border into the state of Colorado, and the town of Cortez.

Our reason for crossing into Colorado was Mesa Verde. It was inhabited by Paleo-Indians around 7,500 BCE, and during the 12th century the famous cliff dwellings were constructed by the Puebloans. A few generations later they were abandoned due to droughts and became a sacred place for the Ute mountain people. It also helps that they appeared in an episode of The X-Files - a hugely contributing factor in me wanting to see them.

Of the available guided tours at Mesa Verde, the only one we could attempt was Balcony House. With a thirty-two foot ladder to climb that James wasn't keen on, it was however the only way we'd get to see the cave dwellings up close.

I spent the morning driving us around the park until it was time for lunch. After this we were able to go on the tour we'd arranged. Our guide for Balcony House was big on talking, and was generally a good guide. He started off by describing the route we'd be taking, did a quick safety briefing, and then after taking our tickets, led the group to start the tour.

Lindsay was looking forward to looking around; but despite my best efforts to help her - she couldn't climb the ladder. She returned to the start to sit and wait for us to finish. I wasn't keen on leaving her alone; but she insisted she'd be okay. After her having made it up the Statue of Liberty it was a shame she couldn't mange this; I really thought she could.

Next up was James - he grabbed hold of the ladder, looked ahead, and made the climb as swiftly as he could. He'd been able to push passed his fear of heights. The guide had said this ladder was the point of no return, so whatever lay ahead of us; we'd have to face those too and couldn't turn back.

Everything we could see was built under the ledge of a cliff. It was an amazing feat of engineering, and the design would have helped keep them safe from the worst of the elements. The buildings themselves were made from carefully carved stone blocks - even some large pits were lined with them.

At the end of the tour we had to crawl on hands and knees through a tight crawl space into a sort of room. From there it was another short ladder climb, and then a walk up the side of the cliff-face to the final ladder which returned us to the roadside. It's amazing what's required sometimes to get photographs, or to make the most of a trip.

Lindsay had been left out in the sun longer than we'd intended as the tour overran by thirty minutes. She was in good spirits though when we rejoined her for the drive to the Four Corners Monument.

We made it there just before closing time - we felt it worthwhile for the chance to be in Arizona, Colorado, New Mexico, and Utah simultaneously.

Whilst most of the parking is in Arizona, there was a sign indicating they had overflow parking in Utah. Utah's pretty big - anywhere in particular?

When we left there, the road was straight for as far as the eye could see: the landscape was barren. We knew this meant it'd be a good idea to get fuel as soon as possible as you never know how far it might be to the next.

Our arrival in Kayenta coincided with the sun finally dipping below the horizon. This small town is so close to the Utah border that unlike the rest of Arizona, they observe daylight savings time.

One thing I learnt on this trip is that early morning runs are not always possible - no matter how much you want to go out. In Kayenta it was too dark, and the roads unlit for running to be safe. In future I'd need to travel with a head-torch.

Breakfast was hard work - we were the first ones there; but the service was slow and the waitress difficult. When she asked what juice we wanted, we asked what they'd got. She didn't know, and wouldn't check, so we had to play a fun guessing game of what they may or may not have. We were however able to order a packed lunch at the same time - a time saver for later. I guess we'd already learnt something on this trip.

Our main job for the day was to see as much of Monument Valley as we could.Although the invading populace took control of most of the land, this small area still belongs to the Navajo. The amazing landscape here was once under the sea; but during the Paleozoic era the ground was forced up above the water. By the Jurassic era, it had hardened into the formations we see today.

The 'Wildcat Trail' was closed indefinitely so most of what was left was a seventeen mile drive around the valley on unpaved road which is not really suitable for anything other than four-wheel drive. Fortunately due to a fluke of circumstances that's what we'd got.

There are eleven official stops around the valley, and other places where it's safe to stop. To see everything we could took around three hours. This place is what I pictured in my mind when thinking of the 'Wild West'.

In the afternoon we drove through the Grand Canyon National Park, and stopped a couple of times along the way for a bit of sightseeing. One stop was without railings - so we could peer over the edge to see the Little Colorado River below.

Whilst I'd been taking photographs, James had disappeared. Lindsay hadn't seen him either, and we started to wonder where he was. What if he'd gotten too close to the edge? This sort of thing does happen; but wouldn't we have heard him if he had fallen? There'd have been screaming, and a commotion surely?

Time passed, and we discovered that despite his fear of heights he'd found his way down onto a lower ledge to get a better view. A relief!

Sunset was edging closer; but even then the car park at the Grand Canyon visitor centre was busy. The centre was closed, so we decided we'd walk along the path to Mather Point. It was nice to get our first proper glimpse into the canyon, but the best views would be yet to come.

Our overnight stay had been in a B&B where the owner cooked us breakfast in the morning. We could have eaten well, but we all decided a light snack would be best. Today we'd got a flight in a helicopter to get through, and I was remembered one of the passengers from the flight over the Nazca lines. Nobody wants to be that person.

We arrived at the Grand Canyon Airport early, and after being transferred to the correct terminal, they took our weights. The waiting time after this was then much longer than anticipated as their computer systems had failed - this meant they couldn't calculate the weight distributions for each flight. They had to ground further flights until it was working.

Forty minutes passed, and eventually things were working again without us needing to offer our services as computer scientists. We boarded the Airbus EC-130 helicopter ready for our aerial tour of the canyon. James and I had paid extra to get guaranteed seats at the front of the helicopter, whilst my sister sat behind us.

The flight started fast and low over the trees so that when we finally crossed over the canyon rim the helicopter could slow down and give us more time there. As we crossed over the rim the pilot started playing the theme from '2001: A Space Odyssey'. I think it was a good choice.

Depending on the scientific study you read, it has taken between five and forty million years for the Grand Canyon to become what we could see from the helicopter. Although the canyon was carved by the Colorado River, it has also been a product of uplift which has brought two billion year old rocks to the surface.

I'd planned this to be the end of our trip so that anything afterwards wouldn't feel underwhelming. Our Grandma had taken a plane across the canyon so we felt we needed to do similar - though I'm glad we opted for the helicopter. This ride gave us time to take it all in, and to get photographs along the way.

When the tour was over we bought sandwiches and drove to Desert View Point. The view was impressive, and a great place for getting a photograph with my legs dangling over the edge of the rim. This was the last proper view of the Grand Canyon we'd get. From that point on we were on our way back to Phoenix to complete our journey of over 2,000 miles.

The morning in Phoenix was completely without plans. We'd dropped the car off at the airport when we'd arrived back in the night, and James would be heading back to Canada shortly after breakfast.

Whilst he was getting ready I went out for a run, and was greeted by a lightning bolt striking the ground in front of me. I carried on for another half a mile thinking that it'd be okay to do so, but common sense prevailed and I ran back to the hotel.

By the time Lindsay and myself had decided to look around Phoenix James had already landed in Toronto, and the temperature here had soared. There wasn't much to see either in this part of town except a bar owned by Alice Cooper. We'd both had enough, and were ready to go home.

30: Nepal

In the years since I started travelling around the world a lot has changed. One of the most notable things was that in the beginning I'd be lucky to find internet access anywhere: it'd usually be expensive if it could be found at all. Now the internet is everywhere, and often free. The internet, or social media to be precise, is how I found out about a company who were organising a marathon in Nepal following their recent earthquake.

On the 25th April 2015, Nepal suffered a magnitude 7.8 earthquake that killed nearly nine thousand people on top of the twenty-two thousand it injured. In addition to this massive loss of life, the damage to the country was significant. It would cost ten billion US dollars: half of their domestic product, in order to rebuild everything.

Our efforts would be focussed around a small community; but I knew little more than that.

On the morning of my flight to Nepal I went out for one last short run. It was through the torrential downpour that had been named 'Storm Angus'; but I felt it necessary. After a roast dinner I headed to Heathrow airport to begin my Himalayan adventure.

Checking in was once again not straightforward. My passport was taken away from me due to a rip in the photo page that had happened whilst I'd been in America. When she returned, the lady confirmed that just this once I could fly with it.

Unable to fly direct, I had to change aircraft in Istanbul. Unfortunately the flights were not that good. On one I was served chicken that was pink inside. I wasn't going to eat that.

The airport in Kathmandu is a small one, and the visa application causes semi-organised chaos within. Firstly, you need to queue to use a machine which will take your picture and requests details for your visa. At this time there were only two machines working and a lot of people needing to use it.

The next step is to queue, and I use that term loosely, for one of the three cashiers who you'll then pay the visa fee to. On the noticeboard it indicated I could pay either US$25 or £20. With the exchange rate at the time, the dollars option worked out a little cheaper. It's pretty common for countries to favour US dollars in currency exchanges as they're more useful to them.

My luggage had long since arrived, and was now sitting alongside the carousel. I met up with Nick from Impact Marathons, and waited for the others to begin our journey.

The driving was similar to busy cities in India and China, so to me the driving didn't seem out of the ordinary now. We'd got one night in Kathmandu, so I took this opportunity to explore a little and to change some money into Nepalese rupees.

I'd never explored a country like this by myself before, and at the start of my travels I wouldn't have dreamed of it. Walk around Cairo by myself? That seemed like madness; but all these years of travel to both developed and developing countries had taught me a lot. The world had changed too, so with an offline map on my phone I was able to find my way to Hanumandhoka Durbar Square. The closer I got the narrower the roads got, and cars were soon replaced with mopeds and bicycles that weaved through the busy streets.

Rickshaws reminded me of Beijing, and in some ways the streets reminded me of China too. It was becoming commonplace for me to find similarities between places. An especially common occurrence was being hassled by people wanting to sell their wares. I've long since learnt that I should keep moving unless I'm interested. It may sound impolite, but the frequency of it means a five minute walk could easily turn into an hour.

When walking down Freak Street I wasn't being hassled as much as I expected to be. I could see other tourists being stopped; but I was mostly left alone. I wondered if it was because I was walking by myself, and wasn't lingering.

The square is one of three royal squares in Kathmandu. After its construction in the Licchavi period, it was the seat of power for numerous Shah Kings between 1484 and 1896. None of the buildings that stand there today are from that time though. In fact, not all of the buildings were still standing after the earthquake.

For tourists there is an entry fee of one thousand

rupees; but locals are allowed to walk straight through as it's one of their holy sites. The money would at least go into the repairs so hopefully tourists and locals alike will be able to enjoy the architecture of these buildings again.

It's a busy square with cows roaming freely in places. Most people there are on foot, but you get the occasional moped driving through as well. I moved around as quickly as I could to get pictures before sunset so I could leave in daylight. It's not uncommon for places to look different in the dark, and this can make finding your way back more difficult.

Back at the hotel I got to know some of the other people who would be running. It was a casual event with waiters wandering around with plates of deep fried vegetables and chicken momos. This was a little like a starter for the evening meal of dal bhat: a staple food for this area. As we ate, a film crew from one of Kathmandu's national news stations arrived to interview Nick about what we'd be doing in the coming days.

We were in the breakfast room at 06:00, and on the road just thirty minutes later to Boudha. Our small group had the earliest start; but we got to relax with some lemon tea before we started.

We were led down a path between buildings to an open space between privately owned buildings. This area was filled with rubbish that had been dumped by the locals instead of them paying for refuse collection.

Although the ones in this immediate area likely could afford the twenty-five rupees, there'd be many that couldn't. Many of the residents also don't understand the consequences of this sort of pollution either, so the action needed to be two-fold: clean-up, and education. It's a lesson I felt some areas back home needed to learn too.

Nobody knew who owned the land so they couldn't be ordered to clean it. Instead our small group of volunteers, armed with face masks and gloves, were there to get it done.

After a couple of hours it felt like we hadn't made a difference - there was so much left. Though when comparing before and after photographs we found we'd made a tremendous difference already. What was left would be done by a couple of hired labourers. There would also be some lights put up, and a guard hired to patrol at night to make sure it remained clean. Sounds like overkill, but that's what they claimed.

Lunch was dal bhat with some variation from the night before. Our goal was to finish lunch as quickly as possible so we'd have time to visit a nearby stupa before our school visit.

The Great Boudha stupa, Boudhanath, is a UNESCO world heritage recognised site; but is one that had suffered during the earthquake the year before. What stood there now was a new concrete structure which had only just been reopened to the public by the Prime Minister that morning.

We completed one clockwise lap of the grounds, and also got to see some of the inside. This stupa is one of the most important sites in Kathmandu, so it was nice that we'd been given the chance to visit it.

We walked from the stupa to a school where we watched a play they were using to educate children on the importance of proper waste disposal. I didn't really understand what was going on for most of it, though the school children were captivated by it. Maybe this education might just work.

For what remained of the day we travelled up into the mountains to Kakani as the sun began to set. When we arrived in the village we were ushered off the bus, and welcomed to the beat of drums as each of us were handed flowers. This was then repeated a second time with dancers that led us to a prayer room for donations.

For the next few days the scout hut there would be the athletes village - surrounded by tents we'd be staying in. On a nearby peak was the 'Sunset Bar' where some of the group were already waiting for us around a large campfire drinking cinnamon and rum punch, and eating momos.

Everyone sat and shared their stories from the day until we were called down to the hut for our evening meal. It was dal bhat again - this would be our staple for the next week.

The tent I stayed in was spacious and shared with just one other runner. There were beds on wooden frames to keep us off the ground, but even then it was cold enough to sleep fully clothed.

Of the challenges that Nepal faces, one of these is access to a clean and reliable water supply outside of the cities. Our plan was to spend the next two days changing this for the people of Kakani by laying a pipeline to a new water supply.

Before sunrise a group of us set off on a two mile

run around the mountains. It shouldn't have been hard work, but the altitude and elevation changes made this a lot harder than normal. This would hopefully get a little easier as the week went on.

After the run I tried the showers at camp for the first time. If the water in general had been described as cold, then first thing in the morning that would have been an understatement. At this time of day the solar-powered water heaters had not collected any power at all. It was certainly a challenge.

Following breakfast we split off into groups, and made our way to the site of the project. The Armed Police Force had already made a start on digging the trench which would eventually cover five kilometres across difficult mountainous terrain. At the front of the group there were people armed with machetes clearing a path through the vegetation.

The APF would tell us what to do, even though the locals could have been doing this themselves. It was others being there that would motivate them, and supposedly provide some organisation - they were better at this work than us though.

We didn't notice the APF disappear; but we did once the rest of the Nepalese workers broke for lunch at 10:30. We were slower, but progress seemed good. In places it was challenging - there were narrow ledges where we'd need to brace ourselves against stronger branches as we worked, but at other times there were branches we needed to cut through with pick axes.

Eventually we encountered a ravine that was too deep to traverse. If we dug down and then back up like we'd done elsewhere then the water would lose too much pressure in the pipes, and if we left it exposed and draped across then the water would freeze in the winter.

Once they'd come to an agreement with the locals, the pipe was rerouted through a small settlement to cross the ravine in a place that is not as deep. For the next hour I hacked away at rock with a pickaxe so we'd be able to lay the pipe on the other side.

In the afternoon I worked on a different section of the pipeline which was on the precipice of a long drop. It meant progress here had to be slow due to the necessary caution. Someone ahead of me slipped, and he fell backwards towards the long drop below. Things could have gotten very bad very quickly, but he was caught up in the pipe we were laying: this combined with the branches of the trees saved him. Since he was already hanging onto the pipe we used it to pull him back to safety.

We carried on as if nothing had happened, and then stopped for the day when we reached the stupa we'd found at lunch. We'd laid only two kilometres of pipe: under half what we needed to do. It felt like we might let down this community.

Once again the day started with a run around the mountains before breakfast. This time it was hill sprints to try and get used to the sort of climbs we'd need to do during the marathon. I'd never encountered hills like it before, but it was kind of fun - especially the focus required for running down hill at speed. It's the sort of focus that would eventually come in useful for Race to the Stones back home.

The days work seemed to be slow to start. I was standing near some exposed pipe, and had a shovel in my hand, so I took charge and got us working to bury it. When the others joined in we caught up with the front of the group in no time at all. Instead of standing around waiting we climbed up off the path, and walked to the village where we could be of more help.

Whilst we'd been in the forest some dispute had started in the village. A local seemed distraught and was preventing the pipe from being laid. We couldn't understand what he was saying though, and he couldn't understand us.

To bridge the communication gap we located Tarjan, a Gurkha from our group, to help with the translating. The villager was getting quite animated, but Tarjan remained calm. We found that the villager was drunk, and was protesting about where the water pipe was going to be located. Things were settled and the pipe-laying continued.

It was hard work, and unlike anything I'd have done back home. How often in our comfortable western lives do we get to use a pickaxe to smash up the ground on the side of a mountain? I certainly don't from the comfort of an office job. I think it was safe to say many of us were breaking new ground in our experiences.

At the end of this day we were told we'd fallen short of the water supply by a whole kilometre. We'd failed the community, but at least now they could continue on by themselves. Our efforts had not been for nothing.

On the final day before the race we could do whatever we wanted. I chose to go for a walk with my camera to see what I could find. School children passed me with the usual "namaste" greeting, and I was amused by one carrying a live chicken. I thought to myself that perhaps that was their packed lunch.

When I returned to the camp I sat and listened to a talk on some of the challenges they face in Nepal. When it was over I headed in the direction of Shivapuri National Park -it was my hope I'd get to see some wildlife. The entrance to this park is a small clearing with a guardhouse.

"No ticket!" one of the guards told me.

"Where do I get a ticket from?"

"No ticket!"

With a combination of hand gestures, and broken English he eventually understood I needed to know where to get a ticket from, and was able to convey enough meaning to suggest the ticket would be from the scout house.

I realised I wouldn't have time for that before sunset - so instead watched a film called 'Mira'. The film is about a Nepalese trail runner who enjoyed trail running and went on to compete internationally. She came second in the Sky Runner Championship in her first year, and is now inspiring young Nepalese runners:some of which would be joining us for the marathon in the morning.

My ankle was mostly recovered from the accident I'd had in Moscow, but I wasn't yet sure how it was going to cope with both the distance and terrain of my first trail marathon. There was a good reason they named this course the "Beast of Shivapuri". It would be testing both physically and mentally with a cumulative climb that is equivalent to climbing Ben Nevis twice whilst at an average elevation of over two thousand metres above sea level. What was I thinking?

I started the day with a bowl of cereal that had been in my suitcase since I'd left home. With warm milk it didn't taste great, but I wanted to be consistent with my pre-race traditions.

When the other marathon runners were ready we made our way to the UN APF parade ground for the start. The local guest houses in the village had opened their doors for athletes, so you could use their facilities if you needed to along the way. It was already getting warm, and would likely be far warmer by the time I finished.

As with any race, people nervously stood around preparing themselves for the challenge ahead, and completed the necessary paperwork.

When the race started, a number of us shot off at a fast pace, and began the downhill stretch to some prayer flags which marked a turnaround point for going back up the road and then off onto the trails. It was after this turnaround point I noticed a large number of runners who had been behind me, who had never passed me, were now in front of me.

When I saw one I knew she asked me how I got behind her, and it became apparent that a group of people had turned off down this road early instead of going down to the bottom of the hill so had cut their route short by just under mile.

The one that had started the mass shortcut claimed

that she'd thought the elites had made a mistake. They hadn't, they'd listened to the race briefing and were following the lead motorbike.

The trails started with some steep climbs, and areas where your feet would get wet. As the terrain got tougher and more technical, the distance between runners increased.

At a waterfall crossing it was necessary to hold on to a rope in order to get across safely. Anyone who slipped without holding on would have been in serious danger. At the very least it'd have ruined their day.

Over the first ten miles of this race I overtook the majority of those that had cut the route short and made good progress in working my way up through the positions. It was never going to last though: sooner or later the terrain would defeat me.

As I was carrying my own water I was able to ignore the aid stations and continue running whilst others paused. I'd even been a stereotypical runner and had jelly babies in my pocket for fuel during the run as well; but lost almost half of them when they fell from my pocket fairly early in the race.

A marathon is far enough that sometimes you have to change your strategy mid-race. This was one of those times. On the second lap of the course I stopped to make sure another runner was okay. He didn't look too good, but insisted he was well enough to walk a few hundred metres back to the nearest aid station.

After that the course started to feel harder. Each hill was feeling tougher, and longer than the previous lap. Where other runners had been around me, I was now alone. With nobody around, the mental challenge of keeping my legs moving was not an easy one. I ran when I felt I could; but it was not easy.

When I eventually neared the finish line I sprinted with almost everything I'd got left. It was done - I'd finished my first overseas race. It'd been more of an adventure than a race, during a week of many experiences. I'd had to jump or stride over boulders and fallen trees, clambered across rocks, crossed waterfalls, and moved carefully along narrow paths.

Upon crossing that finish line they used the red dye of a Sindoor tree on my forehead, and put a garland of flowers around my neck. We all had stories afterwards which we shared and celebrated around the roaring campfire that night. By this point our group had raised £85,000 for Nepalese charities.

The morning after the Nepal marathon was an early start. It seemed too early for what was planned. The four of us who would be continuing on around Nepal for another week needed to be up at 05:00 to get the coach back into Kathmandu. A few others were also there to head to the airport.

The coach driver thought we were all going to the airport, and had not been told that we were going to the trekking office to begin a tour. The driver had no idea where it was, but one of the group was able to direct him somewhere nearby to drop us off. It was then half a mile of dragging suitcases before we found the office.

Nobody seemed to know what was going on, even at the hotel where we were supposed to be staying.

Eventually we called the marathon company, and they spoke to the people on the hotel reception. They sorted things out and told us it'd be another hour until we could check-in to the hotel.

At the end of Mandala Street we found a bakery for lunch. When we returned to the offices we arrived just ahead of those that had been on the later coach.

More time was spent waiting until eventually they were ready to take us on the fifteen minute drive to a tour of Swayambhunath: the Monkey Temple. It gets this name from the number of rhesus macaques that live there, but its Tibetan name means 'sublime trees'.

It's the oldest religious site in Nepal, and important to both Hindu and Buddhist religions which is quite unusual. It's for this reason, in addition to the tourists, it can get quite busy there. It was difficult to tell what there was more of: people or monkeys.

Our guide led us into one of the shops around the stupa, and there they explained to us different painting techniques they used, and demonstrated different levels of mastery. For the more advanced levels they'd have spent decades of their life having repeated the same design over and over.

Our guide asked us if we wanted to see anything else, but wouldn't tell us what else there was to see. *Great guide!* So, we were driven back to the hotel until we were ready to go out for an evening meal.

We used social media to see who else from the athletes village was in town - our group soon swelled from four to twenty-three after we arrived at a restaurant.

In the early hours of the morning we felt a minor earthquake. For those that live in Kathmandu it's nothing unusual, and they didn't seem to even notice it. For those of us that live in England, it's a rarity to encounter them. The last one I'd felt had been in South America.

We walked a mile with suitcases in tow from the hotel to get on a bus that would be the first leg of a 210 kilometre journey to Pokhara. It's a road that a popular motoring show would have people believe is one of the most dangerous in Nepal - though the road they were thinking of is north of Pokhara. Sure this road has dangerous drivers; but doesn't any road?

Over an hour after leaving Kathmandu we stopped briefly at a service station, and by pure coincidence bumped into some fellow runners from the athletes village who were off on their own adventures. I couldn't wait for our own to start. The next time we stopped was at the Trishuli River.

At the river our suitcases were loaded onto a truck that would take it downstream. As it did so we sat and waited for the next thirty-five minutes for another group that would be joining us for some rafting.

We each put on a crash helmet and life jacket, and began practicing what to do for each command. There's not much we needed to know; but white water rafting is hard work through waves that crashed over the boat.

For the first two hours we got drenched repeatedly as we avoided capsizing, and had to steer furiously with the oars. That time passed so quickly, and when we reached some calmer waters passed a sandy beach I thought it was all over. We got off the raft and watched as a black snake struggled to cross the river itself. For us, this was actually just a ten minute break before the hardest section - what the guide described as major rapids. He wasn't joking.

Waves crashed over rocks and the boat, and the steering had gotten even harder as we were now moving faster. One of the last waves struck us with so much force that the boat almost flipped as the front soared through the air with us still in it. We shifted from paddling fast, to hiding inside the raft and bracing ourselves for the jolt we were anticipating. We felt it hit; but we hadn't gone over.

We quickly moved back onto the side of the boat to put everything we had into steering once more. It took everything we'd got left; but we got through the worst of them without leaving the boat.

I'd never experienced anything like it. Again. It seemed like so many of these trips had led me to do things I'd never even thought to try before having got on that plane to Cairo what was now so many years before.

When it was all over, I felt extremely cold from how much body heat had been lost to the river. As it was now mid-afternoon I was also very hungry. We were led from the beach, and across the road into a back room of the Ananta Jeewan Church where we were able to get dry, and change into some warm clothes. Downstairs they'd put on a strange buffet of cold pasta, cold beans, an indescribable spam-like meat, peanut butter, and bread.

Little did we know, the bus we'd been scheduled to take had already been passed - we'd missed it due to the delay in starting the rafting. The guide was trying to flag down a tour bus; but was having no luck. If I'd encountered this situation on my own I'm not sure I'd have known what to do.

Eventually, not having had any luck with tour buses, he was able to get us on a local bus. This was the sort that does not have suspension, and you feel every single bump on the road with some severity. They're the sort of transportation you'd refer to as a 'bone-shaker'. To make matters worse, for those next three hours I had to sit with my heavy camera bag on my knee as there was nowhere else to put it. An elderly lady at the back of the bus was also making phlegmy throat-clearing noises frequently until she was eventually sick.

It was the worst bus ride I've ever taken, and it seemed to last forever. It's the sort of thing the locals have to live with, and it even makes our overcrowded trains seem 'good'.

After an hour into the journey our guide got a call from the porters in Pokhara asking where we were as we were now over two hours late. Our options now were to stay in Pokhara and miss the hike, or to make our way to a guest house and do the hike in the morning. We didn't really want to miss anything, so we agreed to the guest house.

In Pokhara we left the bus, and waited for a jeep that would take us the rest of the way into the mountains to Kande where a guest house had been organised at the last minute. The driver hadn't been told how many of us there'd be or that we had luggage which meant this was even more cramped than the bus had been. So cramped in fact that the guide was sitting in the boot with the luggage around him.

When we arrived, the guide got out first to talk to the owners of the guest house. There were raised voices; but we couldn't tell what was going on. Eventually they led us inside.

On the ground floor, the front of this guest house is open to the elements as it's also used as a shop and cafe. It'd probably seen better days too as years of dirt had built up in places. At the back of the building they led us down dark steps to a corridor of padlocked rooms. What was this place?!

It felt like we'd stumbled into an abandoned asylum from a horror movie. When they opened the first of the rooms I saw two beds with dirty sheets and a thin blanket. It was impossible to know how much time had passed since they'd last had a clean. All of the rooms were the same, so Ben and Keith took this first room.

They opened up a second room which I took, and then a third room for Sam. Once we'd dropped our luggage off in the rooms we locked them back up and headed upstairs for food. There wasn't really anything we could have other than peanut butter pancakes as everything else came from somewhere in the village, and was now closed. It was a day I was glad to have cereal bars on me.

I guess this place sounds bad; but it's this sort of thing that creates stories which we remember forever so they can't be all bad. This was an adventure.

I awoke from five hours of sleep fully clothed. It'd been cold overnight; but not to the degree that Norway had been. If I hadn't been tired from the rafting and shortage of food then maybe I'd have struggled to sleep.

Before breakfast, we'd now got a hike to do. It was a two mile ascent to the Australian base camp for Annapurna, with sherpas passing us along the way. My legs were still a little heavy from the marathon; but the misty views across the valley were incredible. It was worth every tired step, and thoughts of our overnight accommodation were gone.

At the base camp we were led onto the roof of one of the two story buildings. This is where we'd be eating breakfast: on the roof of a building on a Himalayan mountain, and overlooking one of the most incredible sights in the world - clouds parting to reveal mountains and valleys. To make things even more surreal we found there was Wi-Fi available.

After breakfast it was a 4.2 mile descent along a winding path to the village of Dhampus. This was an end to the grassy trail, and the start of hard stone paths. Some of this area made me think of Yorkshire, especially with the moss growing on stone walls.

From the base of the mountain we continued on by jeep to Pokhara, and then into the back of a van to be driven up a large hill to where guides were waiting for each of us.

One helped fit me with a helmet and harness, and attached us both to the parachute we'd be paragliding with. I was told not to look down, and to just run forward.

I ran forwards towards the edge of the cliff until my legs were moving but not making contact with anything. In a matter of hours we'd gone from a climbing up and down part of a mountain, to running off one. It's another thing I'd never even considered doing before - why would you run off a mountain? There we were though: soaring through the air like oversized birds defying gravity.

When you're gliding through the air, catching thermals, time passes quickly. On one of the thermals we circled over it to take us higher and higher, passing close to vultures also riding the thermals, before swooping down over the trees. It was so different to looking down on a city from an aircraft.

"Do you like rollercoasters?" the guide asked me.

"Yes…". It had sounded to me like a loaded question; but before I could think any more about it we veered to one side so that we were over Lake Phewa Tal.

"This will be fun," the guide laughed. With that he began to perform aerial acrobatics over the water. I hadn't known it was possible for parachutes to go upside down.

When we got back into town afterwards, in one piece, the group checked into a hotel and went our own separate ways. I took my camera down to the lake and waited for sunset. My hope was that it'd make a good photograph, but after twenty minutes a layer of mist started to roll over the mountains. The sky had a purplish tinge to it. I realised there wasn't going to be a fantastic sunset:I just had to make do with the light that was there.

That evening the four of us went to the Moondance restaurant, and met up with a number of other marathoners who just happened to be in town that night. I was starting to lose count of how many times we'd met up with people we'd already said goodbye to.

Most of the following day was a bus journey to get us to Sauraha, on the edge of the Chitwan National Park and bordering India. Our only real activity of the day was a village walk - which to me sounded like it'd be boring, but I went along with it anyway. Perhaps I'd be surprised, and I'd got nothing better to be doing.

This walk started with some of the neighbouring buildings - traditional homes made from elephant grass, and was told that they eat copious amounts of chilli all year around as a way of keeping malaria-carrying mosquitoes away from them. I wasn't sure how effective chillies really are; but they have been proven to have health benefits, and were believed to be used as medicine by the Maya. Maybe there was something to it.

The commercial centre of this town was small; but the buildings modern. Beyond this we found our way onto a trail alongside the Rapti River. This is where it started to get interesting - I'd already spotted a gharial and mugger crocodile on the river, and I'd spotted other wildlife to be photographing too.

We reached a sign that read 'No permission without entry', and continued on passed it. I photographed an elephant in captivity, and felt sorry to see it that way; but this was not all that I'd see on this trail. About ten metres in front of me, far closer than any of its African cousins had been in Kenya or Tanzania, was an Indian rhinoceros. It was mostly obscured by the bushes it was grazing from, but we weren't allowed any closer. At most, ten metres was close enough.

The others who had joined our group for this tour were talking loudly, unlike the rest of us who were either being silent or using hushed voices. This agitated the rhinoceros after a while which gave our guide no choice but to take us back to the river and wait for sunset whilst watching another in the distance.

The following day started with an early drive to the riverbank where a dugout canoe was waiting to carry us along the river. The easiest way to imagine these canoes is to think of how a Venetian gondola is steered, then think of the boat being more like a long, hollowed-out tree trunk which when fully loaded has the sides just above the level of the water. It did of course mean we could get very close to the mugger crocodiles. More so than the other crocodile species I'd seen in Australia.

Further along the river we disembarked, and began a nature walk through the trees. There wasn't that much to see really - just a deer, and a wild boar. It was a walk that ended with sadness at the elephant breeding centre.

At a very young age they will take the elephants away from their mother, and then have their food and water restricted. This form of torture is what they do to 'break' them so that they can then teach them to be beasts of burden.

Their torture of these animals doesn't stop there though. The information describes how they are burnt and washed to desensitise the skin, and also how they can sustain injuries during training.

I strongly disagree with what it is they do. They may be protecting the animals from poachers, but in some ways their treatment of them seems worse as they're made to suffer repeatedly. I didn't want to see any more. Even in the elephant bathing area you could see pink scar tissue from where their spiked tools are used to control them.

We were shown elephants in captivity with the older ones chained up by one leg, and no longer able to roam like their instincts tell them to. The females of this species are herd animals and are not used to the solitary life. I saw one calf also chained up and trying to get to one of the other elephants. It couldn't and looked distressed. I got closer to one of the youngest ones; it used its trunk to pull on my leg to bring me closer.

When it found it couldn't pull me into the enclosure it then started to pull on my shoelaces instead. You could tell that despite this harsh treatment, some were still filled with a playful spirit that hadn't yet been broken.

There was the option to ride an elephant, or to take a jeep for the afternoon tour. I'm sure riding an elephant would have been an experience, but I couldn't do it knowing what they had gone through. The jeep tour went on for a long time without us seeing any wildlife. I think maybe it was too commercialised with too many vehicles in a small area.

In the evening we went to the Tharu Culture Program to learn about their culture. It was an hour long dancing performance with some of it looking like fighting kata that may have been originally used to teach warriors.

Already our time was over: we spent most of the next day driving back to Kathmandu. Rush hour in the city made our arrival a lot slower than I'd expected. I noticed one Nepali cleaning windows whilst standing on an upturned bucket which itself was on a ledge over a four story drop. It wouldn't have taken much for him to have fallen.

The place where we'd been dropped off was not the place we'd caught the bus previously, and nobody from the trekking company was there either. We had to figure out where to go, and then make our own way there.

We tried to catch a taxi, but the driver had no idea where Mandala Street was. Fortunately I had a map on my phone so was able to navigate us on foot. It just didn't help that we all had heavy suitcases to carry for two kilometres, and I don't think the others believed I knew where I was going. I probably wasn't all that confident myself. If this had happened when I first started travelling then I wouldn't have been prepared, and would have been clueless about what to do. I got us there without getting lost.

For one last time we used social media to see if any other marathoners were in town, and sure enough a few met up with us at the Electric Pagoda for a final group meal.

The last day was to be a busy one: we'd got a flight with Buddha Air to take us passed Mount Everest if the weather was okay. The flight time arrived and went. The staff there updated the PowerPoint presentation they were using for the departures board to say it was delayed pending a weather report.

Apparently domestic flights are frequently cancelled or delayed depending on how much fog is about. I started to keep a close eye on the time as each delay would eat into the time I'd have between this flight and my flight home. Just as it got to the critical time for me, we were able to board the plane.

My seat was at the front on the left-hand side of the aircraft. I was staring at the peaks trying to figure out which one was which. When I realised which was Mount Everest I quickly took photographs, and just happened to be given the chance to go into the cockpit as the aircraft was turning: I could see it straight on from the front.

To look at it from the air, it doesn't seem special: it could be any mountain, couldn't it? Though we know it to be the highest peak in the world, and one which many people have lost their lives trying to climb. Nature is a force to be reckoned with in any form.

I was back at the hotel after the flight with thirty minutes to spare before I needed to be heading back to the airport with my luggage. The security there was different to any other I'd passed through.

There was a queue for men, a queue for women, and then the business class queue. As the queue for men was twice the length of the queue for women they moved half of the males into the business class queue: even though that one was longer than the queue for women too. They wouldn't let men and women queue together.

I think this is the only time I've ever departed the same airport twice within a six hour time period.

Looking back I'd made new friends, some of which I'd see again on later trips, and others that I'd eventually lose contact with. This was the first time I'd gone anywhere not really knowing anyone, and being there primarily to run and volunteer. It's a very different side to travel.

31: Parks of California and Utah

When I was working on the plans for Arizona, I'd started to make a few notes on a different idea - a road trip around California and Utah to see bits we'd missed. My planning wasn't perfect though as I'd not taken into account needing to get an 02:15 taxi to the airport fourteen hours after completing the Greater Manchester Marathon for the second time.

The taxi driver seemed to think he was the reincarnation of Ayrton Senna due to the way he threw the car into corners at speed. If this had been the only 'drama' whilst travelling then I'd have been pleased.

For this trip I was passing through Frankfurt Airport as I have done many times. Despite the usual extra checks of my camera gear being commonplace for me in this airport, this time was unlike any other time. My camera backpack tested positive for explosives.

Explosives! I didn't understand how that was possible, and I wondered what was going to happen. Of all the things you can be prepared for, how can you plan for this? Would I make my flight?

The official called over some armed security guards

who stood either side of me, clutching their MP5 sub-machine guns tightly. My passport was taken away from me, and the details from it noted down whilst they took details of the flight I was connecting to. He then got me to prove my laptop was working: this is why electrical goods should always be charged before a flight.

Apparently some cleaning products can cause these false positives, particularly screen wipes. Maybe I'd put my bag down on a floor that'd just been cleaned and now had some residue from that.

He re-tested my backpack, and then my laptop. *Please pass, please!* I thought to myself. My legs hadn't yet forgiven me for that marathon - they didn't need this.

This time the test was a negative. It was a relief like no other, and the rest of my journey to San Francisco went smoothly. James was waiting at the car rental desk for my sleepy arrival. It was fortunate he'd be driving the first stretch to Oakhurst.

I'd fallen asleep within minutes of arriving at the motel, and was wide awake before sunrise. I may have just run a marathon but I decided to go for a short, slow run around the town to loosen my legs. I tried my best to keep to the few sidewalks about. It meant I was running up and down the same stretch of road; though I saw it as an opportunity to look out for places we could eat in the evening.

Afterwards, it may have only been an hour drive to the entrance to the Yosemite National Park; but once inside it's still quite a drive into the valley to reach the first of the viewpoints: a panorama of El Capitan, Half

Dome, Cathedral Rocks, and Bridalveil Falls.

We started with the Misty Trail - I could feel the marathon in my legs still as I walked along the undulating path. The rocks were glistening in the sun from the fine mist that was blowing across them from Vernal Falls. It's the sort of trail where you'll get a little damp along the way, and have to watch your footing.

We could have continued on to Nevada Falls, but James was getting hungry and we had no food with us. The nearest place was the Yosemite Store where we could buy everything we needed to make our own sandwiches for days. At least on subsequent days we could spend more time on the trails.

Our next trail actually had some of the winter snow remaining, though it didn't hinder our progress. We thought afterwards we could do the Upper Yosemite Falls; but after speaking to a park ranger we found that it actually takes several hours to complete. It may look a short distance on a map; but there's no context of what the trail is like. So instead we hiked to Mirror Lake.

The drive out of the Yosemite Valley back to the motel in Oakhurst took almost two hours. If we'd realised this travel time beforehand we'd have considered paying more to be closer.

By 10:00 the next morning we were at the trailhead for Upper Yosemite Falls. The start of this feels monotonous with constant switchbacks to quickly gain height. Once it straightens out it takes you across small waterfalls, and also along misty paths alongside the Yosemite Falls where rainbows arc across the spray.

The closer we got to the top, the less shade there was to be found. It was a hot day, and I'd only thought to carry a litre of water with me. It wasn't going to be enough. We hadn't exactly taken our time either: for a trail that takes around ten hours we reached the summit in two and three quarter hours.

The last part of the ascent had been through deep snow, though the summit itself was mostly clear. We went looking for the trail to Yosemite Point, but thought it looked impassable without better equipment. Shorts, t-shirt, and training shoes are not what I'd consider ideal for crossing deep snow. We sat on some rocks for lunch.

Eating has a habit of giving you time to think, and in this time we saw an alternative way down to the river to cross the bridge. The climb on the other side was far steeper, and actually very difficult in the wrong footwear. James however was off like a rocket whilst I was constantly sliding back down.

However, on the way back down after the viewpoint it was James that injured himself: he slipped and cut his arm on a rock. We'd made it across to the other side and began the proper descent by the time it'd stopped bleeding.

My shoes had become sodden from the snow, so every step of the descent was accompanied by a squelch. It was the sort of feeling that started to conjure images of trench foot. My water bottle may now have been empty, but my shoes seemed full.

It had taken seven hours to hike up to the top, explore a little, and return to the bottom. I guess even after a marathon we were still a little quicker than the average hiker there.

The hike meant I didn't bother with running the following morning: my legs were tired enough. All we'd really got time for was the Bridalveil Falls - any other hike would have taken more time than we had. We needed to drive back to San Francisco.

When I took over the driving in Gilroy, there was only ninety minutes of driving left to go, and the sun was setting. The roads seemed familiar, and with good reason: we'd taken these same roads to San Jose on the way back from Los Angeles on a previous road trip.

From the outskirts of San Francisco we encountered rain so heavy that the visibility was almost non-existent. I was struggling to see the lines on the road; and could only see tail lights in front. The concentration required was tiring.

We didn't know this at the time, but the storm had stranded tourists on Alcatraz Island for hours until a brief lull in the storm after midnight allowed for a quick rescue boat.

Our hotel was in the middle of nowhere, and finding somewhere to eat was a struggle. All we could find was a hotel restaurant with terrible service.

Our first full day in San Francisco had a late start in order to avoid rush hour traffic. I packed what I'd need for the day, and left everything else in the hotel where it'd be safe. James on the other hand took his entire camera backpack with him.

We parked near Pier 39 where they charge a 'day'

rate of US$37 for twelve hours. It feels like a bit of false advertising there. At least this wouldn't be too far from everything we wanted to see. We started up Telegraph Hill to Coit Tower - named for San Francisco's first female firefighter.

Heading further into the city from there took us through Chinatown where it did actually feel a little like being back in Beijing or Xi'an. The shops had the same feel to them, and their wares similar. We weren't that far from Union Square so we carried on using my offline map for navigation.

One Cheesecake Factory break later, we were on our way to see more sights; but James did not feel well at all. We rested in a church out of the sun, and decided it'd be an idea for him to retrieve his sunglasses from the car. Time was now short, but we headed in the direction of Fort Mason.

I wanted a photograph of the Golden Gate Bridge, and Fort Mason seemed like the place to get it from without needing to go too far. Time was tight. I went on ahead at a faster pace, and would meet James in the Historical Maritime Park. It was a brisk walk, and was fast enough to overtake tourists on Segways. Sadly it was a waste of time: the bridge was still too far away, and shrouded in fog.

This may not have gone to plan, but it left us with time to get some lunch from the Boudin Bakery - famous for their sourdough, and for James to revisit the car one last time to change his shoes before our tour of Alcatraz.

Alcatraz Island hadn't always been a prison. Once upon a time it had been a fort with a dry moat, and drawbridge to defend against attackers wanting to gain access to the gold of San Francisco's gold rush. This was where the name 'Golden Gate' comes from.

The island never experienced an attack; it's fortunate as the embrasures had been badly designed so that riflemen would have shot each other from either side.

It was Abraham Lincoln who ordered the fort to become a prison. When it closed many years later, it did so due to the proposed cost to bring it up to modern standards. At this time, some buildings were knocked down before native Americans occupied the island. That is until it was designated a National Monument.

A place like this has so many stories to be told, and for our 'behind-the-scenes' tour we'd hear many of the more famous ones, and see some of the places others don't get to. One place we saw was adjacent to the power station where there's a tunnel dug by prison labourers. The Park Service have knocked down the wall at the end of this so it's now possible to see that it led to the workshop.

Above, we moved onto the main prison building. It had once been the citadel; but that had been levelled down to the cellar before the new building was constructed. A locked door was opened for us, so we could move from the visitation area, up some stairs into a chapel.

The walls were painted with the graffiti of native Americans, and draped through a puddle was a power cable. Maybe that wasn't too safe; but it was safe to say the room had seen better days.

Underneath A-block we got to experience the solitude cells in what would once have been a dry moat.

The prisoners would have experienced the sound of rats scurrying across the floor in complete darkness. The lights had been fitted for tourists; but they were turned off for a while so we could glimpse the conditions they'd have faced. It was dark. Very dark.

In the barbershop we were told a story of a violent end to a lovers quarrel, and in the dining hall we were told how Alcatraz had turned a non-violent offender into a killer. There was a common theme here: inmates were either driven to insanity or became killers by the conditions. It seemed the conditions were considerably worse than those we'd seen in the Darwin Gaol.

We went to a number of the evening talks after this; but decided we'd take the 20:40 ferry back to the mainland so we could get food just before our 12-hour parking was up. James went to pay another US$15 for parking, whilst I went to the rental car.

I opened the back up, and noticed glass everywhere. At first I was confused - where had that come from? Then I noticed the hole in the rear window as more glass dropped from it. One of the tinted side windows had been smashed too. Thieves had broken in.

I called James over, and we soon realised his camera bag was gone. He'd lost a camera, lenses, and even his house keys. He did not feel well at all, and wanted us to go straight back to the hotel; but I insisted we call the police first, and then the car rental company before moving anything. A friendly passer-by, who was visiting from New Jersey, heard us and asked if we needed help.

We explained what had happened; he'd seen the same thing further along the coast that morning. He told us how thieves had turned up in an SUV, broken into a vehicle, stole some bags, and then drove off.

He dialled 911, and after several attempts was finally able to get through. Good job it wasn't an emergency. After repeating the details on the call, we were told they wouldn't be sending anyone out, and should dial 311 instead. Reporting it there would give us an incident number needed for the insurance.

The New Jerseyite was horrified that this was the way they handle things in San Francisco, and told them it was little wonder they'd got a rising crime rate. How true that is, I couldn't say. Though in hindsight I'm not sure what sending officers out would have achieved.

Next up was the car rental company: they told us to continue on with our trip with the damaged window. I drove it back to the hotel whilst James spoke to his cousin on the phone. It sounded like he was in shock over what had happened, and I'm sure that although only twenty minutes had passed it was the longest drive of the trip.

It didn't seem like a great idea to be driving that car with glass falling as we drove along; but there was nothing else we could do. It's not the sort of thing we were prepared for. Even the hotel staff weren't interested when we told them we'd parked a vehicle with a broken window in their car park.

We never did get to find somewhere to eat - we ate a couple of biscuits whilst compiling a list of what had been stolen until midnight had come and gone.

We started later than planned the next day in part due to the events of the night before, and partly due to the heavy thunderstorm that rolled in, spewing large hailstones.

James didn't have the stomach to drive, so I took us into the city one last time so we could visit the USS Pampanito: a submarine from the second world war. The tour starts in the aft torpedo room and proceeds from there into the manoeuvring room, the engine rooms, the crews mess and galley, and then the control room. At the other end the tour exits through the forward torpedo room, and out onto the deck.

The sun had come out whilst we'd been in there, and our chances of getting a photograph of the Golden Gate Bridge seemed good. In fact, I didn't have to drive all the way there as I'd thought: we found a viewpoint along the way that would suffice.

When we arrived at the airport they questioned the smashed window, but accepted it once we'd given them an incident number. Whilst waiting for the flight to Utah, James got talking to a couple he'd helped out with some painkillers. They'd overheard us talking about the theft, and told us they were volunteers at the Snowbird ski resort - offering us free tickets for the cable car. Acts of kindness from strangers shows that the world is a kinder place than it sometimes seems.

In Salt Lake City we decided it'd be a good idea to pay extra for a vehicle that could hide our luggage fully. Fortunately due to having flown in on one of their partner airlines the extra was reduced from US$45 to US$15. I never knew this was possible, and would be something to research in future.

The hotel, which resembled a mountain lodge,

wasn't too far from the airport, and next-door was a grill named after aviator Amelia Earhart. Whilst we were eating there the constant rain we'd experienced since arriving in Utah had turned into sleet: hopefully not the weather we'd be experiencing all week.

The morning brought with it a new challenge. The clouds had cleared and we could see the mountains around us; but at some point the sleet had changed to snow and the car was covered in a thick white blanket. We'd got nothing to clear it with except for some gloves James happened to have with him. I guess Canadians are always ready for snow.

To get to Arches National Park we had to first cross the mountains, and in doing so there was a dramatic change in the weather. The snow disappeared, and changed to sand as the sun shone down on us.

San Francisco had taught us to be more careful. We didn't want to leave the car unattended for too long. We also didn't want to leave any camera equipment there, so I found myself carrying my sixteen kilogram backpack for the hike.

We got as far as Landscape Arch before turning back, but also saw some other viewpoints along the way out of the park. Some were very impressive, and it'd have been nice to have spent longer there; but we were three hours away from Torrey, and had little fuel left.

As we left the park the needle edged closer and closer to empty, and for mile after mile there was no gas station in sight. The first one we found was expensive; but what choice did we have? We later discovered there wouldn't have been another for seventy miles.

We arrived at the inn on the other side of Capitol Reef Park just twenty minutes before they were going to stop serving food. It was a rush, but at least we'd had some luck. That night I took advantage of the remoteness of where we were staying to take some photographs of the night sky.

Sunrise in Torrey was earlier than it was during our stay in California. For the next couple of days we'd be hiking around Bryce Canyon, and staying in Panguitch. We felt we'd learned a little from Yosemite, and decided we should start with the farthest point and work our way back across the eighteen miles.

The first viewpoint was Rainbow Point, situated 9,115 feet above sea level. We sat in the carpark next to a mound of snow and ate the sandwiches we'd bought. It was cold out, and quite a contrast to what the weather had been like the day before.

We stopped at every viewpoint on the way back from Rainbow Point to Swamp Canyon Point. At this last stop it was warmer, and we set off on a four mile hike along the Sheep Creek connecting trail. It's an easy one to start with: downhill until it reaches a campsite and the Hoodoo marker. The terrain soon changes: we crossed a dried up creek, climbed over fallen trees, and ducked under others.

There were times when I wondered whether we'd gotten lost in the wilderness; but every now and then there was the telltale sign that we were still on the trail. It took just shy of two hours to complete in the now soaring temperatures. Conditions change quickly there: I could understand why getting lost in National Parks like this can be a real concern. For now, we were done for the day.

Our main hike for the next day was the Navajo trail: part of which we knew was closed; but we were unsure where from. This trail descends through a narrow valley with many switchbacks before levelling out. We followed this for 1.2 miles and found the point where it was closed from was the other end of Wall Street - just 0.1 miles from the end.

A lot of the views we'd seen this day were similar - the same needle-like rock formations from different angles. We'd now seen everything we could in Bryce Canyon along the trails that were passable. So I felt now was the time to go for a run in the midday heat - just an easy eight miles in a town that wasn't really big enough. There isn't really much else to do in small American towns like this.

Instead of spending another morning in Bryce as we'd expected, we were able to make an early start on driving to Zion National Park. Unlike the other parks, this one doesn't allow people to drive through so we had to park up on the road and walk to the entrance. It was already very warm, and the forty-five minute queue to get a shuttle bus to the farthest point was without shade.

At the 'Temple of Sinawava' stop we did the full riverwalk; but couldn't do 'The Narrows' due to the high water level causing them to close the area. The walk is only 2.2 miles, but their map predicts it should take around ninety minutes. Even with many stops for photographs it took us under an hour.

It became a common theme that every trail was one we did far quicker than the map estimated. Seeing what the differences were meant we could make our own estimates for other trails based on theirs.

When we got back to the car, the water we'd left in there was about the temperature I'd drink tea at. It was almost like being in Rome again. Getting into the car wasn't that much fun either; but we needed to get to Hurricane to check-in to the hotel, and find somewhere to eat.

Zion had very little left to offer us. James' fear of heights meant there were certain trails we couldn't take. Despite this we returned to the national park one last time and parked up outside the visitor centre for US$20. The day before had been free, but we'd parked a fair distance away. Today we'd save some time.

The only thing we really had left to do was the Sand Beach Trail - a five hour trail we decided we could do in three. It was far too warm though, and mostly without shade. The sun felt relentless and unforgiving. It was hard work to plod on through seemingly endless mounds of sand.

I was fed up of hiking. Hiking along the sandy trail had been too mind numbing with feet sliding in the loose sand, avoiding horse droppings, and the ever-present sun beating down on us.

I sat at the end of the trail, and poured sand from my shoes. It'd have been comical if I hadn't been so fed up. There was however some relief we'd finished; or at least I thought we had. We found we'd missed the Pa'rus trail, so we took that to ensure nothing spectacular had been missed. We hadn't missed anything.

We should have been spending Good Friday in Zion; but we decided two days had been enough so went looking for other places. The first was Kolob Canyon - covered by the same entrance fee as Zion.

There are a number of trails to choose from, so we decided we'd take the shortest of them: Taylor Creek trail. This one passes two wooden huts from the 1930s, and crosses Taylor Creek many times as it winds through the valley.

The end of this trail is at a place they call the 'Double Arch', though to me it seemed more like an alcove with good acoustics. As we'd heard there was a waterfall beyond, we continued passed the end of the trail along rockier terrain until we reached a crevice in the cliff with a trickle of water within. It might not have seemed much, but it was different and redeemed our opinion of the area.

From there we headed back through Hurricane and into Arizona to get around to a bumpy, unpaved road back into Utah to reach the Coral Pink Sand Dunes State Park. There isn't really that much to do there though unless you have an ATV or dirt bike. It is possible however to go on a short hike, which is what we did.

The first part of this barefooted hike was a mixture of smooth sand, and places with a high concentration of pebbles. We had to keep an eye out for off-road vehicles driving at speed around the dunes even though they mostly stayed away from where people were.

The largest of the sand dunes was steep and was hard work to climb up; but it was worth it for the better view of the park. Climbing it reminded me of a scene from Stargate when they first arrive on Abydos.

It was strange, but despite the name describing the place as pink, all we could see was an orange similar to the hue of their forty-fifth President.

For our final day we headed back to Salt Lake City to do some sightseeing, starting with the Snowbird Resort. The closer we got, the less use the satnav was as it'd not been updated in some time. It was fortunate I'd got a map on my phone I could use to navigate our way into the mountains. Sometimes technology is fantastic.

The temperature started to drop as we got higher, so I was seriously questioning my decision to wear shorts and a shirt. It wasn't my best idea, and it'd only get worse.

The tram, or what we'd call a cable car, is primarily for the skiers; but there were some other tourists taking it up the mountain as well. At the summit there is a fair sized building with a restaurant and other basic facilities. We were there purely to use it as a viewpoint.

The air was almost completely still, and the sun was warm, so walking around in shorts wasn't actually too bad. Though it looked odd when standing next to people who were all wearing thick coats and woolly hats.

Our final sight was the Temple Square back in the middle of the city. It wasn't easy to find some local parking, and the best we could find was US$10 for under an hour. Afterwards we found out that as their machine wasn't working, they weren't charging.

The Salt Lake Temple is a relatively impressive structure for a modern church; but it's one we couldn't go inside as we're not Mormon. We wandered around outside looking for what interesting photographs we could take until it was time to return the car to the airport.

After the drop-off we were told to wait at passenger pick-up six for the airport shuttle for the hotel. Time passed slowly, and it seemed we weren't going to be collected. James called them again, and was asked to wait a little longer. It was getting colder though as the sun was edging closer to the horizon.

Further waiting and telephone exchanges continued for ninety minutes until we spoke to another driver and they told us that airport shuttles couldn't use this stop. We wondered if the hotel had meant door six and not passenger pick-up six as they'd stated.

It was a completely different area; but our suspicions had been correct. The receptionist had made us wait in the wrong place, and the shuttle driver was not happy. He insisted he'd been there waiting for us but didn't seem to understand, or didn't want to understand, that we'd been told to wait in the wrong place. We found it'd been the receptionists first week, and he didn't seem to know the airport at all.

In the early hours of the following morning we took the airport shuttle once more. At the airport I was asked if I could take a later flight for a US$200 voucher; but with two further flights to take with this airline I couldn't see how that would work. If I missed this flight then I'd miss the rest.

The first of these flights was to Houston, and my flight from there to Newark was showing as delayed. It's an airport I've not had the best of luck with so far.

I'd have just thirty minutes to connect internationally, and that didn't seem possible. It was making me a little nervous as I didn't know what I'd need to do, so I went to the service desk to find out. Whilst talking, this buffer dropped to just seven minutes following another delay. It's not possible to disembark, and board another flight in that time - forget the time it'd take to get across the airport. The international flight wasn't going to happen.

The airline's desk was far from helpful: they didn't know how their company would operate in Newark, and wouldn't call them either. She told me the best she could do was to have me on hold for another flight out of Newark; but that my checked luggage wouldn't follow me. She wouldn't tell me why.

What am I going to do? What's going to happen to my luggage - will I eventually get it back? It seemed hopeless.

I sat down and thought about it for a while, and decided I needed to find out what would happen with my luggage. Someone must know. I spoke to a different representative from the airline, and they told me the reservation I'd been given was a waste of time: even the slightest delay would mean I'd miss that one too. I was starting to wonder how I'd ever make it back to England.

He suggested that if I could go to Heathrow instead of Birmingham that they'd get me on a flight to there from Newark with a confirmed seat, and my luggage would travel with me. It wasn't ideal going to the 'wrong' airport; but it was a way home. Hesitantly, I agreed.

A further sixteen minutes of delays proved I'd made the right decision in switching flights. Though my original international flight had now been delayed as well. There was a chance I could still make it.

Upon arrival in Newark the other passengers were kind enough to let me off first so I could run from gate to gate as quickly as I dared to. The gate however had closed at the original departure time. It was time to put the back-up plan into effect: I'd be going to Heathrow. I was going home.

I was incredibly grateful they'd solved the problem; though from then until we landed in the UK I heard constant complaints from passengers. It's amazing what airlines have to deal with; especially in the unfortunate case of the entertainment system not working.

Whilst I'd been at the back of the plane I'd seen on one of the screens that the system had a file system error - it was something I could probably have fixed for them. I doubt regulations would have allowed it, so I didn't suggest it.

It had certainly been an eventful trip; but I made it home with my luggage intact.

32: Morocco

Ten years of travel were almost at and end. It had seen me visiting the seven continents, and experiencing many things. From scuba diving in subterranean caves to soaring over a city on a paraglider.

In the beginning I started off by visiting an Arabic-speaking country knowing nothing of what to expect: I couldn't speak the language, and I couldn't read the road names. It hadn't gone entirely to plan; but I learnt a lot about travelling, and learnt even more in the years since. I was now at ease with travelling by myself as well.

Over the years I've met a lot of people, and one of those is Howard who I know through running, and have done some of his UK trips through his adventure travel company. One of the places he takes groups to is the High Atlas Mountains of Morocco. It felt like in returning to an Arabic-speaking country I had come full circle.

Morocco would be something similar to Egypt, or so I thought; but this time my planning would be better. Before going I loaded my phone up with offline maps, and made sure I had a list of sights and their addresses.

I couldn't take a suitcase with me as it'd be carried

by a mule; so I bought an adventure travel pack, then filled it with everything I needed in vacuum bags and dry bags. The mule would likely have river crossings so I'd need to keep everything dry.

Within days of booking this trip, the Department of Homeland Security in the US announced a travel ban on electronic devices in aircraft cabins. On the American list of affected airports was Morocco. It was rumoured that the UK would be following suit.

If the ban affected the UK it would mean I could only take my camera if it went in the aircraft hold. Travel insurance doesn't cover valuables in these circumstances, and the risk of damage or theft is greatly increased. Days passed by and after nervously waiting it was confirmed that the UK would be implementing a ban, but would not include Morocco. My camera would be safe.

As it'd be a trip with lots of hiking, and off the back of some big races, I decided I'd start the trip in comfort. I drove there, used the valet parking outside the terminal building entrance, and after security went to the British Airways lounge to relax and have lunch. It was a very nice experience and one I haven't really had during my years of travelling.

The flight itself wasn't that different to flying economy though as they use the same seats, but keep the middle ones empty. I took this time to read the inflight magazine that featured an article on hiking through the Toubkal National Park in the Atlas Mountains.

Over an hour after landing in Marrakech I'd gone through immigration, collected my hiking backpack, and changed a little currency. Once the others arrived, Howard introduced me to John, and Deb. To get to know them, I joined them all for pizza.

Our first day of hiking would be from Imlil, a place described as being the Moroccan Kathmandu, to the remote Tizi Oussem. Having no idea what to expect I thought I'd be running from one place to the next: it'd be a few miles and we'd be done by lunchtime. Even after all these years of travelling I get things wrong. These trails were not as easy I thought they might be. At least one in our group was injured so couldn't run, and I didn't want to leave them behind. This needed to be a group experience.

We drove to Imlil and met up with the support team that had been hired: a guide, a chef, and a muleteer. They'd accompany us on our hike across the High Atlas Mountains over the next few days. They'd show us the way, transport our bags, and cook our food when we reached each gîte.

Hassan, our guide, led us to the rooftop of his home for Berber tea whilst Lessem and Mohammad loaded our heaviest packs onto the back of two mules along with food and cooking equipment.

Berber tea, known locally as Berber whisky, is a green tea made from mint leaves and copious amounts of sugar. When it's served, it's poured and returned to the teapot three times to give the tea some air before it is consumed.

The taste is distinctive, and is one I tried to avoid as the week went on. It was too sweet for me; but the teeth of many Berbers suggests they love it. Berbers are a people spread out across northern Africa, with a name derived from the Egyptian for outlander.

It was a relatively steep climb over nearly five miles of terrain to reach the peak of Tizi h'Mzik. The sun beat down on us with little shade for shelter. At this altitude there's a real danger of sunburn - something I really struggled to avoid. The summit was cooler due to the strong winds blowing across the valley, but the danger was still there.

For the descent into the valley I ran ahead with Hassan, passing cyclists that had braved the trails. With my heavy camera backpack it meant I couldn't run as quickly as I normally would, and it meant I couldn't stop as quickly either - something I discovered when I ran into a bush where the path wound tightly. It's better a prickly bush than down into the valley. I was more cautious after that, and walked whenever I felt I needed to.

In Tizi Oussem I was led into the gîte. Back home I might have believed it to be derelict or still under construction; but here it was one of their better buildings. It was open plan and open to the air, allowing dust to be blown across the floor. *So this is why we need sleeping bags*, I thought to myself. It wasn't though: there were proper rooms below us.

Two of the rooms had mats spread across the floor which is what we'd be putting sleeping bags on. Another room was used as a communal room which is where we'd socialise, and eat. The last of the rooms was the kitchen where Mohammad was already preparing salad for lunch.

Following lunch, we were introduced to another

Berber tradition - the hammam. The tradition itself is from all over Africa; but in Morocco it evolved further during the Roman occupation. Here it was a ramshackle hut split into an antechamber for undressing, and a room with a heated floor - the rooms being separated by polythene hanging from the roof.

The floor was being heated by a log fire underneath the building - this made the floor mostly too warm to stand on, but was also warming a cauldron of water in the middle. The tradition of hammam is that you don't pollute the water in the cauldron: you take what you need and mix it with cold water in another small container. Maybe it sounds primitive; but it was the only way we could wash. At any rate, it was already one step ahead of Norway where washing hadn't been possible.

Before the sun had set we headed out into the village to look around, and to give out stationary and sweets to the children there. We didn't get far before a villager invited us into his home for some tea.

Feeling we should accept his hospitality, we followed him home to their kitchen, one unlike any you'd see in England. It was a stone hut detached from where they lived, with branches from nearby juniper trees as a roof. Opposite the entrance was an alcove and chimney where a log fire was heating a pot. We crowded in, and sat wherever we could whilst our host moved a small table into the room between us.

His family brought us homemade bread and walnuts, accompanied by a pot of coffee. Whilst we ate and drank they told us about about an abscess and asked for more hydrocortisone cream.

The local language is a Berber dialect rather than Arabic or French so translations were being handled via Hassan who would translate into French and where possible, English. Hassan had learnt French in school, but his English came entirely from speaking to tourists. Sure I've learnt bits and pieces of languages on my travels - it's only natural; but to pick up a language to the degree Hassan had? Impressive!

We didn't have any of the hydrocortisone cream they wanted; but John offered them some aspirin. It just meant we needed to lead him to the gîte in the dark using nothing but our phones to light the way.

It's in situations like this you realise that in developing countries everything seems magnified - the divide between the poor and the rich is so much more pronounced. So many people live there with almost nothing, and rely on tourists to make a living and to help provide some of the things they need to live.

Some will travel to countries like this and feel fear, and a feeling of being unsafe. I don't think there's any need to - we'd seen with our own eyes that they can be some of the most trusting and kind people you'll encounter. This one had just invited us into his home. We just needed to set aside our western preconceptions, and any prejudice we may have had.

That night we tried our first proper Moroccan dish: tajine. This dish is named after the conical earthenware pot it is served in, and the ingredients can differ depending upon what is available. Ours was beef served steaming with potato, carrots, olives, tomatoes, and courgette. I guess it's a little like a stew.

Having my fill of food, I climbed into my sleeping bag for the first time this trip, and drifted off into the quiet abyss of sleep.

It came as a surprise to have slept better in my sleeping bag than I had done in Marrakech. This was despite the morning call to prayer from the nearby mosque at the crack of dawn.

Once we'd had breakfast, and I'd solved the three-dimensional jigsaw puzzle of repacking, we were on the trails heading to Tizgui. To go up, we first had to go down into the valley where a small stream was flowing. On the other side we began our climb, passing goats along the way. There wasn't really much wildlife to see.

At the summit we took a break for a snack just as we had on our way to Tizi Oussem. The winds here were stronger than ever - it was little wonder it was considered unsafe to climb Mount Toubkal.

For this descent I didn't run: the ground was too loose for me to want to risk it. I did wonder if I was just looking for excuses to take it easy; but in doing so I could enjoy the blues, greens, and reds of this valley.

We crossed the stream a number of times until we encountered buildings. This village was very different to the previous - it felt bigger and more prosperous though apparently appearances were deceiving. This gîte seemed nicer than the last too - they had a terrace where we could sit out in the open air until night fell.

Another day, another hike. We'd hiked ten miles to Tizgui, and had many more miles to cover before we'd reach Tiziane for our next overnight stay. This time there were two calls to prayer - one before the sun had even risen. I was awake long before we needed to be moving.

The trail out of the village took us passed a football pitch on the dusty red ground where the outline was marked with rocks. Trees had been cut down and tied together to make goalposts at either end; the people here are certainly good at working with what little they've got. This being on the side of the mountain, I did feel sorry for anyone having to fetch the ball.

The red shades of the first mountain pass reminded me of Arizona and Utah. It's strange when places begin blurring from one to the other. It's like seeing the world as a single place. Is this what it was like for people that travelled the world in one go? One of my colleagues had done a trip around Europe in his younger years, and other than a few specific things, most of it was a blur from one country to the next.

When we reached the second pass, the mules left us to take a route that would be easier for them. The route we were taking would go through a third pass with a descent along a dried-up river bed. The problem for the mules was that high flood defences had been built that the mules could not easily navigate.

It started with loose stones that would shift underfoot, though this eventually changed into green mounds of sheep droppings that my feet sank into like sand. It wasn't pleasant, and was harder work than the stones; but it's one of those things you have to just deal with and move on.

Down in the dried-up riverbed there were slopes to

climb for each dam crossing: one of which was difficult enough for Hassan to be helping us cross it.

To protect my arms from the strong sun I had to wear my hoodie, but in doing so I was overheating and getting through my water supply faster. Eventually we climbed away from the riverbed, and continued along a road to Tiziane where there was some shade.

This gîte, located over a stable, felt a little 'rougher around the edges' than the ones before. This one was being lived in by the owner; but not all of the facilities were in working order. The shower was a ceramic hole in an outbuilding which you could sit in, and then a leaking knee-high tap could be used for washing. A drainage problem meant it couldn't be turned on for long; though the hot water kept cutting out anyway.

We were led from the gîte to the neighbouring village of Tizi Zougouart where Deb and John once again handed out stationary to the children. This time though they were surrounded: each one tugging and pleading for more and more like a scene from Oliver Twist.

Hassan had seen enough. He took charge of the bag, and continued our tour of the village whilst the children followed him like some strange version of the pied piper.

On our way back to Tiziane the army of children surrounded Deb one last time even though she had nothing left to give. She tried to move out of their way, but fell to the ground. It was fortunate she hadn't been injured. Eventually though, we left them behind.

Back at the gîte we found the dormitories had ill-fitting windows, which did little to block out the cold night.

It was now the anniversary of the Green March, a day in 1975 when 350,000 unarmed Moroccans had marched on the Spanish Saharan region of Sakiya Lhmra. It was a protest against the Spanish government, and was accompanied by demands to decolonise the area so it could be under Moroccan control. In the years since the area remains disputed, and is now known as Western Sahara. It's a border that is inadvisable for tourists to approach.

Our hiking for the day would be far from it: we were going to Imsker. This trek started off with a descent down to the river, and then a climb on road surface to a radio tower. It was a big difference after the trails we'd hiked across so far, but it wasn't exactly tarmac.

During this climb the mules caught up with us, so we were following them for the descent with the sun now at its strongest. I kept my hoodie and cap on to try and protect myself the best I could. Despite my best efforts I was already burnt.

Whenever the mules strayed from the path they were hit with a stick. It can't be an easy life for beasts of burden like this. I liked to think that they were appreciated as much as 'Bill' - the pony in The Lord of the Rings. A trip like this also makes you appreciate what the long walks must have been like for those fictional characters.

Eventually we reached Imi Oughlad, and continued along the riverbed which was a putrid combination of rotten apples, donkey droppings, and water to the start of our final climb. Although short, and not that steep, it felt like the hardest one we'd done. The heat was making it difficult to concentrate, and I found myself staring at my feet instead of taking in my surroundings.

Somehow I found the energy from the top to run the remaining way to Imsker. It was a slow pace to start with, but once we hit the road I decided to run as fast as I dared to with my camera in hand.

The remainder of the afternoon was spent talking with Hassan, and convincing him that people had been to the moon. He'd never heard of Neil Armstrong or the Apollo program. It sounded laughable to him that people could leave this planet.

In the mountains they really do have a very different view of the world. It was during these evening chats we could see other differences in culture too. There was a definite hierarchy amongst those we'd hired, and they seemed too embarrassed to sit, and eat or talk with us until we insisted on it.

Mountain life meant that other than when we'd passed through Imli Oughlad we hadn't really seen any vehicles or heard any traffic in days. It seemed strange to wake to the sound of passing vehicles.

Following our farewells to the muleteer and chef, our trek started by following the road through the village under the shelter of trees, and up into the mountains. To pass the time we started playing games where we picked a subject and then had to name things from it for every letter of the alphabet.

We passed through another village with a newly

built school, though it hadn't yet been finished as it had no sanitation. Apparently the 45th President of the United States had funded the construction of this school; but the money had been siphoned away before completion.

We stopped in the next village for Berber tea, not that I wanted any more of it. I wasn't a fan of the taste; but had drunk it a few times out of politeness. At least we were in the shade for a while.

When leaving this village we passed villagers washing their clothes in a stream that led to the base of our last peak. The path zig-zagged up the side to a height of over 2,000 metres above sea level. The biggest surprise was not just seeing a shop, but also an actual road leading back down. Our climbing was over.

Instead of following the road all the way, we took shortcuts through the switchbacks until we reached the gatehouse for the Kasbah du Toubkal - a place recognised by National Geographic. Here we had the comfort of the Garden House for staying in: an unexpected upgrade as Howard knew the owner. All the food here was included, and we could eat whenever we wanted to. Even the hammam here was nicer, and included as part of the price.

Being in a place like this makes you appreciate how well we live, and how little the Berbers in the mountains have. There wasn't much I could do, but I donated my old running shoes to our guide - his own were falling apart.

Our last full day as a group started with a four mile hike up another mountain. This one took us passed what looked like a damaged crater of an explosive volcanic eruption. It seemed this was an old stratovolcano known as Jbel Sirwa.

Further along this path was another village: Aroumd. We shopped in their co-operative market for souvenirs, and for the last time drank Berber tea when Howard met up with us. Whilst the others looked at large rugs, I bought an ammonite; but refused to haggle. The price was reasonable, and the money would mean more to them than what little I could have saved. I felt an ammonite would be a good souvenir from this country as Morocco is well known for its fossils.

Following a waterfall and watercourse for about a mile got us back to the Kasbah to relax for the remainder of the day. I dropped my camera off there, and headed out for one last run in the mountains; though I didn't really know where I was going. So much of the area looked different to when I'd been going in the opposite direction. Behind the Kasbah it was hard to tell one tree from the next which made directions even harder.

When I got back from my run I decided it was time to try out their hammam. This one was a lockable building you book for thirty minutes at a time. It was far fancier, and comfortable with power sockets on the wall in the main room should you want to charge your mobile or other device. In the centre of four pillars was a tiled pool filled with cold water. This didn't interest me quite as much as the steam room with the heated cauldron. This was far more comfortable.

It was a largely uneventful day I could have spent elsewhere; if I'd planned more I could have tried spending the day somewhere else such as Ouarzazate. It was however our last day as a group, so after a lamb dish to eat we sat and played card games into the night.

We left the Kasbah in the morning, and took a taxi back to the hustle and bustle of Marrakech. Howard led us through Jemaa el-Fnaa, the main square in the Medina of Marrakech, and told us about the famous orange sellers there. They've been known to start fights with each other if one thinks they've caught your eye and then you buy from another.

Adjacent to the square are the souqs-a name which comes from the Hebrew word for marketplace. Everywhere you look there are shops selling similar goods-a little reminiscent of Kathmandu, but far cleaner.

In the souqs we witnessed a fight being broken up. I hadn't noticed one of them was then walking in front of us until the other one caught back up and wrestled him to the ground: slapping each other as they went down.

I stepped back a pace, and watched in surprise at the scene unfolding in front of me. Onlookers got involved and started pulling them away from each other. All we could gather was that one of them may have been a shoplifter.

We exited the souqs into an open square with stalls selling caged animals, and other goods. It reminded me of Raiders of the Lost Ark - maybe we'd see a Cairo swordsman. We didn't, but we did bump into a French couple we'd met in Tizgui. Around this area we also found a terrace cafe that overlooked the rooftops of the souqs and beyond.

From the cafe I left on my own with the intention of meeting up with the group one last time before their trip to the airport. When I visited Egypt I imagined I'd have been uneasy going off exploring by myself; but experiences and having an electronic map changes things.

I started with the Koutoubia Mosque. As non-Muslims cannot enter, I photographed the exterior and continued walking until I reached Bab Agnaou: an ornate gate, and a sign that led me to the Saadian Tombs.

By 1672 the Saadian dynasty had come to an end, and Moulay Ismail wanted no sign of this dynasty to remain. He destroyed the palace, and sealed the entrances to the tombs so they could only be accessed via the Kasbah Mosque. Hundreds of years passed and the tombs were forgotten about until the French General Hubert Lyautey rediscovered them in 1917.

For what is there to see, the entrance fee was massively underpriced: in the UK this sort of sight would have been five to ten times more expensive to look around. The best part is a room with twelve highly decorative pillars amongst the tombs.

Having more time available after this, I went in search of more Saadian history: the El Badi Palace. I found myself walking down random alleyways filled with locals, and mopeds hurtling through them. Eventually these winding passages opened out into a large square, and there was the entrance.

I was now on a mission to see what could have easily taken a few hours in just thirty minutes. There was so much variety in the architecture to see - indications of many rooms with different purposes.

Finding my way back the Jemaa el-Fnaa afterwards was easy, though I was hassled by many shop owners along the way. I'd made it back in time to say goodbye to the others, and to explore some of the food stalls that were beginning to open up. Since our earlier visit, it had now attracted a number of acts such as snake charmers.

Photography in the square must be done with caution: if someone catches you taking a picture of anything they own or do then they'll expect to be paid for it. The performers even have people in the square looking out for this.

Dusk was approaching, and I still needed to find the hotel I'd be staying at. After having one final meal with the others I'd collected my adventure travel pack from where it'd been left, and was now on my own for the remainder of the trip. Having both backpacks now seemed less of a good idea. They were too heavy for how far I needed to walk. In hindsight a taxi would have been a good idea; but I wanted to know the route.

As the last of the light left the sky I arrived at the hotel. It was close to the Opera house, and train station - far from the tourist areas.

Taking a train in Morocco isn't too difficult, though I was cautious to make sure I was on the right train after my Naples experience. The train I took was one which was divided into compartments so had the potential to be relatively quiet.

For most of the journey we passed nothing but barren landscape until we reached Casablanca. Litter lined the sides of the railway. It looked very different to

Marrakech. It looked newer, and more European. That is until you get to the sea where it's more industrialised. I'd made the right decision not to stop there. The only reason I'd considered it was because of a famous film that wasn't even filmed there.

Five hours after setting off, I arrived in Rabat. It's obvious that Rabat is as different to Marrakech, as Marrakech is to Imlil. Marrakech has character in the old buildings and winding souqs of the medina; Rabat feels like a western city. There is a tram system and busy roads: it could easily be a city in France or other French-speaking country.

I navigated my way through the medina to the riad I'd be staying at. This medina seemed cleaner, and newer. There were some that were wearing a red fez as well - the first time I'd seen this iconic hat in Morocco.

The riad seemed ancient. The room I stayed in had large doors as high as two or three people and could only be locked with large bolts and a padlock. The rooms conjured an image of Arabian majesty - I could picture that hundreds of years ago someone would be relaxing on cushions here, smoking a hookah pipe.

I dropped my bags off, and headed back out into the city. The roads were busy, and the sights seemed more difficult to find than in Marrakech. I thought it was possible to visit the Royal Palace grounds; but never found an entrance I was allowed through. This did however take me close to Chellah.

Chellah, from a distance, looks like a castle. It started life as a small settlement called Sala, but the Roman Empire transformed it. When the city fell into ruin, Muslim Arabs took control and built a mosque; of which only the minaret still stands.

Inside there was another link between the places I'd visited: the grave of Abu al-Hassan; a Moroccan sultan of the Marinid dynasty who ruled before the Saadiens. He had died in the High Atlas Mountains after being exiled, but was buried here.

I then walked to Hassan Tower and the mausoleum of Mohammed V - the tower being part of what had been intended as the largest mosque in the world. It had been a commission of Sultan Abu Yusuf Yaqub al-Mansur, the same sultan that converted Chellah into a necropolis, and had started reconstruction of the Kasbah of the Udayas.

The entire site is surrounded by walls with ceremonial guards on horseback at each entrance. The tower itself was closed; but tourists were allowed to enter the mausoleum protected by ceremonial guards.

Inside the mausoleum you can look down from the balcony to see the tomb of Mohammed V below. It's become more of a family tomb - his son Prince Abdallah was buried there in 1983, and his other son King Hassan II was buried there in 1999.

I left as the sun was setting, deciding on a five kilometre walk to get some pizza. It felt even more western in that part of the city, and the sunset gave me photographic opportunities I hadn't expected. Sometimes these ideas are worth it.

After breakfast served on the terrace of the riad, I was on my way to the Kasbah of the Udayas. I was surprised how easy it was to find without needing a map to get out of the medina.

Just inside the entranceway was where I encountered the first of what are known as faux guides - ones which are not wearing the badge of an official guide, and are usually (allegedly) trying to scam tourists. He was hanging around at the entrance and started talking to me, as soon as I realised where the conversation was going I told him, "I don't need a guide" and walked off.

I started with the gardens, though they weren't really worth the time. I started to realise I had three hours here, and wouldn't need anywhere near that. I walked slowly, and started to explore some of the alleyways - some painted white and blue, and some white and red. I'd never seen use of colour like this anywhere I'd been before.

As I passed a shop being set-up I encountered another faux guide.

"I live here, let me show you around"

"I'm good, thanks"

"Do you know the area?"

I looked down at the map I had in my hands, and looked back as I walked away, "yes".

"No you don't!" he shouted after me.

Sure I might not know it personally, but my map knew the area pretty well. I'd got so much time to spare I wanted to walk down every alleyway, knowing that many of them would be dead-ends. Any one of them could be worth a photograph.

The north-easternmost part of the Kasbah is an open courtyard with a view across the Bou Regreg River to Salé. I'd got time to cross the bridge over there if I'd wanted to; but didn't know of anything worth seeing. It felt the time would be better spent exploring the older buildings in Rabat.

A path wound away from the courtyard, and along the coast passed a beach and a cemetery, and eventually a lighthouse. After going as far as I could, I returned back to the Kasbah and walked south along the river instead.

I'd not been walking long when I started to hear a number of gulls approaching. This noise got louder and louder, and I wondered what was happening. I spotted an old man that was wheeling something along, and all of these birds were flocking towards him. The cacophony of noise was loud, and the sky was filled with wings. It was like watching Alfred Hitchcock's 'The Birds'. Rather than stick around, I kept on walking.

I ran out of places to go eventually, so returned to the Kasbah to sit in the garden. No matter where I sat, I found myself surrounded by stray cats: a very common sight in Morocco.

When I left I found the large gates of the Kasbah had been opened to reveal an art gallery inside. Before this I'd had no idea there was actually something on the other side - my research indicated it was just another entrance. It was another reminder to not believe everything I read about places.

After collecting my luggage from the riad, I made my way to the train station early. I heard an announcement mentioning the train number I was taking, and then 'vingt-cinq minutes'. If I'd understood correctly, it meant the train had been delayed. I'd already wasted two hours in the train station - I'd really overestimated how much time I'd need in Rabat. Could I have spent the last two hours any better in Marrakech?

It was dark when I arrived back at the hotel in Marrakech, though it'd be a while before I could sleep - I could hear loud shouts from outside. I looked out from one of the public balconies and could see people chanting in the streets, blocking traffic, and mopeds circling the junction and blowing horns.

I checked the news to see if there were any reports of things going on. Morocco had just beaten Ivory Coast, getting them into the World Cup. Here the celebrations were peaceful in nature; but in Brussels the Moroccan residents had caused a riot that made it onto BBC News. These celebrations continued on until the early hours of the morning.

There were two places left for me to see before heading home. I managed to find my way from the hotel to Jemaa el-Fna with ease; but needed to use my map to find Bahia Palace.

The style of this palace was incredibly different to El Badi: it was built in the 1860s by Grand Vizier Si Moussa using the best craftsmen that Morocco had to offer. It's a palace of traditional zouaq roofs, and carved stucco coated walls combined with mosaic tiles.

On my way out I decided to use some time to explore the Mellah: the old Jewish neighbourhood. The alleyways there differ greatly from the medina as here the buildings are residential. Every alley I walked down, it seemed people thought I was lost. It was however an insight into how people live in Marrakech.

My next stop, via the meandering alleyways, was a theological college known as Ali Ben Youssef Madrasa. It was founded in the fourteenth century, and remained open until 1960 when it had lost too many students to a college in Fez. What's interesting about this place is the architecture: the courtyard is an amazing example of Arabian style.

I made my way to the Jewish cemetery through what I'd been told were the rougher parts of the city. Every few minutes I'd have someone tell me, "the main square is that way," pointing back in the direction I'd come from, or calls of "there's nothing here". To me there was. This was a shortcut, with some shade, and potential photographic opportunities.

I'd read that this cemetery is possible to look around, and usually requires giving the guard a tip; but in this case it was a fixed amount of ten dirhams. Most of the graves are bright white mounds of plaster, though there were also some that were the colour of sand, and were crumbling.

The damaged ones allowed you to see how these graves were constructed: a rectangular arrangement of bricks with a layer of plaster rounding them off to create a slight dome. It looked like the entrance fee was being used to help restore the remainder.

The time had come to begin my journey home. When I got to Jemaa el-Fna I was clipped from behind by a cyclist; but wasn't injured. I continued on to the hotel to collect my bags, and booked a taxi.

The airport required me to prove I didn't have a drone packed, just as I'd needed to upon arrival. They also checked boarding cards and passports with such frequency it seemed almost like an obsession.

The flight home was pleasant, with much of it spent talking to one of the airline attendants about how after fifty miles of hiking in the High Atlas Mountains my ten years of travel had now come to an end.

I got to use a lot of what I'd learned from previous trips whilst also learning new lessons along the way. It proves that even after ten years and seven continents, the learning and experiences don't end.

Seeing all these places brought new perspective about the world, and the people in it. There is no 'us' and 'them', there is just one world which we all live in, where we may have different beliefs; but have the same basic needs. In the countries where they have the least you can meet some of the politest people of anywhere, and they'd still invite you into their homes and share what little they have.

Maybe things didn't always go to plan on these trips; but it was always an experience I wouldn't change. With so many more countries in the world left to see, whenever I'm asked, "how was your holiday?" I reply with, "it wasn't a holiday, it was an adventure."

Lightning Source UK Ltd.
Milton Keynes UK
UKHW020936060320
359895UK00015B/1017

9 781714 463923